The Economics of War

PRENTICE-HALL ECONOMIC SERIES

E. A. J. JOHNSON, EDITOR

PREDECESSORS OF ADAM SMITH, *by* E. A. J. Johnson, Ph.D.

PLANNED SOCIETY, *edited by* Findlay MacKenzie, Ph.D.

MODERN BANKING, *by* Rollin G. Thomas, Ph.D.

ELEMENTS OF MODERN ECONOMICS, *by* Albert L. Meyers, Ph.D.

THE THEORY OF PRICES, *by* Arthur W. Marget, Ph.D.

LABOR PROBLEMS AND LABOR LAW, *by* Albion G. Taylor, Ph.D.

A HISTORY OF ECONOMIC THOUGHT, *by* Erich Roll.

MODERN ECONOMIC PROBLEMS, *by* Albert L. Meyers, Ph.D.

SOCIAL PROBLEMS, *by* Carl M. Rosenquist, Ph.D.

THE ECONOMICS OF WAR, *by* Horst Mendershausen.

The Economics of War

By

HORST MENDERSHAUSEN

*Colorado College
and
National Bureau of Economic
Research*

New York : 1940
PRENTICE-HALL, INC.

COPYRIGHT, 1940, BY
PRENTICE-HALL, INC.
70 FIFTH AVENUE, NEW YORK

ALL RIGHTS RESERVED. NO PART OF THIS BOOK MAY BE REPRODUCED IN ANY FORM, BY MIMEOGRAPH OR ANY OTHER MEANS, WITHOUT PERMISSION IN WRITING FROM THE PUBLISHERS.

First Printing...........October, 1940

Printed in the United States of America

To P.

Preface

The economics of war is a rather distressing subject. Besides explaining the phenomena of economic life, the economist attempts to devise ways of bettering human society by increasing the leisure and material wealth for all. War is not a direct way toward this goal; in general, it leads in the opposite direction, toward poverty and harder work. For this reason, war economics is, as I have said, a distressing subject.

Yet war is a reality in our times, and the nations cannot escape it by refusing to think about it. The less thought they devote to this unpleasant reality, the more they will suffer from it. Since preparation for war and actual warfare present important economic problems, economic analysis has to be applied; economists must attack these problems. The more successful their analysis, the greater will be their contribution to efficient action in a national emergency.

In this book I have attempted to outline the various economic problems presented by war. My aim has been to provide a general theoretical survey of the war economy coupled with short accounts of the practical experience which major wars have provided up to our own day. Therefore, the reader will not find a chronicle of events of war-economic nature in this book. The problems of the war economy are taken up in the order in which they naturally occur to a person who wants to study systematically the economic aspects of war preparation, warfare, and war liquidation. I hope that the execution of this program will fulfill at least the elementary expectations of a critical reader.

In the preparation of this book I have profited from the large number of specialized studies which were carried out after the War of 1914 to 1918, particularly those published under the auspices of the Carnegie Endowment for International Peace. I did not succeed in discovering any theoretical investigation of the war economy in its entirety, published in the English language, except Professor Pigou's remarkable *Political Economy of War*.

During the winter semester 1939–1940, I gave a course in war economics at Colorado College and a series of public lectures.[1] I benefited from the criticism of my students and listeners.

In the preparations for this book I found most valuable assistance from several friends and collaborators. The criticism and suggestions of Professor E. A. J. Johnson (New York University), of Professor O. Lange (University of Chicago), and of Dr. A. Wald (Columbia University) helped greatly to improve both the content and the presentation of the argument. My student and assistant, Miss N. Emerson, took all of the tedious clerical work on her shoulders and executed it brilliantly; she also prepared the diagrams and the index. Miss K. Waters helped a great deal in straightening out stylistic difficulties. My wife patiently went over the manuscript. Numerous blunders in logic and style were eliminated because of her vigilant criticism. I am greatly indebted to all these kind helpers, and I express my sincere thanks to them.

The Bankers Trust Company and Random House, Inc., controlling the publications of H. E. Fisk: *The Inter-Ally Debts*, and of the Inter-Parliamentary Union, Geneva: *What*

---

[1] These lectures ("Four Lectures on the Economics of War") were published in the *Colorado College Publications*, General Series No. 225, Studies Series No. 29, Colorado Springs, March, 1940.

PREFACE

Would be the Character of a New War? respectively, kindly allowed me to reproduce statistical tables from these books.

I should like to draw the reader's attention to a terminology adopted in this book. The War of 1914 to 1918 is designated as the "World War" or the "first world war." The war which broke out in September, 1939, is referred to as the "present war" or the "second world war."

—Horst Mendershausen

Contents

	PAGE
INTRODUCTION: WAR ECONOMICS, ORIGIN AND NATURE	1

The origin of war economics. What is war economics?

Part I.
WHAT A WARRING NATION NEEDS
(The Economic War Potential)

CHAPTER

1. MAN POWER 11
   Size and composition of the population. Density, productive efficiency, and political homogeneity of the population.

2. RAW MATERIALS AND THE PROBLEM OF SUBSTITUTES . . . 21
   What is a raw material? What is an accessible raw material? Regeneration of used materials. Substitutes. Subsidization of substitute products. Resources of certain powers. Foodstuffs. Coal and iron. Other metals. Textiles, rubber, and oil.

3. FACILITIES OF PRODUCTION, DISTRIBUTION, TRANSPORTATION, AND FINANCE 48
   Productive equipment. How a country's productive equipment can be prepared for war. How the transportation system affects warfare. Distribution. Money: the sinews of war?

4. ECONOMIC MOBILIZATION 69
   Inadequate mobilization in the World War. The tasks of government. War and democracy.

Part II.
THE WAR ECONOMY

Chapter	Page
5. Military Versus Civilian Demand	85

The upsurge of military demand. Resisting civilian demand. Order in the chaos.

6. Factors Limiting National Output 96

The soldier-worker ratio. Badging and debadging. Labor's rights and the exigencies of war. Dilution. Declining productivity. Experience in the present war: War economy versus muddling through. What can be done to bring wartime output to a high level?

7. War Finance 119

The scope of financial needs. Distribution of the war burden. Can the cost of war be imposed on allied or neutral countries? Taxation, the "heroic way." The temptation of loan finance and inflation. War finance in the past. War finance in the present war. The Keynes plan of "deferred pay." Summary.

8. Priorities and Price Control 145

Why previously considered measures are insufficient. Meaning and functioning of priority schemes. How can priority be enforced? Treatment of nonessential industries under the priority scheme. Control of prices. How prices rose in the first and the second world war. Multiplicity of causes producing the boom. Price control in the first and the second world war. Technical problems of price control. Control of wages.

9. Rationing of Consumers' Goods and Government Operation of Industry 179

Rationing of consumers' goods. The technique of rationing. Government operation of industry. Summary.

CONTENTS xiii

Part III.
INTERNATIONAL ECONOMICS OF WAR AND THE SITUATION OF NEUTRALS

CHAPTER   PAGE

10. FOREIGN TRADE AND SHIPPING IN WARTIME 203
Imports and exports of belligerents. Regulation of foreign trade and shipping in belligerent countries. Inter-allied coördination. International law of maritime warfare and its fate.

11. THE WAR ECONOMY OF NEUTRAL COUNTRIES 226
Precarious neutrality. Norway's fish drama. "Bunker pressure" and tonnage agreements. Economic supervision and rationing of neutrals. Neutral war economy.

Part IV.
POSTWAR ECONOMICS

12. THE POPULATION AFTER THE WAR 255
Victor and vanquished alike. War, father of epidemics. The "hollow classes." Economic consequences.

13. ECONOMIC DEMOBILIZATION 270
Prewar conditions are history. Demobilization of men. Exhaustion of the nation's real capital. Conversion of industries to peacetime activities. The struggle over the continuation of war controls. Re-establishment of international exchanges. Summary.

14. POSTWAR FINANCE 291
Termination of war finance. Reconstruction finance. Settlement of internal war debts.

APPENDIX

Table   I. Economic War Potential . . . . *preceding page* 305
Table II. The Cost of the First World War to the Belligerent Governments 305

	PAGE
Table III. How the First World War Was Paid For	306
Table IV. Deaths Caused Directly and Indirectly by the First World War	307
Diagrams. The "Hollow Classes'" Caused by the First World War in Recent Age Distributions of Various Nations	*preceding page* 309
INDEX	309

The
Economics of War

INTRODUCTION

War Economics, Origin and Nature

When society passes from peace to war, fundamental changes occur in men's purposes and activities. A new purpose appears, that of winning the war. Whether war is waged for the maintenance of political and economic freedom, for conquest, or any other reason, winning the war becomes a social aim. Let us assume that for one reason or another the great majority of people accept the new purpose. As a result, all human activity has now to be measured by new standards. Everybody is confronted with the inquiry: "Are your doings instrumental to victory?" Many people will discover that although their activities were socially useful in peace they do not help to win the war.

Thus, the occupational pattern will be upset. Some men will leave their jobs and enroll in the fighting forces; others will shift from the production of peacetime goods to that of munitions; still others will exchange leisure for work. Under the compulsion of a new purpose, society has to work out a new pattern of occupations.

War economics may be defined as the study of the ways and means by which the wartime pattern of the division of labor is brought about. More accurately speaking, we must say "allocation of resources" instead of "division of labor." For there are not only human activities to be reallocated; everything that society possesses, all natural resources and instruments of production, every productive agent must be employed for the prosecution of war. Hence men will have to change their jobs to satisfy the requirements of war, while raw materials, power, buildings, and machines will have to be put to new uses.

The Origin of War Economics

Although war economics is as old as war itself, as a special field of interest *war economics* did not emerge until the twentieth century. Why should this branch of investigation be so much younger than its subject matter? The answer is not hard to find. In societies consisting of a number of relatively small highly self-sufficient units (families, villages, manors, or even small princedoms), the problems of war economics did not affect society as a whole; they appeared and they were solved for the most part within those self-sufficient units. When a medieval European prince wanted to go to war, he ordered his vassals to appear with their armies. The vassal-knights, if they followed the order, called upon their peasants, and the peasants left their homes equipped with what armaments they possessed, their best fighting dress and provisions. War compelled the peasant families and villages to rearrange their economic life. It affected also those unfortunate people through whose territory the armies happened to march, taking away food and whatever else appeared desirable. Perhaps the knights had to procure a certain amount of small arms; perhaps the prince had to acquire heavier equipment such as ships and artillery. Thus the question may have come before the authorities from whom to get these things, whom to have produce "munitions." On the whole, however, the equipping and maintaining of the armies and the care of the "home front" was none of the prince's business. War economics was not a problem for the highest social authority; it did not concern society as a whole, even though it may have affected every village.

War is no longer fought by plumed knights. The small self-sufficient units have disappeared; men have become cogs in an intricate economic machine. They have become specialized and interdependent within a framework that goes far beyond the limits of their family, their village or town, and even their country. Political power has shifted from knights to princes, from princes to kings, emperors, and presidents. Society has come more and more to be organized on a national basis, with central governments of ever-increasing autonomy. In our times, when governments call men to war, there are scarcely any people who can bring arms with them. On the other hand, the departure of the soldiers from home leaves their families without breadwinners. Therefore, modern central government faces at once certain problems of war economics: how to obtain arms, how to make people produce arms, how to collect money to pay for the arms, and how to support the families of soldiers.

Larger social bodies could afford to fight with larger armies and navies. Larger armies required a higher degree of organization, specialization, and discipline. Consequently, armies were put into uniforms. The feeding of large masses of men could no longer be left to the chance of finding plentiful booty. The technique of warfare advanced with the development of techniques of production. Large masses of standardized small arms such as rifles, gas masks, and helmets, complicated equipment such as tanks, airplanes, and battleships became prerequisites of an army. Today nobody expects the individual soldier to procure such equipment, nor will anybody believe that it could be turned out overnight without considerable productive effort. The problem is now of social scope. The government has to buy huge quantities of food and fighting equipment.

Where will these goods come from? Will the nation's

productive power provide them automatically? If not, how can the production be organized? Obviously, the government cannot ask the producers of war goods to give them away free. If it did, nobody would produce an object of military interest. Hence, huge sums have to be appropriated by the government. From whom and by what methods shall they be collected?

The economics of war has become a social science dealing with the economic problems that government and citizens have to solve coöperatively when the nation becomes involved in war. Just as economics in general owes its existence to the increasing interdependence of individual economic activities, so does its special branch of war economics. And while the increasing scale of production units, technical progress, and so on, stimulated general economics, similar developments in the field of warfare created a need for the application of economic thought to the special problems of war.

What is War Economics?

Let us now survey the field of war economics. At the beginning, it will be well to specify what kind of war we are talking about. This book deals with *international* wars. It is true that many of the problems we are going to take up are also of interest for civil wars; but our main interest will be concentrated on wars between nations or groups of nations. Furthermore, we are mostly concerned with the economics of *modern major* wars. Wars of the past and minor wars of today may, however, occasionally provide interesting illustrations for the development of the general idea.

Any nation upon going to war possesses a population which owns a certain quantity of material resources. We call this stock of human and material resources the *economic war potential.*[1] In Part I of this book we are going to discuss the elements of this economic war potential, and how it can be built up. There is first the population, its size and its distribution by age and by occupation. Raw material resources at the disposal of a nation are a second important element of the war potential. To the extent that important materials are not available within its own, within allied, or friendly neutral territories, the problem of substitutes arises. We see that a nation's war potential in raw materials is not exclusively provided for by nature. It depends also on the civilization, technical level, and other properties of the nation. This is still more obvious when we come to factories, railroad systems, distribution facilities and the like. The important industrial bases for a modern war may, and to a large extent do, appear simply as results of peaceful economic development. But in part, they are created just for war purposes. Finally, we shall examine certain auxiliary elements of the economic war potential, such as the financial status of the nation.

In a war, the side which has the greater economic war potential is likely to gain the upper hand. But even the strongest war potential does not *assure* victory. Quite apart from the quality of a country's military and political organization—both of which lie at the margin of our subject matter—the nation's capacity for quick adaptation to new conditions enters as an important factor. An economic war potential may or may not be put to full utilization, depending upon the nation's capacity for adaptation and organization.

This brings us to Part II, in which we shall deal with the transformation of a peace economy into a war economy. As

---
[1] W. Oualid defined war potential *(potentiel de guerre)* as "the present degree of aptitude for and the facility and rapidity of possible adaptation to the requirements of war." *(What Would Be the Character of a New War?* Enquiry organized by the Inter-Parliamentary Union, Geneva, New York, 1933, 119.)

the nation's economy passes into war it experiences a sudden and extraordinary change in the demands for goods and services. It is true enough that in a modern economy like ours changing demands are the rule rather than the exception. But as compared with peacetime changes, the voluminous and urgent war orders accompanied by strong reactions in civilian demand appear as a real revolution. More guns are demanded and less household furniture, more army cloth and perhaps fewer silk stockings. But just when war orders require an enormous productive effort, factors appear that limit the national output. Times of excess capacities in man power and equipment are then forgotten, and the belligerent country is faced by shortages in both fields. On the one hand the government is responsible for these troubles; on the other hand it has a part in their solution through the diversion of purchasing power involved in war finance. Simultaneously, it has to distribute the financial burden of war in one way or another over the various classes of people.

But in modern wars, the roles of government in the war economy are not exhausted with the giving of orders for materials and collecting purchasing power. Much more intricate functions have to be fulfilled in the control of production and distribution, such as the fixing of priorities, price control, and rationing. We shall see whether or not far-reaching government interventions into the economic system can be avoided. As in general economics, our foremost point of inquiry has to be: How can the available human and material resources be put to the most effective use, or how can the maximum return be obtained from the economic effort of the belligerent nation?

War does not affect only one single national economy. It is an international event. Therefore, in Part III, we shall consider the international aspects of war economics. Economic relations between enemies are largely interrupted, with complete and undisguised warfare taking the place of commercial conflict or forms of partial warfare practiced before the outbreak of hostilities. Allies, however, will draw closer together. New commercial and financial relations will come into existence. Special problems of international war economics are raised by the existence of neutral countries. Neutrals play a role, sometimes a very important one, in the war economy of the belligerents. On the other hand, the neutrals' economic system is affected by war shocks of various kinds.

The end of the war brings the end of war economics. An adjustment to peace conditions has to be attempted. But the economy emerging from the war will differ from that preceding the war, just as the war-scarred veteran differs from the young recruit. Part IV will deal with the postwar economics. War has left its deep impression on the population. Marriages have been postponed, children who would have been born had there been no war have not seen the light of day; invalids have returned from the battlefields. Similarly, the nation's real capital has suffered. Railroads have deteriorated, houses have been left unrepaired. Territorial gains or losses affect both human and material resources. A system of internal and external debts is inherited by the postwar generation. Industry emerges from war with a structure ill-adapted to peace conditions; trade relations have been disrupted and pressed into abnormal channels. All these conditions present grave problems. The problems may be solved; or, left unsolved, they may lead to depressions and new international conflagrations.

This in brief is the outline of the course our discussion will take. In following it, we shall draw on factual material of present and past wars.

SUGGESTED REFERENCES

(Clark, J. M., Hamilton, W. H., and Moulton, H. G.; editors):
Readings in the Economics of War, Chicago, 1918, chapter VIII, articles 1 and 2.

Sombart, W.: *Krieg und Kapitalismus,* Munich, 1913.

PART ONE

WHAT A WARRING NATION NEEDS
(The Economic War Potential)

CHAPTER 1

Man Power

The significance of the human war potential cannot be overestimated. Of all prerequisites to successful warfare a strong population was earliest recognized by governments. In the seventeenth and eighteenth centuries European princes undertook population censuses in order to ascertain the human war potential at their disposal. While these rulers were mostly interested in the available number of recruits, today nations view population as a war potential from two sides: how many *soldiers* and how many *producers* has a nation at its disposal? In our times too, the interest of bellicose governments in large population is obvious. Varied measures are designed to stimulate marriage and procreation such as marriage loans and benefits to large families in countries like Germany and Italy. There is of course no *necessary* correlation between such policies and belligerent, imperialistic intentions. Yet in the cases mentioned a correlation is generally believed to exist.

SIZE AND COMPOSITION OF THE POPULATION

At first glance, it would seem appropriate in a discussion of national population power to start with the total population of the nation. Yet this may not be the total reservoir of human forces. Obviously, nations that possess colonies may draw on those populations for working and fighting purposes. This indeed is an established practice. During the World War Britain and France used numbers of Indian and North African men on the battlefields and in factories. It is not even necessary that these auxiliary forces be drawn from regular colonies; they may be taken from allied, subjugated, or "protected" countries, or from the enemy, as prisoners of war. In 1918, for example, sixteen and four tenths per cent of the coal miners in the German Ruhr district were prisoners of war. In addition, deported or freely hired workers from the occupied areas in Belgium and France were employed.[1] In the present European war, Germany uses more than one million Polish laborers on German farms and numerous Czech workers in industrial plants. In June, 1940, she began importing thousands of Danish unemployed workers. Plans were under way for employing Greek workers in French factories.

Let us concentrate our attention on the population of the belligerent country proper. Other factors being equal, we may say that the larger a country's population, the greater its war potential. Since there is work of tremendous magnitude to be done at home and at the front, the larger the number of people over whom it can be spread the better.

If we look a little closer into the matter, we see that it is not all of a country's population that constitutes an asset for war purposes. One might perhaps say that in order to be ideal for the purposes of a war a population should consist of men only, twenty to fifty years of age and trained in all essential civil or military occupations. Unfortunately, such a population would be rather short-lived and uninteresting. No general staff can sidestep the fact that the nation will go to war with roughly fifty per cent females (of all ages) and about another twenty-five per cent of boys and old men.

---

[1] F. Friedensburg: *Kohle und Eisen im Weltkriege und in den Friedensschlüssen*, Berlin, 1934, 66, and F. Passelecq: *Déportation et Travail Forcé des Ouvriers et de la Population Civile de la Belgique Occupée (1916–1918)*, Paris, 1928, *passim.* See also below, p. 107.

Only about twenty-five per cent of the total population will ordinarily consist of men of the best working and fighting age.[2] (Let us define the working age interval as from fifteen to forty-nine years. This is a rough approximation of reality.)

Still it would not be entirely correct to say that these twenty-five per cent alone represent the nation's human reservoir for warfare. Most of the women and a good number of the old, perhaps even some of the children, may contribute to the productive effort at home. As a verse popular in Civil War times put it:

> Just take your gun and go,
> For Ruth can drive the oxen, John,
> And I can use the hoe.

During the World War, many women gave up all or part of their household work to hold jobs on farms, in factories, and in transportation systems—jobs that had previously been held by men. Others, in particular old people, devoted time to knitting warm clothes for soldiers. In Germany, children collected waste materials, as they do once more in Nazi Germany. Youngsters, oldsters, and women are even drawn into military occupations. Women are employed in the ambulance service; Soviet Russia is reported to have female fighting units; in several countries women and old men act as air raid wardens; and toward the end of the World War, the German army enrolled even boys seventeen years of age for active service. Therefore, we may come closer to the facts by assuming that in addition to the nucleus of twenty-five per cent of able-bodied men at least another twenty-five per cent of the total population is available for

---

[2] The percentage of men fifteen to forty-nine years old in the total population: United States (1935): 27 per cent, Greater Germany (1938) and United Kingdom (1937): 26 per cent, Italy (1936) and France (1936): 24 per cent. (Source: *Statistical Yearbook of the League of Nations, 1938/39*, 32–34.)

productive and military service. The remaining group of fifty per cent or less, consisting of children and old people, largely constitutes a burden as far as the economics of war are concerned.

Actual populations differ in still another respect from the military ideal. The able-bodied men and women are not equally able to take up every occupation, military or peaceful. Most of them are trained or at least accustomed to particular jobs. In part, these jobs are necessary in war as well as in peace. This is particularly true for productive occupations in the narrower sense of the word: farming, mining, manufacturing, and transportation. The situation is sometimes different with respect to certain occupations in trade. Here we find, under the prevailing conditions of imperfect competition, a number of occupied people that appears excessive when most effective utilization of man power is sought. Therefore, one problem is how to direct people from service and trade occupations into tasks more important for the war economy. Even in production proper, considerable shifts of employees may become necessary in war. In Great Britain from 1914 to 1918, for instance, the following increases and decreases occurred in the number of employees:

PERCENTAGE CHANGE IN THE NUMBER OF EMPLOYEES IN GREAT BRITAIN,[3] 1914 TO 1918

	Males	Females	Total
Government services [4]	+52	+634	+151
Metal industries	+21	+279	+ 57
Commerce	−35	+ 88	+ 6
Transportation	−20	+602	+ 4
Hotels, theaters	−38	+ 32	− 5
Textile industries	−29	+ 4	− 10
Building	−48	+361	− 42

[3] H. Makower and H. W. Robinson: "Labour Potential in War-Time," *Economic Journal*, December, 1939, 659.
[4] Including arsenals, docks.

In fields like government services and metal industries the number of both male and female employees increased. In commerce, transportation, hotels, and theaters, the increase in the number of female workers approximately offset the decline in the number of males, while in the textile industry and particularly in building it did not, so that the total number showed a decline. Assuming the same relative changes in employment as then and a need of calling 3,800,000 men to arms, Makower and Robinson set up the following estimate for the present war: As compared with the peace year of 1938, about 4,100,000 women would have to enter British industry, while 3,000,000 employed men would have to leave it, joined by 800,000 unemployed, to form the fighting forces. This brings us to a problem of first importance, namely, the diversion of people from peacetime to military occupations. How shall the able-bodied population be divided between front and workshop in order to ensure the most effective utilization of the human war potential?

The answer depends on various factors. First, what kind of warfare is contemplated? Are military operations planned to be predominantly aggressive or defensive over a certain period of time? What is the enemy's strength? Second, to what extent must the country rely on its own output for the feeding of the war machine, to what extent can allies or neutrals be counted upon? The answers to these questions, which obviously can only be estimates, determine the proportion of people to be mobilized. Various estimates have been made of the ratio between the number of soldiers and the number of workers at home necessary to supply army and civilian population with products. They range between 1:5 and 1:20. For the United States during the World War this ratio seems to have been in the neighborhood of 1:8.[5]

---

[5] S. T. Possony: *To-Morrow's War*, London, 1938, 93 ff. See also below, p. 97.

In order to get some idea of the magnitude of the military drain on a country's human resources let us look at the figures for the first world war. According to estimates of the United States War Department, the number of mobilized men during the years 1914 to 1918 was approximately as follows:

NUMBER OF MOBILIZED MEN
1914 TO 1918 [6]

Germany	11,000,000
Total, Central Powers	22,800,000
British Empire	8,900,000
France	8,400,000
Russia	12,000,000
Italy (from 1915 on)	5,600,000
United States (from 1917 on)	4,400,000
Total, Allied Powers	42,200,000
Grand Total	65,000,000

In other words, Germany had about eighteen per cent of her total population under arms, France twenty-one per cent, the British Empire (considering whites only) sixteen per cent, and the United States four per cent. Remembering that the number of men of working and fighting age amounts to about twenty-five per cent of a population, we find that in France and Germany only about one fourth of this nucleus was left at the disposition of the war economy; in the United States, much less affected by the war, more than three quarters of the population nucleus was left to productive tasks.

Returning to the division of a country's population into occupational groups, we face this question: Is there any optimum distribution by occupations as far as the needs of the war economy are concerned? One can answer this question in the affirmative; but to determine what this optimum distribution is remains a hard task. Again, scale and

---

[6] Source: *World Almanac*, 1938, 702.

type of warfare, geographical position, and many other factors would have to be considered in order to reach an approximately exact answer. Generally speaking, one can underline the importance of a large force of skilled industrial workers. They are needed in the production as well as the use of modern fighting equipment.

Modern mechanized armies require men familiar with the use of automobiles, trucks, and airplanes. To provide these armies with the necessary quantities of standardized guns, shells, tanks, and so forth, workers are needed who are well trained in the operation of semiautomatic machines. Industrially developed countries will on the whole have an advantage over predominantly agricultural countries in this respect. The 130 million Americans of today can furnish more of these qualities than the 170 million inhabitants of Soviet Russia.

Apart from the size of the population and its distribution by age and by occupations, other elements play a role in determining the population war potential of a nation. Let us now consider the density of the population, its general working efficiency, and its political homogeneity.

Density, Productive Efficiency, and Political Homogeneity of the Population

At first glance it appears difficult to state whether a densely or a sparsely distributed population is more advantageous for war purposes. In densely populated countries, which usually are countries of highly developed industry or intensive agriculture, the process of military mobilization can be carried out more quickly. Forces for defense or attack can be concentrated in a shorter time. On the other hand, such countries are generally more vulnerable to aerial attacks. Huge, sparsely populated spaces like those of Russia have in the past proved to be obstacles to invasion, and the absence of communications due to swamps and deserts are probably still today hindrances in the way of a mechanized invader. Of course, these obstacles are just as bothersome for the massing of attacking forces. This could be observed for instance in the Russo-Finnish war of 1939. Consequently, in order to appreciate the advantages and disadvantages of a dense population we find ourselves again referred to the type of war to be waged and other specific circumstances.

It is easier to evaluate the role of the *productivity of labor*.[7] The more the average worker of a country is able to produce per day, the more will the country's population weigh on the scale of war potential. Strictly speaking, we would have to count as two men a worker who in a day's work produces an output double that of another worker in the same occupation. There are quite considerable differences in industrial productivity between nations. Such differences may be due to differences in industrial training and work discipline, in workers' health and coöperation, managerial ability and other *subjective* factors. They may also be caused by *objective* factors such as differences in equipment at the disposal of the worker or by differences in working hours. Again, industrialized nations will have an advantage; but it is certain that even in such nations special attention has to be devoted to improvements of productivity. We shall come back to this problem in Part II of this book.

Finally there is *political homogeneity*. It is obvious that a people unanimously supporting the warfare of its government will produce a war effort superior to that of an equally strong but politically divided nation. Lack of political unity in a nation may be due to the presence of subjugated minorities or social classes or to other factors. The pres-

---

[7] Here, and in the following, the (general) productivity of labor in a given country is defined as the volume of output of a unit of average human labor performed under conditions of training and equipment customary in the country.

ence of a large politically and economically unsatisfied peasant class in Poland and of suppressed minorities such as the Ukrainians contributed to the weakness of the former Polish state. The deep-rooted disagreement between the Flemish and the Walloons weakened the war-waging power of the Belgian nation.

Lack of political agreement on the war aims is frequently found where a dominant country draws its colonies into the war. Colonies that are involved in a struggle for independence are likely to manifest their opposition to the "motherland's" policy. A good example is British India. With its population of 350 million people—about double that of all the remaining British Empire—India represents a tremendous potential force. Nevertheless, it does not appear that Britain is able to mobilize a significant part of this force in a military or economic sense. The reason lies in the fact that India wants to become independent, while the British government has not even granted her dominion status.[8] It is reported that the leaders of the Indian movement for independence resented Britain's declaring war on Germany "in the name of India," and threatened passive resistance. Furthermore, Britain has failed to stimulate the development of essential war industries in India.

Keeping in mind the factors, aside from mere numbers, that make for a country's population power, let us look at the first two lines of Table I in the Appendix showing the number of people at the disposal of various powers and power groups.

With 91 millions, Greater Germany possesses a population about equal to the white population of the United Kingdom and the French empire taken together. The inclusion of the remaining peoples of these and the Belgian and Dutch empires would have given the Western powers

---
[8] In August, 1940, India was promised "free and equal partnership" in the British commonwealth at the conclusion of the present war.

a decided superiority in numbers. But it seems very problematic to what extent the 600 million colored people in these empires can be counted upon in the war with Germany. The defeat of France in 1940 has eliminated 42 million Frenchmen from the western phalanx and rendered the position of the 70 million people in the French colonies highly uncertain. Germany, on the other side, might be able to put to use about 100 million people in conquered countries, plus 44 million Italians and any allies she might find in the future. As long as the fronts are not finally formed and the degree of coöperation of colonial and conquered peoples with the main powers not definitely determined, it remains difficult to say which side in the present war possesses the larger population power. But it is certain that within the boundaries of Europe Germany and Italy have an overwhelming superiority over England.

SUGGESTED REFERENCES

Clark, J. M.: *The Costs of the World War to the American People,* New Haven, 1931, chapters X and XI.
(Speier, H. and Kähler, A.; editors): *War in Our Time,* New York, 1939, chapters IV and XII.
What Would Be the Character of a New War? Enquiry organized by the Inter-Parliamentary Union, Geneva, New York, 1933, chapter III.

CHAPTER 2

Raw Materials and the Problem of Substitutes

It is universally recognized that the economic strength of a nation at peace, and much more so when at war, depends on the raw material resources at its disposal. There can be no doubt that a country having access to all the materials necessary for its industries is in a stronger position than another which may find its supplies limited. Such statements appear commonplace. The logical conclusion then would be merely to list the treasures of raw materials at the command of the various nations and to compare them.

But our problem does not resolve itself so easily. Looking a bit under the surface, we find ourselves faced by some arresting questions. What is a raw material? What is an accessible raw material? Can a nation not do without a certain material by using regenerated substances or substitutes? These questions make us realize that our problem is much more intricate than it seemed at first glance. But we must not shy away from such complications; for there is not much use in finding all-too-simple answers to imaginary all-too-simple problems. Unfortunately, in this survey we must be brief. The reader interested in a more complete discussion of specific raw material problems is therefore referred to the plentiful literature on this subject. A partial bibliography appears at the end of this chapter.[1]

---

[1] The comprehensive studies of Ferdinand Friedensburg: *Die Mineralischen Bodenschätze als Weltpolitische und Militärische Machtfaktoren*, Stuttgart, 1936, and of B. Emeny: *The Strategy of Raw Materials*, New York, 1937, merit particular attention.

What Is a Raw Material?

Let us now look at the first of our four questions: What is a raw material? We may start with a classification. Usually we distinguish between basic foodstuffs and basic industrial materials. Basic *foodstuffs* (as fish, game, and wild fruit) are obtained by collecting certain gifts of nature. Other basic foodstuffs (as farm products) are obtained by certain processes of transformation. The most important raw materials of the foodstuff variety are grains, potatoes and other vegetables, fruits, meats, dairy products, coffee, sugar, tea, and vegetable fats. Basic *industrial* materials are largely obtained by collection processes, such as mining. Some, however, come into being by means of transformation processes, in agriculture or other lines. The list of important industrial raw materials is long and varied. It may be subdivided into the metallic minerals, including the various metal ores, the nonmetallic minerals, and finally the organic substances. Among the nonmetallic minerals are those of the fuel category, as, for example, coal and oil; and those of the fertilizer group, such as phosphates, nitrates. The organic substances include such materials as timber, rubber, fibers (wool, cotton, silk, hemp, sisal, and so forth), hides, animal foods, and medicinal materials.

But are these items used as raw materials in all types of societies and at all times? This is certainly not the case.

While 80 million *Japanese* will point today to the necessity for large supplies of gasoline and crude oil, the present 80 million *Javanese* may easily get along without them. While Eskimos will insist on fish as the essential component of their diet, the Hindus may not care to have any, and *vice versa* with rice. . . . In 1850, Chilean saltpeter as fertilizer was practically worthless; in 1900 it was an invaluable treasure of international importance; by 1920 it was on its way to oblivion.[2]

---

[2] K. Brandt: "Foodstuffs and Raw Materials," in *War in Our Time* (H. Speier and A. Kähler; editors), New York: W. W. Norton & Company, 1939, 106–107.

These and many other instances show that certain articles are important raw materials only at certain times and in certain types of society. As the economic system changes, the list of important raw materials is transformed. Materials which have been merely uninteresting, or even bothersome, become important bases of industry: "In the sixties of the last century the State of Pennsylvania passed laws against the pollution of creeks and rivers with gasoline, which was then a useless waste product; only kerosene counted, which is today itself a by-product." [3]

Dealing with the nations most industrially advanced today, we find our problem relatively simplified. The industries of these countries use more or less the same materials. Therefore, in comparing their respective war potentials in raw materials, we may consider a well-circumscribed group of articles. Yet when we come to the problem of substitutes, we shall face again the dynamic character of the list of important raw materials.

What Is an Accessible Raw Material?

In general, we may say that an accessible raw material is any material found in the territory of the nation. This holds true at least when the national territory is not invaded, nor made unsuitable for production through enemy action. Of course this may happen. During the first world war, France and Belgium were largely unable to exploit their iron ore and coal mines in the regions invaded by Germany, while in the beginning of the present war the coal mines of the Saar territory, lying under the guns of the Maginot line, were kept idle. In 1914 to 1918, however, a most astonishing feature of warfare was the apparent reluctance of both

---

My italics. (Only 71.5 million people are supposed to have populated Japan, 67.4 million the whole of the Netherlands Indies, at the end of 1937. Cf. *Statistical Yearbook of the League of Nations, 1938–39,* 17.)

[3] *Ibid.,* 108.

belligerent sides to subject the enemy's heavy industries to artillery or aerial bombardment.[4]

However, presence of a certain material within the territory of a nation may have more than one meaning. The exploitability of resources depends on their location, considered along with the value of the product, their concentration and physical accessibility, and the technique of exploitation. We shall see, for example, that exploitable deposits of aluminum ore (bauxite) are relatively few. Yet as much as eight per cent of all mineral substances on earth is metallic aluminum.[5] The difficulty is that the present technique does not permit an economical use of these widely distributed riches.

Are materials located in colonies or territories of allied or neutral nations accessible to the belligerent? In peace times, there are no difficulties in importing raw materials from abroad as long as the importer is willing to pay their price. In war times, however, transportation is obstructed by blockade, the lack of shipping tonnage, and the congestion of railroads. Lack of control of sea lanes may jeopardize imports from colonies or neutral sources. This was the situation in which Germany found herself during the first world war. Her direct imports of copper, cotton, and foodstuffs from overseas were eliminated by the British blockade. Since it is not always certain which side will control the sea lanes, estimates of a nation's raw-material potential that take account of its colonial possessions are necessarily somewhat uncertain.

Restricted quantities of foreign raw materials may be *made* accessible for a war emergency through excessive imports in peace times and the building up of more than normal stocks. Importers or traders of raw materials usually have stocks on hand. In addition, the government may

---

[4] P. Noel-Baker: *The Private Manufacture of Armaments*, New York, 1937, 42–46.
[5] Friedensburg: *op. cit.*, 40.

set up special schemes. Government-supported storing of imported raw materials of all kinds is reported to have taken place in Germany on a large scale. Great Britain had accumulated a little more than normal stocks of wheat, oil, and other materials during the year preceding the present war, and even some neutrals have followed this policy. Of Italy it has been said that in order to be able to follow an independent war policy she would have to stock an amount of coal corresponding to at least one year's consumption,[6] not to speak of oil, fats, and other important materials. In this country, the War Department set up a list of *strategic raw materials* of which more than normal imports were recommended. In a critical analysis of this list, Brooks Emeny came to the conclusion that purchase of a large stock would be particularly justified in the cases of manganese, chromite, and tin, and to a lesser extent for antimony and tungsten. For a number of other materials, such as rubber, mercury, mica, Manila and other fibers, and hides, Emeny suggested a continuous checking of commercial stocks in order to avoid the danger of subnormal provisions in case of emergency.[7] At present (summer, 1940) emergency re-

---

[6] At present that would amount to about seven times her domestic output.

[7] B. Emeny: *The Strategy of Raw Materials*, New York, 1937, 166–167 and *passim*.

On January 30, 1940, the *Army and Navy Munitions Board* approved the following definitions and lists of strategic and critical materials:

Strategic materials: Strategic materials are those essential to national defense, for the supply of which in war dependence must be placed in whole, or in substantial part, on sources outside the continental limits of the United States; and for which strict conservation and distribution control measures will be necessary.

Critical materials: Critical materials are those essential to national defense, the procurement problems of which in war would be less difficult than those of strategic materials either because they have a lesser degree of essentiality or are obtainable in more adequate quantities from domestic sources; and for which some degree of conservation and distribution control will be necessary.

Strategic materials (14)

Antimony	Mercury	Rubber
Chromium	Mica	Silk
Coconut Shell Char	Nickel	Tin
Manganese, ferrograde	Quartz Crystal	Tungsten
Manila Fiber	Quinine	

serves are being formed on the initiative of the Federal Government. In July, the Government in coöperation with rubber manufacturers set up a special corporation for the purchasing, storing, and handling of a rubber reserve.[8] Before the first world war, formation of special stocks of materials does not seem to have taken place in any of the major belligerent countries.

Regeneration of Used Materials

Can a nation not do without certain raw materials by using regenerated substances or substitutes instead? Let us look first at the possibilities of replacing raw materials by regenerated substances. Such possibilities exist in a good many fields. Iron ore, for instance, may be replaced by scrap iron. Even in peace times, scrap iron is used in the making of new iron and steel. Certain changes of the production process are required when the proportion of ore and scrap is changed; but the technical possibility exists. Industrially developed countries generally have a considerable supply of scrap iron on hand and are thus able to help themselves over a shortage or ore, at least for some time. A certain amount of old iron may even be collected from battlefields that are filled with enemy shells and destroyed equipment. During the first world war, transition of steel production from an ore to a scrap basis made it possible for France to continue producing steel after the loss of her

---

Critical materials (15)

Aluminum	Iodine	Platinum
Asbestos	Kapok	Tanning materials
Cork	Opium	Toluol
Graphite	Optical Glass	Vanadium
Hides	Phenol	Wool

For a discussion of the situation with respect to these materials, see Army and Navy Munitions Board: *The Strategic and Critical Materials* (mimeographed), Washington, D. C., March, 1940.

[8] *The New York Times*, July 7, 1940, Financial Section.

mines and blast furnaces in the east and northeast, while England and Germany were enabled to keep their steel output on a higher level than their declining pig-iron production would have permitted.[9]

Another example can be found in the case of rubber, which is of particular interest to the United States. For its supply of crude natural rubber this country is entirely dependent on overseas sources: the Malay States, the Netherlands Indies, Ceylon, and Brazil. Yet for a relatively short war emergency, the huge domestic stocks of old rubber together with other domestic sources may well suffice.[10] A similar situation may be found in some other fields.

Substitutes

Another, and perhaps a more interesting, way of replacing a customary raw material is by substitution. A raw material may be found to take the place of the one previously used, or synthetic production of an article resembling the old one may be taken up. There are, however, certain erroneous ideas in this connection. Substitution is sometimes considered as a process by which a good and cheap article is replaced by something of either lower quality or higher price, or both; and many people look with suspicion on the substitute articles, often designated by the German word *Ersatz*. We should realize that there is by no means a necessary correlation between the introduction of substitute articles and inferior quality or higher price. On the contrary, a good deal of what we call "technical progress" is nothing but a sequence of substitutions, in the field of raw materials as well as elsewhere.

As we have seen before, the list of goods destined for

---

[9] F. Friedensburg: *Kohle und Eisen im Weltkriege und in den Friedensschlüssen*, Berlin, 1934, 70.
[10] Emeny, *op. cit.*, 132–138.

human or industrial consumption is not fixed once and for all. In peace times, a dynamic economy shows a bewildering variety of substitution processes. Generally speaking, a raw material is replaced by another or by a synthetic product of equal quality when the new article becomes relatively cheaper through the development of resources or techniques that lower its cost of production or distribution, or as a result of an increase in demand. When cotton cloth became cheaper than woolen cloth during the eighteenth and early nineteenth century, it replaced wool to a great extent. The water frame, the cotton gin, the steam engine, and other factors led to this development. But cotton in turn did not remain king forever. In rayon it found a powerful competitor and substitute. Similarly, coke was substituted for charcoal in the smelting of iron ore. Water as a direct source of power gave way to coal-generated steam; electricity replaced steam power in many fields; and water power finally found a new usefulness in generating electricity. Tomorrow, "Uranium 235" may lead to an elimination of coal and oil as sources of energy.

It is frequently held that such peacetime substitution processes are of an entirely different character from those attempted in the preparation for war or during a war. Substitutes for war purposes, it is said, provide neither cheaper nor better articles. They are just makeshifts that can find a market only because of tariff or other protection in peacetime and the absence of competing imports during war. Can we accept such a statement?

The statement is too sweeping. It is true that in the emergency of war substitutes have been devised without regard for cost or qualitative requirements. Thus substitutes used for copper and nickel during the first world war in the making of German ammunitions, substitute greasing materials, and substitute foods proved to be of inferior quality. But on the other hand two facts must be stressed.

First, experience shows that under prewar and war conditions certain substitutes have been developed which, after a short period of experimentation, were acceptable from the points of view of quality or price, or both. Second, it is dubious whether the usual peacetime criteria of economical production can be applied at all under war conditions. These arguments deserve examination.

First, there are cases in which substitutes have taken the place of former materials because of their qualitative superiority or comparative cheapness. One example may be found in the field of synthetic nitrates, the production of which was markedly developed during the World War in beleaguered Germany. Made out of air, they replaced Chilean nitrates successfully during and after the war, in both the German and other markets. Another example is synthetic rubber. During recent years, Germany's chemists developed the so-called *Buna* which is supposed to be superior, in certain respects, to natural rubber, while costs do not seem to be extraordinarily high. The article is manufactured out of coal, chalk, and other materials. The interest which this synthetic product had created in England and in this country before the outbreak of the present war makes it not unlikely that a good substitute, satisfactory in cost and quality, will finally emerge. Other examples may be found.

It should be noted in this connection that numerous circumstances have to be taken into account in determining the price differential of a customary raw material and its substitute. If the two articles are not produced under unit costs that are independent of output, the volume of output enters as a determining variable. While the cost of production of the substitute may be excessive at an output X, it may be cheaper at a larger output, say 2X. Furthermore, it matters whether the raw material is produced under competitive or monopolistic conditions. It is reported in *The New York Times* [11] that the present cost of production of crude rubber is around six or seven cents a pound, while the selling price in this country is about twenty-two cents. Monopolistic conditions control the production of crude rubber in the Far East. The same report asserts that American producers of synthetic rubber could operate profitably at a market price of twenty-two cents, but not at six or seven cents. They could compete with the rubber monopoly in the Far East if the latter maintained its present selling price; but they might not be able to stand a price war on the level of six or seven cents. In the first case, synthetic rubber would appear an acceptable substitute; in the second case, it would not—if only for the reason that the crude-rubber monopoly could undersell it at will. Finally, the selling price of the raw material may fluctuate considerably with business conditions; the price of rubber, for instance, fluctuated during the last twenty years between three cents and $1.50. Under such circumstances the analysis of the price differential between two materials cannot result in a clear-cut general answer. Only conditional answers can be given, based on certain assumptions with respect to volume of output, trade practices, and general business conditions.

Subsidization of Substitute Products

Second, there is the question whether peacetime criteria of economical production should be applied under war conditions. Let us first define what we mean by peacetime criteria of economical production. In an economic system like ours the decisive questions asked by the producer before embarking on the production of a new article are: *Will it bring a profit? Will this profit stand comparison with profits I might earn in other fields?* Profitability is

---
[11] June 9, 1940, Financial Section.

sought in each and every economic pursuit. Where it cannot be found, projects are discarded. What are the factors determining the profitability of production? They are the price of the product and the costs of producing it. The price of the product depends, in part, on the valuations which purchasers set on the product, the costs, on the valuations which producers set on the factors of production. Under a system of private enterprise these valuations tend to be faulty from a social point of view. Individual purchasers take account of their individual wants; but they neglect any collective wants that may exist besides. An individual purchaser of gasoline may have perfect knowledge of what a certain quantity of gasoline is worth to him in comparison with quantities of other consumption goods; but he will probably fail to take into account a national need of enlarged gasoline production for defense purposes. It is characteristic of typically collective wants that they can only be satisfied for all individuals making up society (or a social group) or for nobody. Once they are satisfied, it is impossible to exclude anybody from benefiting.[12]

Similarly, individual producers take account of the cost items they have to pay for; but they do not take account of any costs to society which do not find expression in their own cost accounts. An individual producer of private cars who refuses to build military airplanes does not include in the production costs of the cars an allowance for the loss of security that his action causes to the nation as a whole.[13] The failure of collective wants and costs to find expression in the prices under a system of private enterprise renders

---

[12] Examples of essentially collective wants are national security, traffic security, a high general educational standard. Satisfaction of these always requires state intervention. *Cf.* G. Cassel: *The Theory of Social Economy*, New York, 1924, 66–72.

[13] Examples of essentially collective costs are the upkeep of the unemployed and disabled, losses due to insufficient preparation for natural and social catastrophes. See also A. C. Pigou: *The Economics of Welfare*, London, 1932, chapter IX.

the price system imperfect. This imperfection may be tolerated by society as long as the neglected social considerations are of minor importance; but society cannot suffer it in times of war—or of preparation for war—when collective wants and costs overshadow individual wants and individual producers' costs.

For society as a whole production of a commodity is economically reasonable if the *social* valuation of output exceeds *social* costs at the margin, where social valuations (costs) represent the *sum* of private and collective valuations (costs). For certain production processes the *social* valuation of output may exceed *social* costs while the *private* valuation of output falls short of *private* costs. From a social point of view it is desirable to carry out these processes in spite of the fact that they cause losses to the individual producer. It is obvious that subsidization out of public funds has to be employed in order to induce the individual producer to operate on a deficit basis. He cannot in fairness be expected to carry the entire loss caused by the imperfection of the price system. This loss has to be distributed in some way over all members of society.

To give an example: Germany produces synthetic gasoline from coal. Probably this gasoline is no better than that derived from natural oil and actually is more expensive. Germany, however, possesses very small supplies of natural oil and is dependent on foreign resources. Some of these, in Rumania and Russia, can be reached by land or river routes. But on the whole, Germany's oil supply is considered highly precarious. We know that oil is a very important raw material in a modern economy, and in particular for a modern army, air force, and navy. A Germany preparing for war should therefore be expected to pay a much higher price for domestically produced gasoline than the prevailing world price. Since, however, such exorbitant gasoline prices would have seriously curtailed gasoline consumption and civilian motorization, the government had to subsidize the synthetic production of gasoline. It had to help carry on a losing business at the expense of other parts of the economic system. In this particular case, the distribution of the losses was partly effectuated by duties on imported gasoline, partly by other revenue measures. A limited increase in the price and a corresponding restriction of the private consumption of gasoline were accepted. It was logical to start this whole process in times of peace, so that production experience would be acquired and plants would be ready in wartime.

Generally speaking, we find that if the aim of economic policy lies in the optimum preparation for war conditions or in certain other specific directions, unprofitable industries may very well be tolerated. One might classify them along with fortifications and other military investments, which do not possess peacetime economic value yet constitute necessary equipment in a world of limited peacefulness.

Of course, it must not be forgotten that production at a deficit means the sacrifice of other more economical possibilities. When artificial wool is made out of wood in a deficit process, a profitable use of wood for building or other purposes may be forsaken. The more deficit operations a country affords, the more sacrifices it will have to make. From the point of view of the war economy, limits for "deficit substitute production" are reached when other essential needs begin to suffer. In other words, if substitutes must be produced uneconomically under present cost conditions, it has to be ascertained whether and to what extent high-ranking needs on the scale of war essentials would be jeopardized by such a program. A tragi-comic situation would have arisen, for example, if Germany's production of *Zellwolle* out of wood had called forth an over-all shortage of timber and made necessary voluminous timber imports over sea lanes controlled by Great Britain. Fortunately for the German government, the timber problem had been solved through the annexation of Austria and Czechoslovakia and the invasion of Poland and Norway. Before these expansions took place, the German timber situation was rather serious. Up to twenty-five per cent of peacetime domestic consumption depended on imports from abroad (1937); and "mining" of domestic forests appeared to be the only solution in case of a major war on two fronts.

We come to the conclusion that serious thought has to be given to the problem of substitutes. To a country that in times of war is cut off from raw material supplies the development of substitutes may be a question of life and death. It should be attacked with the whole economic structure of the country in mind and with the aim of evolving as economical substitutes as possible. A country, on the other hand, that counts on keeping open its peacetime sources of supplies, has no urgent problem of substitutes. Still, such a country should not entirely neglect the possibilities of substitutes. For we remember that some substitute articles represent important technical advances. A rich country forsaking such possibilities, because of lack of initiative on the part of its industrialists or because of monopolistic restraints, renounces chances of rendering its economy more efficient. And in the struggle of empires every little bit of efficiency that can be thrown into the balance will count.

Resources of Certain Powers

After having examined the general problems of raw materials and substitutes, let us now turn to the actual resources of particular powers. We cannot attempt to give a comprehensive survey. Only the high lights of the situation will be shown.

How shall we measure the raw material power of different countries? The problem may be approached from several different angles, each one providing us with a particular kind of information. First, we might measure, at least as far as minerals are concerned, the national treasures in the subsoil. Two factors, however, militate against such a procedure: (1) our knowledge of the quantity and quality of subsoil resources is generally vague; (2) these treasures do not determine exclusively the amount of raw materials available over a short period of time, and from the point of view of the war potential it is only the short period that counts. For a few years a country relatively poor in resources might well compete in output with a rich country by imposing a higher rate of exploitation.

Second, we might measure the national *output* of raw materials, taking data from recent peace years that showed a high degree of business activity. In this way we would attempt to estimate the productive capacity in various materials. This attempt has been made in Table I of the Appendix. In defense of such a procedure it could be said that warring nations are generally unable to dig new mines or to enlarge their agricultural output significantly in a short wartime period. Therefore, their productive capacity will generally not greatly exceed the maximum output reached shortly before the war. However, productive capacity is not the only factor we are interested in. We might like to know how this capacity compares with the needs of various countries for raw materials. In that case, we should supplement our information on output capacity by data on the degree of self-sufficiency in certain raw materials.

This is indeed a third way of measuring the raw material power of different countries. But it involves considerable difficulties. Suppose we know peacetime output and peacetime consumption of a certain material in a country. These data will tell us something about the degree of self-sufficiency in peace times. Can we draw conclusions from that about the degree of self-sufficiency under conditions of war? This is highly questionable.

First, the degree of self-sufficiency which we compute by comparing domestic output and domestic consumption of a certain article in a certain country may be apparent only. Suppose, for example, that in a large country one region possesses large supplies of coal while a far distant region is rich in iron ore. Transportation of these bulky materials from one region to the other is highly expensive. But there may be a foreign country adjacent to our coal region which is in need of the coal, while our iron-ore region adjoins a foreign country with large coal supplies. Then, under conditions of free trade, or reasonably free trade, our country may be apparently self-sufficient in coal and iron ore while in practice all of its coal is exported and all of its iron ore is imported. If such a country were suddenly forced to combine domestic coal and iron ore, tremendous problems would arise. Costs of iron smelting would increase, transportation difficulties would appear. Conditions of this kind can easily occur.

Second, apart from the fact that a certain area rich in materials may fall into the hands of the enemy or be put out of use through its proximity to military operations, the war situation may deeply influence production or need. Thus, in peace times, England is certainly more than self-sufficient in coal; nevertheless, she experienced a shortage of coal during the first world war. Many reasons contributed to this surprising situation: rising needs of the domestic war industries and of her allies, mobilization of miners, declining efficiency and strikes of the remaining crews, lowered quality of the coal produced, losses of coal ships, difficulties in obtaining the timber needed in coal mining, and railroad bottlenecks. Consequently, peacetime self-sufficiency may go hand in hand with wartime shortages. As far as foodstuffs are concerned, it has been estimated that in order to be counted as self-sufficient in war, a country would have to produce about 140 per cent of its peacetime consumption, because large-scale military operations are likely to result in a decline of output of about 20 per cent, while needs may well increase by 20 per cent. Such tendencies must be kept in mind.

Foodstuffs

Of the major powers of Europe, Germany and particularly England have to wrestle with serious problems of food supply in times of war. In recent years, England's dependence on imports amounted to about two thirds of her home consumption, Germany's from one fourth to one fifth. Under the Nazi regime, Germany has made desperate efforts to reduce her dependence on foreign foodstuffs; but the result has not been decisive. Serious defects in self-sufficiency still appear, particularly in the field of meats, dairy products, and fats. Germany's expansive moves, however, opened up considerable possibilities of bridging the gap, at least for a short period of time. Denmark and Holland are Europe's larders, Poland is a strong producer of sugar and potatoes (see Table I). It remains to be seen to what extent Germany will be able to extract foodstuffs from these countries. Much will depend on the degree of coöperation she will get from the peasant populations of the invaded territories and on such other factors as the amount of fodder and fertilizer supplies available to the countries of intensive agriculture. But since the farmers in the conquered countries will have to earn a living, production of foodstuffs is not likely to decline enormously. Over and above that, the huge livestock supplies of Denmark, Holland, and France represent a reserve on which the Germans can draw in an emergency by slaughtering without regard to the future.

England's food situation is more serious. In 1934, the following percentages of home consumption had to be imported: wheat flour, 84 per cent; butter and cheese, 83 per cent; sugar, 75 per cent; fruit, 72 per cent; meat, 53 per cent.[14] Only with respect to fresh milk, potatoes, and some vegetables was there anything like self-sufficiency. It is true that the dominions, colonies, Argentina and other neutral countries are well able to satisfy most of England's import needs, but mastery of the seas is a prerequisite for England's imports. The German occupation of Denmark and Holland has cut off important supplies of poultry, bacon, eggs, butter, cheese, meat, and vegetables. And the more perishable these articles are, the more difficult their replacement; for a perishable commodity is not easily shipped over long distances. For various reasons England has not made a major effort to prepare an approximate self-sufficiency in foodstuffs for war times. First of all, the task would be tremendous. Though a good deal of hunting grounds and other waste lands could be brought under the plow, the reduction in import needs would not be significant. Furthermore, England has endeavored to maintain good relations with her dominions, which are agricultural-surplus-producing countries. Another reason lies in the costliness of British crops: Imported wheat and sugar cost about forty per cent less than the home-grown varieties.[15] The burden of tariffs and subsidies on the British economy would be terrific, if an attempt were made to replace all food imports by home-grown produce.

---

[14] J. B. Orr: *Food, Health and Income,* London, 1936, 54.
[15] K. A. H. Murray: "Food Supplies in Peace and War," *Lloyds Bank Limited Monthly Review,* October, 1938, 489.

In the course of the first world war, England was able to increase the share of domestically produced food products. But after the emergency had passed, the area of cultivated land declined again and the country returned to the policy of relying on imports for the satisfaction of the most important food requirements.[16]

Another European country with insufficient domestic food supplies is Italy. In spite of the astonishingly low per capita consumption of "protective" and relatively expensive foods such as meat, milk, butter, and eggs; in spite of repeated "crop battles" of the Fascist regime, serious gaps persist in Italy's supplies of meat and fats.

The United States is actually or potentially self-sufficient with respect to most important foodstuffs.[17] Only with respect to sugar and tropical plant products such as cocoa, coffee, bananas, and tea does a serious need for imports exist. As long as trade lanes to Central and South America can be kept open, there will be no problem at all for the first four of these articles, while tea imports presuppose open lanes to Asia.

Coal and Iron

Coal and iron may be regarded as the most important industrial materials. Coal is needed as fuel and as a source for many other substances such as coke, gas, tar, and tar derivatives. Iron is the leading metal in our modern economies, and it is also the basis of military equipment. The importance of iron for warfare was realized a long time ago:

Amongst other objects of interest which Croesus, king of Lydia, showed to Solon of Athens, was his countless treasure; and to the question as to what he thought of his power, Solon replied, "that he did not consider him powerful on that account,

---

[16] T. H. Middleton: *Food Production in War,* Oxford, 1923, 334 and *passim.*
[17] Emeny, *op. cit.,* 185.

because war was made with iron, and not with gold, and that some one might come who had more iron than he, and would take his gold from him." [18]

While warfare is likely to have stimulated the production and use of coal and iron, these materials in turn have developed and revolutionized the technique of warfare.

A large output of coal and iron is one of the prerequisites for a major power. Looking at Table I, we recognize the leading position of the United States, Germany, and the United Kingdom in the production of coal; that of the United States, Soviet Russia, Germany, Great Britain, and France in the production of pig iron and ferroalloys. But while countries with large coal supplies are likely to have an extended production of pig iron and steel, they do not always have a broad basis of iron ore. Only in a few instances are coal and iron ore found side by side. The huge empires of the United States and Soviet Russia are, in peace times, self-sufficient in coal as well as in iron ore, but the smaller countries show a remarkable inequality in their provisions.

PRODUCTION OF COAL AND IRON ORE
AS PER CENT OF APPARENT CONSUMPTION [19]

Country	Coal	Iron Ore
United States	104	98
Germany	123	30
Great Britain	136	70
France	71	140
U.S.S.R.	103	107
Italy	3	76
Japan	108	65

Great Britain is more than self-sufficient in coal, but has to import large amounts of iron ore from Spain and Scandinavia. The same is true for Germany, the iron-ore de-

---

[18] Niccolò Machiavelli: *The Discourses*, chapter X.
[19] Averages 1925 to 1929, U.S.S.R. 1929 to 1932. Source: Emeny, *op. cit.*, 177.

RAW MATERIALS AND SUBSTITUTES 41

ficiency being only more marked. In recent years, however, efforts have been made in Germany to improve upon the degree of self-sufficiency in iron ore. For the end of 1937 this degree was estimated to lie between forty and forty-five per cent.[20] Exploitation of poor ores has been started on a large scale by government initiative *(Reichshüttenwerke Hermann Göring)*, and this is expected to raise further the percentage of domestic supplies. Before the conquest of France, however, Germany had to deal with a pronounced deficiency in domestic iron ore. Imports from Sweden, exploitation of some fields in Luxemburg and utilization of scrap iron were then expected to fill the gap. Before the German invasion of Norway, Sweden split exports of her high-grade ores between Germany and England in a ratio of approximately two to one. It should be noted that the iron-ore situation of Germany in 1939 was much less favorable than the one which faced Imperial Germany in 1914 to 1918. Then, most of the *Minette* ores of Lorraine were at Germany's disposal. In 1913, Germany produced seventy-six per cent of her iron-ore consumption at home, fifty-six per cent in Lorraine alone.[21]

In France the situation is the opposite. Her deposits in Lorraine give her a strong surplus in iron ore, while the coal fields around Lens near the Belgian frontier are relatively meager. In peace times there used to be a voluminous exchange of iron ore and coal between Germany and France, involving Lorraine as ore supplier, the Saar and Ruhr basins as coal suppliers, and the Rhine with tributaries and canals as a convenient medium of transportation. The recent war between Germany and France, and the occupation of the Lens coal fields made it necessary for France to rely temporarily on English coal, while Germany tried to dispose of some of her surplus coal in Italy. On both sides,

---
[20] H. E. Priester: *Das Deutsche Wirtschaftswunder*, Amsterdam, 1936, 270.
[21] Friedensburg: *Kohle und Eisen* . . . , 135.

difficult problems of transportation appeared. They came, however, to a quick solution through the German victory over France. The iron ore of France is now at Germany's disposal, and the iron works in Lorraine can be supplied with Ruhr coke. Shipments of coal from Germany to Italy are likely to be facilitated by French canals and rivers now available for traffic between the two countries.

Of little quantitative importance but necessary in the production of high-quality steels are the ferroalloys, manganese, chromium, nickel, tungsten, vanadium, and molybdenum. The United States is an important supplier of molybdenum, low-grade manganese and vanadium, Peru of vanadium, Canada of nickel, China of tungsten, Soviet Russia and Brazil of ferro-grade manganese, Rhodesia of chrome ore. These metals are distributed over the world in such a way that no country is self-sufficient in all of them.[22]

OTHER METALS

Among the nonferrous metals, copper, zinc, lead, tin, and aluminum are the most important. They are needed for various peacetime and wartime needs: copper for electric equipment, shell linings, and the like; aluminum and magnesium for lightweight metal in aviation and other fields; tin for canning; zinc and lead in the munitions and chemical industries. How are the various powers provided with the ores of these metals?

In copper, only the United States is self-sufficient, but England and her allies possess important treasures in the Belgian Congo, Rhodesia and other colonies. Germany and Italy have a decided shortage. The German domestic production may satisfy between ten and twenty per cent of the needs. Soviet Russia could help here, but she is far from self-sufficiency herself.

---

[22] See Emeny, *op. cit.*, *passim.*

In zinc, the United States, Germany, and Italy are self-sufficient. Britain has rich deposits of zinc ore in her empire, particularly in Canada and Australia. In lead, the situation is about the same for Britain. Germany and Italy are not self-sufficient, but Yugoslavia holds an important auxiliary position. The United States is about self-sufficient.

None of the major powers is self-sufficient in tin, the world's supplies coming mostly from the Malay States, the Netherlands Indies, and Bolivia.

In aluminum ore, France is the only major power satisfying her domestic needs and retaining an exportable surplus. Italy and the United States are nearly self-sufficient. Germany has to import nearly a hundred per cent of her bauxite, but large supplies are at hand in Hungary and Yugoslavia. The rich deposits in France have now become available to Germany. British Guiana, the Netherlands Indies, and Curaçao in the West Indies are the most important colonial suppliers of Britain.

Textiles, Rubber, and Oil

All the major European powers with the exception of Soviet Russia depend on foreign supplies of cotton and wool. The dependence is most pronounced in the case of cotton, the United States, British India, Egypt, and Brazil being the world's largest suppliers. With respect to wool, the situation is somewhat different, Great Britain and Italy covering about one fourth of their needs. But the world's most important suppliers again lie outside Europe: Australia, Argentina, New Zealand, the Union of South Africa, and, last but not least, the United States, which is more than 50 per cent self-sufficient. Obviously, there are other textile materials of importance, such as flax, hemp, jute, and silk, each of which fulfills specific needs; and finally the synthetic fibers, rayon and synthetic wool. In view of her dependence on foreign supplies for wool and cotton, Germany has made attempts to foster the home cultivation of flax and hemp, thus redeveloping old German occupations. Furthermore, synthetic production of textiles has developed. But at present Germany can scarcely supply more than one fourth of her total needs of textiles (one third, if account is taken of the utilization of rags). Therefore, a pressing demand for imports persists, which can only temporarily be overcome by the depletion of stocks.

With respect to natural rubber the world depends nearly exclusively on British and Dutch possessions: the Malay States, the Netherlands Indies, and Ceylon. In view of the significance of rubber for the motorization of armies, it is therefore not astonishing to watch the gigantic effort made in blockade-threatened Germany to evolve a substitute product. It has been found in the so-called *Buna* article. Conflicting opinions have been given about the quality of this product; but it seems that in several respects it does compare favorably with natural rubber.

Let us conclude our survey of key raw materials with a survey of the oil situation. Already during the first world war, oil was a strategic material. Since then its importance has grown considerably with the motorization of land armies, the expansion of air forces, and the transition of navies from coal to oil fuel. Today it may be ranked equal in importance to coal and iron.

The world's treasures of crude petroleum are very unequally distributed over the various countries. More than half of the world supply is found in the United States. The rest is split up among Soviet Russia, Venezuela, Iran, the Netherlands Indies, Rumania, Mexico, Iraq—ranked in the order of their output—and a few minor producers. With the exception of the United States and Soviet Russia, no world power is self-sufficient. For the sake of oil supplies alone, fighting for the mastery of the seas might appear worth while to a belligerent European nation. Cut off from the high seas, Germany cannot count on suppliers other than Russia and Rumania, and it is highly doubtful whether either of these countries can contribute enough to keep the German war machine going over a number of years. Rumania's output alone would be insufficient. In addition, the major sites of Rumanian wells are owned by English and Dutch investors. During the first part of the present war, many attempts were made by the Allies to prevent the flow of oil to Germany. The interruption of traffic on the Danube River because of winter ice added a further obstacle. If in order to overcome the political difficulties Germany were to invade Rumania, she might find herself again confronted by the situation she encountered in 1916. Then, in the face of the approaching German army, English engineers destroyed a number of oil wells. It might appear better policy for Germany to "synchronize" the Rumanian government and to make it control the whole oil industry.[23]

As far as Russia is concerned, the first question is whether her government will be willing to part with a significant amount of oil. During recent years, Russian demand for oil has seemed to outgrow her supplies. The transportation problem would appear also, and in intensified form; for the Soviet railroad system is not well developed. A pipe line from Baku or some Black Sea port to the German frontier might, however, solve the problem just as the pipe lines from the Mossul fields to the Mediterranean made Iraq's oil easily accessible to the Allies.

In view of these facts, it is understandable that Germany

---

[23] Shortly after the collapse of France, a pro-Fascist government was formed in Rumania. On July 24, 1940, it confiscated the British-owned Astra-Romana Oil Company, the largest oil firm in Rumania. Since the beginning of the war this firm had steadfastly refused to supply Germany with oil. The confiscation has made its output available to Germany.

has concentrated upon a domestic solution of her oil problem. On the one hand, it is certain that considerable stocks were built up before the war. On the other hand, synthetic production of oil from coal has been promoted, and far-reaching attempts have been made to replace oil as a motor fuel by gasses of many kinds. Germany is reported to have covered in 1937 about sixty to seventy per cent of her domestic consumption by domestic production.[24] Since the increase of consumption to be expected under active warfare is likely to exceed the productive capacity of such additional sources as the Polish wells and the stocks found by the German army in Denmark, Norway, Holland, Belgium, and France, oil deficiency constitutes a major difficulty for Germany in a long war. This explains Germany's emphasis on speedy victory to a large extent.

We meet here an interesting correlation between a country's raw-material equipment and its military strategy. It does not hold for oil only, but for all important raw materials. A country poor in raw materials will probably try to force a decision of the war at an early moment, while a rich country can afford to keep on the defensive side and to face a prolonged war. In this way, it can bring its material superiority to bear on the enemy. But since it is not impossible to win even a major war in a few months, the poor country has a real chance of victory. Obviously, if the country rich in materials allows the enemy to win in the short run, it cannot expect to conquer in the long run. Treasures of raw materials become a decisive factor in warfare only if they are converted into actual military power.

SUGGESTED REFERENCES

Army and Navy Munitions Board: *The Strategic and Critical Materials* (mimeographed), Washington, D. C., March, 1940.

---

[24] Priester, *op. cit.*, 270.

Emeny, B.: *The Strategy of Raw Materials,* A Study of America in Peace and War, New York, 1937.
Friedensburg, F.: *Die Mineralischen Bodenschätze als Weltpolitische und Militärische Machtfaktoren,* Stuttgart, 1936.
─────: *Kohle und Eisen im Weltkriege und in den Friedensschlüssen,* Berlin, 1934.
Leith, C. K.: *World Minerals and World Politics,* New York, 1931.
Possony, S. T.: *To-Morrow's War,* London, 1938.
Priester, H. E.: *Das Deutsche Wirtschaftswunder,* Amsterdam, 1936.
(Speier, H., and Kähler, A.; editors): *War in Our Time,* New York, 1939, chapter V ("Foodstuffs and Raw Materials," by K. Brandt) and chapter VI ("Autarchy," by E. Heimann).

CHAPTER 3

Facilities of Production, Distribution, Transportation, and Finance

In the survey of the economic war potential of nations two elements were distinguished: population power and raw-material equipment. Now we come to an element which in a certain sense is a synthesis of the two, the nations' equipment of man-made instruments of production, distribution, transportation, and finance. But this equipment is by no means an automatic consequence, although it is an outgrowth of the two former elements. We know of countries, China for example, densely populated and amply provided with raw materials, which possess relatively few mines and factories; moreover, China has an undeveloped railroad system, and lacks other features of an industrial country. On the other hand, there are countries with industries, fleets, and banks of world importance, which are relatively poor in key raw materials (Italy, for example, or the Netherlands) or in human beings (Norway). In evaluating the nations' economic war potential we cannot content ourselves with a study of population and raw-material power. We have to see to what extent the nations have been able to provide themselves with the economic equipment fundamentally important in time of war. The war between China and Japan has shown how lack of such economic equipment condemned a populous and basically rich country to the role of a chained and powerless giant.

Our task, then, consists in enumerating and evaluating

the various types of economic equipment that count in a nation's war potential. We cannot promise to tell the whole story; it is too long. But drawing on recent economic history we shall point out a few essential requirements.

Productive Equipment

The first demand that warfare makes on the productive equipment of a nation is that it be adequate for the needs of the armed forces and the civilian population. Small powers, satellites in a belligerent phalanx, may depend largely on the production of the leading powers and still conserve their usefulness for a military alliance. During the World War, for instance, Bulgaria and Turkey on the one side, Serbia and Greece on the other, were far from producing the munitions used by their armies. For these as for most of their war expenditures they depended on Germany and the main Allied powers, respectively. (See Table III of the Appendix.) The leading powers, however, taken as a group, cannot shift their burden of the productive war effort over to others.

Since productive equipment is of various kinds, its aggregate volume is only one aspect of its usefulness. In order to be of maximum usefulness for warfare, the various types of equipment must be provided in the right proportions. Classifying roughly, we may divide the productive equipment into the following three groups: mining, manufacturing, and agriculture. The grouping may be considered comprehensive if we include quarries under mining, and forestry, fishing, and hunting under agriculture. Equipment in these various fields must, as we said, be provided in the right proportions.

In each of the three groups we find a large variety of equipment: buildings, tools, and machinery of many types. It is imperative that all these innumerable devices should be available in sufficient quantities in time of war. If they cannot be kept available in the form of stocks, a belligerent nation must be able to produce them on short notice. This would be an insuperable task, however; a nation cannot wage a major war and *simultaneously* build up its productive equipment. The equipping of the national economy must be undertaken before the outbreak of hostilities. Two ways of solving the problem are open to a nation.

The first way is to let competitive private enterprise, coupled with a certain degree of government supervision, try to achieve the maximum degree of economic development. An economic system is thus likely to arise which will be characterized by a comparatively high degree of productive efficiency and adjustment to national and international competitive conditions. Productive equipment under this system is likely to be very well adapted to peacetime efficiency. Whether it is well adapted to war conditions is another question. It may be, or it may not be.

One probable shortcoming of such an economic system is the underdevelopment of lines of production which are of little importance in times of peace and of others which are important but more efficiently operated by foreign countries. An example of the first type are the munitions industries in the specific sense of the word. They will almost certainly be underdeveloped in such a "free" national economy. An example of the second type are the dyestuff and glass industries in the United States before the World War. In this respect, the economic system of the United States, grown up under relatively free conditions, was found to be insufficiently prepared for war.

At the time of the outbreak of the [first world] war in Europe, the American glass industry was supplying the domestic market with a large proportion of its window glass, bottles, lamp chimneys, and pressed glassware. The up-to-date American mills were equipped with excellent automatic and semi-automatic glass-blowing machinery. We were dependent upon Germany and Austria, however, for certain special but very important glass products. These included chemical or laboratory glass ware, important not only in our universities but also in the research departments of many of our great industries, and optical glass of the highest grade, used for lenses of field glasses, range finders, and periscopes.[1]

After the blockade of Germany had set in, some time elapsed before American industry was able to replace the imports of these articles. At present the gap in the American glass industry is certainly less marked. Yet German patent control still seems to be dominant in the optical glass industry and financial restraints are thus put on the supply of military optical equipment by American producers.[2]

The dyestuff situation was more serious. In 1914, Germany held monopolistic positions in several branches of the chemical industry. For instance, she was producing three fourths of the world's supply of coal-tar dyes. These German products, used as raw materials in such industries as textiles and printing, were indispensable in numerous manufacturing activities in other countries.

Dyes are made from intermediates, which in turn are made from crude coal-tar products. The making of these products, and particularly the manufacture of the intermediates, involves in many cases technical knowledge of the highest order. Secrecy and protection through patents of the processes elaborated by German chemists after many years of intensive and painstaking research made competition difficult. The intermediates were the keystone of Germany's dye monopoly.[3]

In view of these conditions, the effects of the interruption of German supplies were catastrophic to this country as well as to others. In 1915, stocks of dyestuffs at American textile

---

[1] W. S. Culbertson: *Commercial Policy in War Time and After*, New York: D. Appleton-Century Company, 1919, 22.
[2] *The New York Times* of June 2, 1940. See also Army and Navy Munitions Board: *The Strategic and Critical Materials*, March, 1940, 27.
[3] Culbertson, *op. cit.*, 34–35.

mills grew smaller and smaller, and various economy measures had to be taken. Culbertson reports that light shades became common in many lines of goods and designs were so changed as to have small figures printed on white backgrounds. It was more than a year before a new American industry of dyestuffs and increased use of natural dyes had banished the specter of a dye famine. At least a certain number of colors could be made satisfactorily. After this country's entry into the war, the last restrictions imposed by German patents were finally removed. This illustration shows that a peacetime economy left to itself may, even in a country of so high a degree of natural self-sufficiency as the United States, exhibit serious gaps when suddenly confronted with the exigencies of war.

There is obviously a second way of providing a country with the productive equipment needed for war, and that is by means of methodical preparation under government control. Through tariff protection, subsidies to industries, and other types of stimulating measures, the government may attempt in peace times to provide a high degree of self-sufficiency. In recent times, Germany and Italy have gone very far along this way. Before the outbreak of the present war, their national economies were, for many purposes, war economies. But there is no major country in the world that has not, at least partially, embarked upon this course. Naturally, whether it is realized or not, such a course implies certain economic sacrifices through diminished international division of labor.

Furthermore, such an anticipatory practice puts a larger responsibility on the government. Once it takes the nation's economic future into its own hands, it needs a higher degree of continuity, insight in economic matters, and initiative than if it were restricted to the proverbial role of the "night watchman" under *laissez faire*. Comprehensive surveys of the country's productive capacities and probable war needs have to be made and far-reaching decisions must be taken. Particular attention has to be devoted to the probable *bottlenecks* of the industrial system, that is, the branches which through insufficient output may cause widespread disorganization. These potential bottlenecks are likely to be found among the industries producing producers' goods: machines, tools, and raw materials. At present for instance, it seems that the expansion of American airplane production may be held up by inability of the producers of machine tools and motors to fill the quickly rising demand of the plane factories.

In 1935, the productive capacities of the main industrial nations compared as follows:

SHARES OF THE WORLD CAPACITY OF PRODUCTION [4]
(1935)

Country	All Branches of Industry (Percentage of World Capacity)	Producers' Goods Industries (Percentage of World Capacity)
United States	44	52
Great Britain	10	8
France	7	7
Germany	11–12	11
Italy	3	?
Soviet Russia } Japan	14	15
Total for the countries included in this table	89–90	93

How a Country's Productive Equipment Can Be Prepared for War

The ways in which a government may stimulate the adjustment of productive capacities to war needs are manifold. Advance planning of wartime orders and their allocation to

---

[4] Source: Institut für Konjunkturforschung: *Industrielle Mobilmachung*, Hamburg, 1936, 76 and 79.

individual plants help private industry to arrive at an adjustment by itself. So do *educational orders* of small quantities of military equipment, which are designed to familiarize manufacturers with the problems they have to expect in war. Such orders help to mitigate the confusion which sudden changes of production plans are bound to cause in factories. During the first world war, ignorance of war requirements and inexperience in the execution of new tasks proved to be serious obstacles. They can easily be reduced.

Small orders, however, are unlikely to help develop the experience in mass production which is essential in war times. In order to develop this effectively before the outbreak of war, the government would have to embark on a large-scale armament program. Since, however, certain complicated arms, such as planes and tanks, are subject to a high rate of obsolescence, production in advance may be bad policy. There remains the possibility of selling large stocks of arms, accumulated in peacetime, to civil war factions or other foreign purchasers of second-rate equipment. A neutral country in a major way may keep its armament industry on a large-scale production basis by selling equipment to belligerents.

More fundamental problems arise if the existing productive equipment is found to be entirely insufficient to satisfy war needs. This is likely to be the case for the munitions industries proper. The government may attack the problem by mapping out a system of industrial transformation. Such a system would predetermine the use of the facilities of certain nonessential industries for the making of munitions. The experience of the first world war provides useful lessons in how to prepare industries for the transition. Then, producers of automobiles, elevators, and stoves had to start producing shells; others shifted from building private yachts or gramophones to coöperating in the construction of hydroplanes; still others changed from sewing machines to machine guns, from locomotives to artillery, or from ladies' waists to signal flags. Similar, though not necessarily the same, changes may become desirable in another war, and steps may be taken to prepare manufacturers for them.

In some fields, however, it may appear necessary to construct new plants and to equip them for war production. As examples the "shadow factories" of Great Britain may be cited. Under its prewar armament program, the British government stimulated the creation of certain factories, particularly of aircraft, with the intention of postponing their full utilization until the outbreak of hostilities. In Germany, plants for the production of substitute articles were erected before 1939.

How the Transportation System Affects Warfare

The extent and the quality of a nation's transportation system are of highest importance in war times. The existing facilities have to be used for the transportation of troops, munitions, and other supplies to the front. Simultaneously, they have to take care of the shipment of merchandise between producers and from producers to consumers. Finally, a certain amount of mail and passenger traffic has to be moved. During the World War, the transportation facilities of all belligerents were insufficient in many respects, and serious trouble was often caused by bottlenecks.

The most important instruments of land transportation are railroads and automobiles. In the War of 1914 to 1918, the *railroads* played by far the greater role of the two. Although the automobile has considerably increased in importance since then, the railroads still have the larger share in the transportation of merchandise. What features of railroad transportation determine its usefulness in war times? First, there is the density of the network; second, the degree to which it is satisfactory from a strategic point of view. The two do not necessarily go together. France, for example, has a well-developed net of railroads, but it radiates from Paris. Every region of the country can be reached easily from Paris, but direct communications between the various regions are in many cases insufficient. This may prove inconvenient if, for military reason, heavy direct transports from one region to another become necessary. When Paris was taken by the Germans, the limitations of the French railway system were promptly felt.

Further important features are the quality of the roadbed and the volume and quality of the rolling stock and of station facilities. Since during war all railroad equipment is subject to enormous strain because of extraordinary requirements, enemy action, and the difficulties of maintenance, a country expecting to wage a war will do well to keep its railroad equipment in good condition in peace times. This may be very difficult, particularly in large countries or in countries whose heavy industries are momentarily occupied with other tasks. The shortcomings of the Russian railroad system have become proverbial, but even a country as industrialized as Germany experienced acute difficulties during the period of rearmament preceding the present war.

An organizational problem of the railroads that has frequently attracted attention is the degree of centralization of management. In countries where the railroads are under the direction of various private companies, the difficulties of wartime transportation may be greatly increased by the lack of centralized management. The distribution of equipment over the various networks, train schedules, and other measures are likely to be worked out more satisfactorily if the management is unified. In Chapter 9 we are going to see what measures have been taken in countries with nonunified railroad nets to insure the unity of command in war times.

TRANSPORTATION, FINANCE

The line entitled "Railroads, goods carried" in Table I of the Appendix gives an idea of the peacetime strength of railroad systems in the various countries.

Automobiles and trucks are extremely important in supplementing the railroads. Because they are more easily adaptable to continuously changing transportation conditions, they are particularly useful in maintaining communications between railroad centers close to the front and the front itself. They may be called upon to replace railroad transportation when lines have been interrupted or are congested. An outstanding example of automobile transportation during the first world war was the conveyance of French troops from Paris to the battlefield of the Marne in requisitioned Paris taxis. Good roads are a prerequisite for speedy transports by automobile.

Realizing the importance of a large automobile supply in war, several countries have encouraged private automobile production in peace times. Germany in particular has gone far along this line. In addition, the National Socialist government has undertaken the construction of a network of superhighways in Germany and Austria. Their location clearly indicates that strategic considerations governed the minds of the planners.

Table I of the Appendix contains figures indicating the number of passenger automobiles, busses, and trucks in use in various countries in 1938, as well as automobile production. In both numbers in use and production, the Franco-British alliance showed a definite superiority over Germany and Italy at the beginning of the present war. At present (July, 1940) the British Empire matches the facilities available to the German-Italian block.

Special types of land-transportation facilities may alleviate the burden on railroad and automotive traffic. *Pipe lines* for oil reduce the volume of tanker business to be done by railroads, trucks, or ships. *Power lines* constitute valuable instruments for energy transportation, relieving the railroads of transports of bulky energy containers such as coal. They are of particular importance in countries well equipped with water power or such low-grade fuels as lignite and peat.

Passing on to *water transportation,* we find two groups of essential equipment: (1) internal waterways and ships usable on them, and (2) the merchant marine operating on the high seas. It is obvious that a well-developed river and canal system provided with the necessary equipment in the form of barges, tractors, and so forth, may prove to be of great assistance to land communications, particularly in the handling of bulky materials. Apart from the relative cheapness of river transportation, its lower vulnerability to air attacks speaks in its favor. It is easy to understand why the Danube was given so much attention in the news during the first six months of the present war. The freezing of this river during the winter interrupted the preferred lane of shipments of Rumanian wheat and oil and other materials from the Balkan and Black Sea regions to Germany. Later, the policy of the Allied governments of chartering all available barges and thus withdrawing them from service for Germany created a problem. Germany attempted to solve it by transferring barges from the Rhine, where military operations interfered with their use, to the Danube. The importance of this river to Germany during the first world war has been described by one of her leading generals in this way: "The military successes achieved in Rumania . . . are an advantage that cannot be overestimated. The Danube means everything to us." [5]

The *merchant marine* is useful to all belligerents in so far as it acts as an auxiliary to the navy. Furthermore, it is

---

[5] General Groener to correspondents of *The New York Times* in December, 1916; reproduced in *Readings in the Economics of War,* Chicago, 1918, 201.

necessary for overseas transports of merchandise and men. In the first and in the second world war, destruction of part of the German merchant marine and prevention of the rest from operating, as well as tenaciously maintained shipping communications on the part of the Allies, gave the latter an advantage of the first order. It is therefore understandable that numerous countries have come to consider the merchant marine an industry of national importance, and that they have attempted in many cases to insure its strength by shipping subsidies.

Measuring the gross tonnage of the merchant vessels of the major seafaring nations in 1938, we arrive at the following result: the United Kingdom ranks first, though its superiority is less marked than it was in 1914; then follow the United States, Japan, Norway, Germany, Italy, France, and the Netherlands. As Table I of the Appendix shows, the tonnage of the British Empire in the present war (about 21 million gross tons) is about treble that of Germany and Italy combined. If one adds to the British tonnage that of Norway, Denmark, Holland, Belgium, and France,[6] the merchant fleet at Britain's disposal becomes more than four times as strong as that of Italy and Germany combined (32,600,000 to 7,600,000 gross tons). This situation gives England a considerable advantage in the field of overseas transportation—at least as long as her navy and air force can safeguard the traffic of merchant vessels.

It should be noted, however, that the present shipping situation is not quite so favorable for England as these figures would seem to indicate. It is true that as long as France was her ally England was able to interrupt German shipping almost entirely, and it is possible that Italian ship-

---

[6] This procedure is not entirely correct, since Germany has seized part of the merchant marine of the countries invaded by her. Most of these countries' ships, however, were on the high seas or in foreign ports at the time of the German invasion and were brought under British control.

ping outside the Mediterranean will undergo the same fate. But on the other hand, wartime conditions have proved bothersome to English shipping. First, there is the submarine danger, now increased by Germany's dominance over the coasts of her victims. During the first ten months of the present war, submarines have not taken as high a toll of merchant vessels as they did in the days of the most active U-boat warfare during the first world war. Still, the damage they are doing is not negligible, and the threat which their mere existence is exerting has led to the institution of the complicated, expensive, and inefficient convoy system. Instead of leaving harbors whenever they are loaded and weather conditions not too unfavorable, ships going to and coming from English ports have to wait until a whole merchant fleet is ready for the voyage. Then they are taken out under protection of naval vessels and accompanied through more or less extended danger zones. The number of ships forming a convoy varies. During the first world war, when the same system was in force, the number was in some cases as high as forty. But the more usual number was twenty to twenty-five.[7] It is easy to see why such a system is complicated. It is expensive in so far as it implies longer intervals between the loading and discharging of ships, and inefficient because of the lower degree of utilization of shipping space, congestion of harbors, and so on. The convoy system is said to have diminished the efficiency of the British merchant marine by half.

Besides the effects of enemy action and of protective measures against them the increased difficulties of navigation without an international weather report system, the requisitioning of ships by the armed forces, and other factors handicap the commercial utilization of the merchant marines.

Finally, the importance of *air transportation* should be

---

[7] J. A. Salter: *Allied Shipping Control,* Oxford, 1921, 122.

mentioned. It is the youngest branch of transportation, but the development of numerous airports and large fleets of commercial planes has become extremely significant. First, these airports and planes provide reservoirs on which a country's air force can draw. In times of parachute-troop warfare, large transport planes are very useful to the air force. Second, the airplane provides the speediest transportation of passengers or merchandise and therefore plays a role in the hinterland.

Of the European countries, Germany and Italy lead in the volume of merchandise and passenger traffic by air.[8] They as well as other countries subsidize civil aviation in various ways.

Distribution

Facilities for the storing of commodities play a notable role in the nation's economic war potential. Since the production and flow of commodities are subject to sudden interruptions in war times, and particularly since overseas imports are precarious or largely impossible, the formation of stock piles takes on a greater importance than in times of peace. Facilities have to be provided to store more than normal quantities of foodstuffs, industrial raw materials, and semimanufactured goods. These facilities are of various kinds: dumping spaces, grain silos, oil tanks, and so forth. Peacetime industry and trade provide them to a certain extent. But the greater the necessity for the formation of special wartime stocks, the larger the need for excess capacities. Storage for war purposes may also require equipment of specific quality. Oil tanks have to be camouflaged against enemy airplanes, munitions dumps may have to be built underground. In view of these special require-

---

[8] Cf. *Statistical Yearbook of the League of Nations, 1938/39,* 205.

ments it appears necessary for the government to assist manufacturers and traders in making provisions for wartime storage, and eventually to undertake construction of adequate storage centers on its own account. If such precautions are not taken, stocks of valuable merchandise may deteriorate. That has happened, for example, to a large part of the cocoa crop of 1939. *The New York Times* of June 2, 1940, reported:

> Last fall the [British] Food Ministry required the whole crop of British West Africa plus parts of the West Indian crop, totaling 400,000 tons, or three fifths of the world supply. Thus far only half of these supplies has been sold, the United States being the chief buyer. Part of the surplus became unmarketable through inadequate storage.

Though little statistical data is available, it is known that the German and Italian governments had devoted much attention to this problem before the outbreak of the present war. It has also been given attention in England.

Other features of the war potential relating to distribution facilities are essentially of an organizational character. Preparations for war, for example, may consist in the education of retail traders for their role in the rationing of consumer goods and the control of prices.

Money: the Sinews of War?

The proverb that "money is the sinews of war" expresses a popular fallacy. It is frequently believed that stores of money render a country strong in times of war. This is certainly not true as far as stores of national paper currency are concerned. If their volume were an indicator of belligerent strength, the technology of the printing press would be the only concern of war economics, and Germany would have won the first world war. In the realm of the domestic economy of a warring nation, it is not money that counts, but productive power and stocks of useful goods.

Yet if we reduce the scope of that old proverb sufficiently, we find that it tells some truth. First, nations *which are not cut off from foreign supplies* may have use for stores of *international* currency or of other valuables for which there is an interest in other countries. Second, the *organization* of a nation's public and private finances is of importance for a war emergency.

Let us first consider the problem of storing valuable objects. It played an important role in medieval war preparations. Precious metals and jewels formed the war chests of princes and cities. When war broke out, foodstuffs and military supplies could be obtained through traders in exchange for these valuables. As time progressed, war chests changed their character. Today they take mainly two forms: (1) national stocks of gold, generally centralized by the government or the country's central bank, sometimes held inside the country, sometimes in safer places abroad; (2) stocks of internationally marketable securities. The purpose of these accumulated treasures is the same as that of their medieval predecessors, namely, to provide foreign commodities and services at a time when the domestic economy is not able to offer useful goods in exchange. To fulfill this purpose, they have to consist of the right types of valuables. Gold may do very well as long as foreign-trade partners are accepting it. Foreign securities may be easily salable in their countries of origin, but perhaps not in a third country. Domestic securities may appear very acceptable to foreigners as long as the country's chances to win the war seem good. Consequently, how valuable a nation's war chest is will depend on many circumstances, some of which cannot be foreseen.

The gold reserves of the world's central banks and governments have experienced a considerable reallocation during the last years, the United States providing the chief point of attraction. In December, 1934, this country held thirty-nine per cent of the world's monetary gold reserves; France followed with twenty-six per cent, the United Kingdom with eight per cent. In March, 1940, the United States owned more than seventy per cent, France's share having declined to about ten per cent.[9] Under the impact of this tremendous shift, accompanied as it has been by the spread of the barter system in international trade and a growing preference of foreign countries for commodities instead of gold, the utility of this country's huge gold stocks has been seriously questioned.

. . . while gold will no doubt be a useful wartime asset for other countries of the world it would be of no use at all to us. Gold has value because the United States buys it. To use it we would have to cease to buy and begin to sell. As far as can now be seen, the cessation of our purchases of gold would alone be enough to make it depreciate very greatly. Any sales we might make would depress its value still more so that it would yield relatively little purchasing power.[10]

But there is no doubt that up to now the gold stocks of England and France have effectively served as war chests. Under the cash-and-carry policy adopted by the United States in 1939 the Allies were able to exchange gold for airplanes, other munitions, and commodities.

Less is known about the international distribution of securities than about that of gold reserves. But it may be of interest to record the results of recent studies of the amounts of foreign securities owned by the Allies at the outbreak of the present war. According to the Federal Reserve Bulletin of December, 1939, the United Kingdom, France, Canada, and other British and French countries

---

[9] *Federal Reserve Bulletin*, May, 1940, 468. See also E. A. Goldenweiser: "The Gold Problem Today" in the same *Bulletin*, January, 1940.

[10] F. D. Graham and C. R. Whittlesey: *Golden Avalanche,* Princeton: Princeton University Press, 1939, 116.

owned at the end of August, 1939, dollar balances of $1,265,000,000, readily negotiable American securities (common and preferred stocks and bonds) of a market value of $1,420,000,000, direct and other investments in this country of $1,540,000,000; this amounts to $4,225,000,000 worth of American titles, in addition to their central gold reserves of $5,755,000,000. Besides these treasures, the Allied countries possessed large amounts of securities in their dominions, colonies, and other countries. Britain's portfolio of dominion and colonial securities alone has been estimated at 861,000,000 pound sterling.[11] But Britain may part with these assets only under extreme pressure; for, as Einzig reminds us, "they constitute a very valuable link between the Motherland and the Empire."[12]

These are considerable amounts. Theoretically, they would enable the United Kingdom and France to finance twice their aggregate yearly imports ($6,788,000,000 in 1937). What role these treasures are actually going to play in the present war depends on many factors. Will England be able to draw on France's holdings? How will the volume of the British imports develop? What proportion of them can be paid for with exports or foreign credits? Will it be possible to sell large quantities of securities without causing a decline in their value? Will the British government and capitalists be willing to renounce "strategic" securities of their empire, and will other people be interested in investing in parts of this empire at a moment when its fate is being decided on the battlefield? On the way in which these questions will be answered depends the actual significance of the treasures for the British government and its allies.

Before the present war the Allied governments took steps toward a coördinated realization of the foreign securities

---

[11] *The Economist*, London, August 12, 1939, 307. At a rate of exchange of 4:1, this amount corresponds to $3,444,000,000.
[12] Paul Einzig: *Economic Problems of the Next War*, London, 1939, 85.

held by the residents of their countries. More than a week before the outbreak of war and the institution of exchange control in Great Britain, registration of a large number of securities with the Bank of England was decreed. Sale and transfer of these "restricted securities" was made subject to official permission. In February, 1940, the British Treasury ordered British owners of sixty selected American stocks to turn them over to the Bank of England at current prices. In April, another hundred American stocks and bonds were called up.[13] The British government has attempted to sell these securities in the American market gradually in order to avoid their depreciation.

Besides the nations' stocks of internationally negotiable values other factors of financial character deserve mention in an appreciation of the economic war potential. One is the standing of the nation as an international debtor. While the strength of its creditor position partly determines the volume of possessions on which a nation can draw in case of war, its standing as a debtor influences the volume of foreign credits obtainable. The ease with which the Allied powers obtained credits in this country during the first world war and the difficulties they have to overcome today after defaulting on their previous debts illustrate the importance of this point. Therefore, if a country expects to find foreign financial support during a coming war it is in its interest not to deceive any present creditors it may have.

But the elements making for a nation's financial war potential do not lie only in its relations with foreign countries. Various interior conditions can facilitate or handicap the deployment of the fullest economic effort in a coming war. The existence of a well-developed system of taxation, capable of being expanded to meet war needs, must be counted as a favorable factor. Another one is a good

---

[13] *Federal Reserve Bulletin* of March and May, 1940.

record of the government as debtor toward its own citizens. While the volume of the internal prewar debt of the government should not be of any great significance for its chances to borrow more in time of war, it matters whether or not the government has honored its obligations during the past. This consideration is of importance in all countries where owners of capital are relatively free in the disposition of their funds. It can be neglected, however, when such dispositions are controlled by the government, as is the case in present-day Germany. General efficiency of the nation's monetary and banking system must be counted as a further favorable condition.

We come therefore to these conclusions. A large number of economic institutions and relationships are found to be of significance in the determination of a country's economic war potential: its production equipment, its transportation, its system of distribution, and its financial position. It can be said that many of the factors that make a country's war economy strong are elements of its general economic development. To a large extent, a strong peace economy means also a strong war economy, provided that efficient use is made of the existing potentialities. But we find also that in certain respects specific preparations for war must be made. Certain types of equipment and organizational preparedness do not grow automatically in time of peace. They require a specific, organized effort.

SUGGESTED REFERENCES

Baruch, B. M.: *American Industry in the War,* A Report of the War Industries Board, Washington, D. C., 1921.

(Clark, J. M., Hamilton, W. H., and Moulton, H. G.; editors): *Readings in the Economics of War,* Chicago, 1918, chapters IX, 4, and XIII, 3.

Graham, F. D., and Whittlesey, C. R.: *Golden Avalanche,* Princeton, 1939, chapter VI.

Heckscher, E.: "Importance of the Financial Forces of a Country for Carrying on War. Possibility of Obtaining Credits Abroad," in *What Would Be the Character of a New War?* New York, 1933, chapter VIII.

Kindersley, R. M.: "British Overseas Investments, 1938," *Economic Journal*, Vol. 49, December, 1939, 678–695.

Pratt, E. A.: *The Rise of Rail-Power in War and Conquest, 1833– 1914,* London-Philadelphia, 1916.

United States Department of Commerce, Bureau of Foreign and Domestic Commerce: *Foreign Investments in the United States,* Washington, D. C., 1937.

Walker, E. R.: *War-Time Economics, with Special Reference to Australia,* Melbourne, 1939, chapter III.

CHAPTER 4

Economic Mobilization

When M-day comes, a nation's war potential has to be transformed into actual war energies, just as the energy stored in a charge of dynamite has to be changed into an explosive force when the moment comes to destroy a rock. The social effort required at this moment must be comprehensive, proportionate, and speedy. It must be comprehensive, because a major war requires the deployment of all energies, military and economic, industrial and agricultural. It must be proportionate, because millions of individuals have to be coördinated and no effort, once it is recognized as essential for victory, must be hindered. Finally, it must be speedy, because the nation that can muster its forces earliest not only gains an initial advantage over the enemy but can also avoid the distressing losses that result from blundering and belated action.

Every person acquainted with problems of management will agree that mobilization requires unified management. Even in national economies based on private initiative there is today scarcely any objection to unified management of *military* mobilization. Who would believe that millions of individuals would on their own initiative leave jobs and homes in order to form an army? Many might do so, but their number would almost certainly fall short of the requirements of a major war. Today, voluntary conscription can solve the problems of minor military expeditions only. Who would believe that men could gather quickly enough to ward off enemy action that might be expected any time, even without an official declaration of war? Who would leave to the millions of citizens the task of determining the relative strength of the various branches of military service? No one contests the government's obligation to take charge of military mobilization.

But military mobilization is only part of the problem. It is ineffective without *economic* mobilization. The question arises: Does everybody agree on the necessity of putting the task of economic mobilization in the hands of government? We find considerable difference of opinion on that point.

Inadequate Mobilization in the World War

At the beginning of the World War, governments were unprepared to undertake an economic mobilization. Their "War Books" contained numerous provisions to be taken in the military field; but they had not much to say about measures of economic character. What were the results?

Russia: "The mobilization of the army was carried out with great speed but regardless of economic consequences. The policy of the Russian government seemed to be the simple one of calling to the colors great numbers of soldiers (20,000,000 men were mobilized) who should be sent to the front without delay, without adequate equipment, and without thought of the effects upon the industrial organization back of the lines. As a result of this policy the first months of the war completely dislocated the economic life of Russia." [1] Indiscriminate military mobilization, or as

---

[1] From an article of S. N. Harper, reproduced in *Readings in the Economics of War* (J. M. Clark, W. H. Hamilton, and H. G. Moulton; editors), Chicago, 1918, 202. The figure of 20,000,000 seems exaggerated; see above, p. 16.

we might call it *overmobilization,* took place in several countries besides Russia. It helped create unemployment among those who were not mobilized. In France, for example, many small employers were mobilized in the first days of August, 1914. They closed their shops, and their employees found themselves out of jobs at a moment when they were supposed to begin a major production campaign.

France: "The first effect of the war was almost a complete disorganization of French industry. Labor was suddenly taken away from the quarries, limekilns, cement-works, paper-mills, iron-works. . . . Various schemes were devised to answer the needs of the moment. The first was to take men out of the army and send them to industrial work. This was done with great caution during the winter of 1914–15. The proportion of the men thus taken increased more and more during the year 1915 and reached its fullest extent in 1916. . . . All this recalling of mobilized men was effected at first according to the need, and without method. By degrees it became clear that the output would be greater if these soldier-workmen were assigned to the plants or factories where they were working before the war." [2]

Germany: "On August 4, 1914, when England declared war, the terrible event which has never happened before occurred, and our country became a beleaguered fortress. . . . Three days after the declaration of war I could not bear the uncertainty of the position any longer, and I announced myself at the War Office, where Colonel Scheuch received me in a friendly manner. I told him that our country was provided with the necessary material of war only for a limited number of months. He agreed as to my calculation of the duration of the war, and so I put this question to him: 'What is being done, what can be done, to

---

[2] From an article of R. Blanchard in July, 1917, reproduced in *Readings in the Economics of War,* 188–190.

prevent a shortage of supplies?'... I was told that I could get the statistics in six months."[3]

England: At the outbreak of the war, the President of the British Board of Trade "was Mr. Walter Runciman, formerly a member of a well-known shipping firm, and a determined opponent on principle of Government trading. ... His policy, which for more than two years became the policy of the Government, was to trust as far as possible even in war time, to private enterprise for the maintenance of civilian supplies; to give assistance in minor matters ... but above all to give confidence that there would be no state trading and no regulation of prices. ... Prices, indeed, of food as of other necessaries, continued to rise steadily. This led to Parliamentary questions and to a discussion which occupied the House of Commons on 11th and 17th February 1915. ... [Prime Minister Asquith] was able to show that though prices of cereals had risen 75 per cent and those of food generally 25 per cent above prewar levels, they were still below the heights reached in 1871; he seemed to hope that they would stay there. ... The President of the Board of Trade was more practical. After expounding the dangers of state action and of any attempt to regulate prices, he suggested that the line of escape from rising prices must be found in raising wages. He started the vicious circle with an official blessing on its wild career."[4]

United States: Before this country entered the war in 1917, people had ample opportunity to study the effects of *laissez faire* in war. Yet the degree of unpreparedness of the government for economic mobilization did not stand far behind that of the European powers. In the words of Georges Clemenceau: "The United States declared war in

---

[3] From an article of W. Rathenau in January, 1917, reproduced in *Readings in the Economics of War,* 197.

[4] W. H. Beveridge: *British Food Control,* London, 1928, 6, 8, and 9. (Reprinted by permission of Yale University Press.)

April, 1917. It was only in March, 1918, that their industrial mobilization found its final form. Even in the land of quick decisions, the routine of peace days struggled hard to live." [5] There were no agencies competent to deal with the economic problems of war. The military authorities themselves were in no way prepared. "Our so-called General Staff was a purely military group; not a Great General Staff. It had made no study, and, as a body, had no comprehension, of the fact that in a modern war the whole industrial activity of the Nation becomes the commissariat of the army." [6] And when the agencies of economic mobilization finally emerged it became obvious that their powers were too limited and too vast at the same time, that they worked at cross-purposes. The basic handicap was the idea that business should go on "as usual." This idea prevailed in most countries during the first years of their belligerency.

It is not astonishing that the effects of this policy were disastrous. The really surprising thing is that both sides adhered to it for so long. Germany was the first power to abandon the idea of "business as usual." The transition was marked by the *Somme* and *Hindenburg programs* of 1916. The World War might have ended differently if Germany had undertaken her economic mobilization in 1914 or 1915.

Why is the omission of a government-controlled economic mobilization an error? Why can private enterprise not manage this mobilization just as well? The reason lies in the incompatibility of the guiding principles, controls, and checks inherent in the private economic units, and the nature of the task. The economic mobilization has to be as comprehensive, proportionate, and speedy as the military one. A nation's aggregate of private firms is not able to satisfy any of these three requirements automatically.

---

[5] G. B. Clarkson: *Industrial America in the World War*, New York, 1923, xxii.
[6] *Ibid.*, 111.

During the last decades, doubts have become increasingly stronger regarding the capacity of *laissez-faire* capitalism to make complete and most efficient use of a nation's resources. It has been pointed out in defense of this system that it is able to provide a most efficient allocation of resources. Interindustrial differentials in profits, interest rates, and wages distribute the marginal units of all factors in such a way as to equalize their returns in various occupations. Enlightened criticism of the capitalist economy has not failed to acknowledge this; but it has also drawn attention to the numerous and systematic deviations of modern economic systems from the ideal *laissez-faire* economy: the existence of monopolies and quasi-monopolies and their political implications, the relative immobility of factors of production. In addition to this, no attempt has ever been made to demonstrate that the profit incentive and other automatic controls of the capitalist economy would bring about *most speedily* the optimum allocation of capital and labor. The advantages of this economy have been defended for the long run only. It has been contended that "over a number of years" everything will come to an optimum adjustment.

Whether or not this holds true for the present-day economic system can be left out of consideration here. But a fact that we cannot brush aside is the essentially short-run character of the economic problems of war. The emphasis on speedy solutions is one of the main features of the war economy. In time of peace, things may be different.

Let us suppose for a moment that the government does not undertake any economic mobilization. War begins. Suppose the military administration needs many tanks and orders them from automobile manufacturers. Since the need is urgent, the government may be compelled to pay almost any price for its order, and the manufacturer following his long-standing commercial principles would act against his own interest if he did not charge the highest price he could obtain. Still, he might not be inclined to expand his output of tanks indefinitely; for he knows that the war will be over sometime, perhaps in a year. A plant that he might build today would be useless then. If the government does not undertake extraordinary financial guarantees, he may think it better to be cautious and let the government get its tanks from somebody else. Or, if the demand for private automobiles shows no immediate decline, he may continue to devote the major part of his plant, labor, and raw materials to the production of private automobiles. Or finally, if he decides to use all the resources at his disposition for the production of tanks, he may attempt to get hold of an unreasonably large amount of raw materials which will increase the difficulties of other branches of war production.

Let us turn to the other side of the picture, the situation of a skilled mechanic in an automobile factory. What foolish things may he do if his part in economic mobilization is left to his own decisions? First, he may enlist in the armed forces, while industry has a greater need for his work. Second, he may decide in view of rising wages to work fewer hours. Suppose that before the war he earned fifty dollars a week and that he would now be able to earn one hundred dollars for the same amount of work. If he has a great preference for leisure, he may find it more advantageous to work every second week only and to have the same monthly income as before. Or third, he may go on working full time, raise his income by a hundred per cent, and spend it on a new car which will increase the demand for civilian goods and give an incentive to the manufacturer in our first example to devote more materials to their production.

Notice that all the things we let our manufacturer and our mechanic do were not foolish at all from the point of view of *laissez-faire* capitalism. We let them make their own choices. Yet their actions would be foolish in one sense or another in the framework of the war economy. They would cause insufficiency of military supplies, inadequate reduction of goods for civilian needs, or an unreasonable bidding-up of raw material prices and wages. Put to operative tasks, these individuals might do splendid service; but if they were left to themselves, there would be a good chance that the transformation of the peace economy into a war economy might be neither speedy nor smooth. Nor would there be any instrument in their power to assure the right behavior of their fellow manufacturers and workers. In other words, they could not provide a comprehensive and proportionate economic mobilization.

It might be argued that over a fairly long period businessmen could be brought to a correct allocation of their resources by means of extraordinary profit inducements. If the government paid *any* price for munitions and let businessmen reap all the profits they wanted to make, it might conceivably achieve the necessary reallocation and utilization of resources.[7] However, such a course would scarcely be politically possible in a democratic society. A rising price level, the appearance of war millionaires, and the impoverishment of receivers of fixed incomes would bring about widespread opposition. And if the government attempted to decrease this opposition by taxing war profits heavily, it might defeat the original purpose of inducing businessmen to reallocate and utilize the resources at their disposition. Little if anything could be done to avoid price inflation and its concomitants.[8]

In attacking the problems of economic mobilization a capitalistic economy of the modern type is burdened with four distinct handicaps. In so far as it is a system of *laissez*

---

[7] See below, pp. 189–198.
[8] See below, p. 146.

faire, (1) it tends to neglect collective wants; [9] (2) it does not guarantee the necessary speed of adaptation; (3) its procedures of adaptation place a democracy under heavy political strains. In so far as the economic system shows monopolistic deviations from the *laissez-faire* ideal, these three handicaps will be accentuated rather than mitigated; and they are supplemented by a fourth: insufficient output.

The Tasks of Government

We see now more clearly the incompatibility of the rules and controls governing individual independent economic units and the requirements of economic mobilization. The latter can be met by centralized management only, which is based on ample knowledge of the potential energies of a nation and requires sufficient powers to direct and coördinate them.

What are the tasks of the government in economic mobilization? Let us attempt to enumerate them briefly. In later chapters (Parts II and III), we shall discuss them in greater detail.

1. *Classification of Economic Activities According to Their Importance in War Times.* The task consists in establishing a ranking of industries according to their importance in war.

2. *Coördination of Military and Economic Mobilization.* The task consists in preventing the labor force of essential industries from being depleted and in avoiding "overmobilization," frictional unemployment, and other disturbances. Certain classes of workers, especially certain age groups, have to be declared unavailable for military service. Soldiers must be recruited mainly from nonessential industries and occupations.

---

[9] See above, pp. 31-32.

3. *Distribution of Production Orders.* Producers have to be provided with orders that will enable them to settle down to their tasks. Apart from orders to produce, orders to expand existing plants have to be given at an early moment, and it has to be decided to what extent orders shall be given to inefficient producers.

4. *Financial Measures.* The government has to provide the revenue to pay for its purchases. Increased taxation, borrowing, and printing of money have to be considered. Simultaneously, the government has to employ effective means of curtailing civilian purchasing power.

5. *Priorities.* On the basis of the established ranking of industries, the distribution of available raw materials, transportation facilities, and labor forces must be influenced in such a way as to satisfy the various needs in order of their importance.

6. *Foreign-Trade Control.* To prevent exports of essentials and to prevent superfluous imports, the government must take control of all international trade and financial relations. Transactions may be subjected to licenses. Shipping may be brought under government control.

7. *Control of Prices and Costs.* Price policies and costs of business must be subjected to supervision. Soon it may become necessary to fix prices and wages. Principles to be followed have to be agreed upon, and the administrative apparatus should be set up at once in order to ascertain the cost situation of producers.

8. *Rationing of Consumer Goods* may be introduced gradually or suddenly, on a large or a restricted scale according to the degree of scarcity of products. Rationing of transportation facilities, raw materials, and labor falls under the heading of priorities.

9. *Conscription of Factors of Production.* It has to be decided to what extent workers shall be conscripted and to what extent plants shall be put under government manage-

ment to ensure speediest adaptation. The problem has to be solved on the basis of information about the degree of voluntary coöperation that can be obtained. These are in brief the major tasks that confront a government if it is to realize the nation's war potential.

In the United States, the necessity of adequate economic preparation for war has been realized as a result of our World War experience. Though problems of preparedness did not interest the general public after the Armistice, they continued to occupy Congress, the War Department, the American Legion, and individual specialists. From 1931 on, a series of *Industrial Mobilization Plans* have been published by the War Department. The most recent edition is the *Industrial Mobilization Plan, Revision of 1939,* which was issued under the joint authority of the Secretaries of War and the Navy. It outlines a system of measures designed to mobilize the nation's economic resources in time of a major war and to prepare the military divisions of the government for their wartime tasks.[10]

War and Democracy

Since, in a democratic country, adequate government agencies may not be found in operation at the outbreak of war, they will have to be created. In creating them, the nation should keep three things in mind: first, that it is the government's legitimate task to direct economic mobilization and, consequently, that prerogatives of private business and labor should be sacrificed to the extent that they conflict with the unity of management; second, that the various war-economic agencies should be well coördinated in order to avoid conflicting planning or mutually defeating orders; third, that business and labor leaders should freely

---

[10] The books by Cherne, and Tobin and Bidwell listed under "Suggested References" at the end of this chapter analyze the origin and content of the Plan.

coöperate with these agencies and voluntarily exchange the role of directors for that of operators. Only if these conditions are fulfilled will the government-controlled war economy becomes an efficient machine. Examples are not lacking to show that an obstructed, sabotage-ridden, and ill-coördinated economic mobilization can lead to the most serious waste of energies and even jeopardize victory.

Dictatorial countries are in a more advantageous technical situation as far as economic mobilization is concerned. Even in peace they have numerous economic control mechanisms in operation. Investments, production, foreign trade are governed by state decisions, and the population is accustomed to a large extent of government interference in economic matters. Therefore we can expect such countries to carry out a much speedier economic mobilization. The lead that they may gain in this way over democratic adversaries is a factor to which the latter should give serious consideration.

Trusting that their superiority in war resources would give them an advantage in a long war, Britain and France showed in the first six months of the present war much of the same lack of economic mobilization that entailed such disastrous consequences in the first world war. The German offensives in Scandinavia and on the western front have revealed a serious deficiency of all kinds of fighting equipment on the part of Britain and France. Suddenly, the Allied leadership began to realize that the war might be lost before their superior economic war potential had become effective. Governments and general staffs were re-formed, and a more active policy in economic matters was introduced. France, however, could not be saved any more. By now (August, 1940) it appears dubious whether Great Britain can recover the ground she lost during the quiet months of the winter 1939–1940, a battle lost not in the field but in government offices and factories.

Democratic nations may overcome the technical handicap which they are likely to have in comparison to dictatorial powers. A democratic country possesses a great political war potential in the fighting spirit of a free people. If the nation realizes the need of comprehensive economic mobilization, this political factor may turn the balance of military power in its favor. It is therefore of greatest importance for the government of a democratic country to mobilize the political war potential. This is not only a problem of propaganda; but to a much higher degree it is a matter of economic and social policy. There will be no popular enthusiasm for a war if privileged minorities are permitted to sabotage the nation's war effort and simultaneously to profit from it, or if civil liberties are abolished indiscriminately under the pretext of war necessity.

The sacrifice of civil liberties must be minimized; in particular, the freedom of criticism must not be suppressed. Free criticism is a powerful corrective of inefficiencies in economic mobilization. The curtailment of liberties must be focused on the privileges of influential groups which handicap the fighting power of the nation. The abolition of the right to hold slaves contributed to the unity and economic strength of our nation. A curtailment of the power of private monopolies is likely to produce similar effects. If the government of a democratic nation is able to undertake the wartime controls of economic activity without infringing too heavily upon the economic interests and the political liberties of the majority of the people, it will not only obtain the strongest support but also "snatch from the exigency of war positive social improvements." [11]

The failures of France and Great Britain in the present war find their explanation not so much in an excessive degree of popular liberties as in the absence of democratic

---

[11] J. M. Keynes: *How to Pay for the War*, New York, 1940, preface.

control over influential and privileged groups and the hesitation of the governments to assume economic leadership.

From the necessity of government control of economic mobilization we must not conclude that the government has to *operate* all businesses or to regulate them in all minute details. On the contrary, this would lead to a bureaucratic and inefficient type of war economy. To achieve an efficient war economy the government should restrict its activity to the issuing of general rules or guiding principles, and it should to a high extent rely upon citizen coöperation. Only where it cannot be obtained, are stricter forms of control necessary. Intelligent coöperation of citizens is much more likely to be found in democratic than in authoritarian countries, provided the democratic government does not forfeit the confidence of the people.

We must now turn our attention to the actual working of a war economy, within belligerent nations (Part II) and in the international field (Part III).

SUGGESTED REFERENCES

Cherne, L. M.: *Adjusting Your Business to War,* New York, 1940, chapters IV and V.

(Clark, J. M., Hamilton, W. H., and Moulton, H. G.; editors): *Readings in the Economics of War,* Chicago, 1918, parts V and VI.

Industrial Mobilization Plan, Revision of 1939, A Study of Methods for the Effective and Equitable Utilization of the Industrial Resources of the United States in Time of War, 76th Congress, 2d Session, Senate Document No. 134, Washington, D. C., 1939.

Popper, D. H., and deWilde, J. C.: "Wartime Economy of Britain and France," *Foreign Policy Reports,* July 15, 1940.

Tobin, H. J., and Bidwell, P. W.: *Mobilizing Civilian America,* New York, 1940, chapters I–V.

PART TWO

THE WAR ECONOMY

CHAPTER 5

Military Versus Civilian Demand

Sudden economic changes are painful. In ordinary times, the economic system moves slowly. Repetition and routine work dominate, and what change there is proceeds gradually and in individual firms or industries. Producers produce for a rather stable demand, and their methods of production follow established customs. Many circumstances make modern capitalism a rather unruly machine as compared with the economic regime of the manor or the medieval town. Capitalism must weather technical changes and the business cycle, new discoveries and social crises. But the system as a whole—the majority of demand and supply schedules—changes in a relatively slow fashion.

The Upsurge of Military Demand

Things are different in the period of transition from peace to war. Suddenly new demands appear, of a volume unknown before and of extraordinary urgency. Military forces have to be equipped, fed, clothed, and transported. Their equipment has to be renewed at a rate that varies with the intensity of fighting. To a certain extent the goods that the armies consume are ordinary civilian consumption goods: bread, meat, socks, shirts, and gasoline. Available supplies of these can easily be transferred from civilian to military use. But a much larger number of goods are of more or less specialized character: uniforms,

MILITARY VERSUS CIVILIAN DEMAND

helmets, fighting equipment, military radio sets, and field kitchens. Here appear new tasks for industry.

Every general staff makes estimates of the quantities of goods needed in war. These estimates must of course be conditional; they will depend on the strength of the forces to be mobilized, on the distance over which they have to be transported, on the length of the war and the nature of operations. It is obvious that more of everything is needed to equip a force of four million men than one of half a million. A study of American history in 1917 will illustrate the significance of this difference in all details. The nature of military operations is of no smaller importance. Considering the needs of a modern army (excluding navy and air force) in a one-year war along a 1,000-kilometer front in terms of metal requirements only, S. T. Possony arrived at the following estimate: [1]

IRON AND STEEL REQUIREMENTS IN A WAR OF ONE YEAR

	Alternative I: Defensive on Land Offensive in the Air	Alternative II: Offensive on Land and in the Air
	(in thousand tons)	
Arms	750	2,800
Ammunition	7,000	25,500
Fortifications	8,000	9,000
TOTAL	15,750	37,300

It should be noted that the offensive type of warfare requires more than double the quantity of iron and steel needed for the defensive type.

It is not our intention here to record the variety of estimates that have been made of the quantities of materials needed in future wars. Nor do we plan to make new estimates. It may, however, be of interest to study some of the needs that the first world war created in this country.

---
[1] S. T. Possony: *To-Morrow's War*, London, 1938, 56.

The demand of the American army for clothing was much larger than one would expect by considering the four million mobilized men as so many civilian consumers. Soldiers wore out their shoes five times as fast as civilians. In 1918, the army purchases of blankets were two and a quarter times, those of wool socks one and a half times as great as the entire American output in 1914. The length of supply lines and the rapid wear to which army clothing was subject at the front helped to create the enormous demand.

The stream of supplies going forward to an army may be likened to the water delivered against a fire by an old-fashioned bucket brigade. For every pailful thrown on the fire there must be many that have been taken from the source of supply and are on the way. . . . The rule generally followed for clothing was that there should be for each man at the front a three months' reserve in France, another two or three months' reserve in the United States, and a third three months' supply continuously in transit. Wool coats, for example, last about three months in active service. Hence for every coat on a man's back at the front there had to be a coat in reserve in France, a coat in transit, and a coat in reserve in the United States. For every man at the front four coats were needed, and needed as soon as he went overseas. Two million men overseas required something like 8,000,000 coats, and required them immediately.[2]

Similarly the army needed larger quantities of foodstuffs than those corresponding to the normal rations of just as many civilians. This was due not only to the soldiers' good appetites, but also to the unavoidably wasteful distribution of goods at the front.

Millions of rifles, hundreds of thousands of machine guns, thousands of pieces of light and heavy artillery, and the corresponding ammunitions were needed. At the beginning of the war, rifles and light artillery were available in quanti-

---

[2] L. P. Ayres: *The War with Germany*, A Statistical Summary, Washington, D. C., 1919, 50–51.

ties sufficient to equip an army of 500,000 men. But when a much larger expeditionary force was formed, there appeared an immediate demand for huge quantities of this equipment. In several lines, American industry was unable, despite all efforts, to satisfy the demand. The Allies had to help out with artillery, tanks, and airplanes, but when this happened, American industry faced a larger demand from the Allies for raw materials, motors, and other articles.

On the declaration of war the United States had 55 training airplanes, of which 51 were classified as obsolete and the other 4 as obsolescent. When we entered the war the Allies made the designs of their planes available to us and before the end of hostilities furnished us from their own manufacture 3,800 service planes.[3]

In order to evaluate the volume of military demand it is necessary to take account of the replacement needs of modern equipment. They too depend of course on the intensity of fighting. During the World War, airplanes were estimated to last between one and two months on the average, tanks three months. Nowadays, a monthly loss of twenty-five to thirty per cent of the plane and tank complement under conditions of active warfare is assumed by military experts.[4] In 1932, a Russian author estimated that an attacking army during one month of operations would have to be re-equipped nineteen times with the standard quantity of ammunitions.[5] Ordinary wear and tear, lack of facilities for repair work, and enemy action create large replacement needs also for guns and for transportation and sanitary equipment.

The military demand for this variety of finished products

---

[3] *Ibid.*, 99–100.
[4] Possony, *op. cit.*, 28.
[5] F. Trutko, quoted in: Institut für Konjunkturforschung: *Industrielle Mobilmachung*, Hamburg, 1936, 22–23.

MILITARY VERSUS CIVILIAN DEMAND

finds its repercussion in the field of raw and semifinished materials. Of the demand for these materials a high percentage emanates from military sources. Professor F. W. Taussig impressively described the situation prevailing in this country during the World War:

> Almost the entire supply of many important articles was wanted for government use—partly by the United States Government itself, partly by contractors working for the Government, partly by the Allies. . . . When things were at their height, the total non-private demand for iron and steel absorbed 85 per cent to 90 per cent of the tonnage. This was the maximum; but at no time between the autumn of 1917 and the autumn of 1918 was the [nonprivate] demand for less than 60 per cent. . . . Nine-tenths of the nickel was taken, during the war period as a whole, for government and Allies' use, and at least as much of the aluminum. . . . Of the coarser cotton fabrics, as much as 60 per cent was at one time taken by the Government; of the country's entire output of cotton manufactures, as much as 30 per cent.[6]

The same is true for zinc, mercury, copper, pine, spruce and fir lumber, acids, and so on. During a period of twenty-five months from April, 1917, to April, 1919, the American government required military goods and services at the rate of one million dollars an hour.[7]

As we saw before, military demand is distinguished by its urgency. This renders its volume still more disturbing to industry. The urgency of the demand makes it impossible to introduce the new production program slowly, to complete earlier private orders, and to adjust equipment and labor force gradually to new conditions. The resulting difficulties can of course be minimized by putting the nation's industry on a war basis before hostilities actually begin; but this is, as we have seen before, a very expensive undertaking.

---

[6] F. W. Taussig: "Price-Fixing as Seen by a Price-Fixer," *Quarterly Journal of Economics*, February, 1919, 211 and 212. Reprinted by permission of the President and Fellows of Harvard College.

[7] Ayres, *op. cit.*, 131.

Resisting Civilian Demand

Still, the adaptation of industry to its new tasks would be comparatively simple if civilian demand declined instantaneously and by amounts corresponding to the increase in military buying. Indeed, one of the essential problems that must be solved by the country's economic general staff is that of bringing about a speedy and large curtailment of civilian demand; for this is by no means certain to take place automatically at the outbreak of war. The purchasing agents of the government are most likely to confront two difficulties: first, industry's slowness in adapting itself to the new kind of demand; second, the competition of the civilian consumer's dollar.

The outbreak of the war finds consumers engaged in the execution of their various expenditure plans. Mr. Jones is building a house, Mr. Green is buying an automobile, the Millers were just married and are buying household equipment and furniture. Some consumers may even expand and accelerate their purchases on hearing the news of the war. Staple foods, canned goods, shoes, and clothing may be demanded in larger than usual quantities, because people expect them to become scarce and dear. Ordinary buying plus hoarding of goods may seriously curtail the amount of supplies available for military purposes. Government appeals or early rationing of goods may render the struggle of the civilians for goods less effective. Yet it will not be an easy task to make civilians refrain from buying in their customary way.

As the war goes on, there will be further stimuli to civilian demand. They will tend to keep this demand on a high level unless measures are taken to prevent their effects or the appearance of the stimuli themselves. Unemployment will vanish, because military and industrial mobilization re-

MILITARY VERSUS CIVILIAN DEMAND 91

quire everybody's services. Shortages of labor will appear in certain occupations that are in particularly high demand, and wages will tend to rise in those occupations. The total wage bill of the country may decline because of the call of workers to the colors; but the per capita income of the civilian population will not necessarily go down. The average civilian may in times of rising money wages and employment have a larger amount of money to spend. And he will try to get his money's worth of consumption goods.

Simultaneously, incomes from capital and management are likely to increase. War business may be costly, but if prices are not kept stable, profits are going to increase because of greater margins. The urgent demand for military goods creates a seller's market. Manufacturers and traders will certainly not renounce the advantages of this situation automatically. Since the volume of business is likely to increase for many of them, there will be a second reason for profits to rise. Like the worker, the manufacturer will try to get his money's worth of goods, the only difference being that a large part of his profits will not be devoted to the purchase of consumption goods but to that of new machines and larger amounts of raw materials for expansion purposes. In peace times the investment of profits in new enterprise has nothing objectionable to it; on the contrary, it is considered the duty of capitalists to invest. But are conditions the same in war? Will not the machines that are bought to replace or to supplement other machines prevent some tanks or planes from being built? Will not leather bought to produce more ladies' shoes compete with the army's demand for boots? Should not shipping space taken by imports of foreign wines and fashion articles be reserved for imports of rubber or nitrates? Can industry be allowed to build new factories, hire new workers to produce civilian goods?

One may readily answer that civilian demand must be curtailed and any means designed to curtail it must be endorsed. Some shrinkage will be unavoidable because, as we shall see, the possibilities of industry to expand output are far from being unlimited. Yet we must keep in mind two things: first, that the civilian population must be assured of a reasonably satisfactory level of living, and second, that the border line between essential and unessential needs is sometimes difficult to determine. Civilians must be provided with essential foodstuffs to keep them healthy, fuel to keep them warm, and clothing to replace outworn goods. They may, on the other hand, be compelled to stop all purchases of durable consumer goods, such as houses, automobiles, refrigerators, vacuum cleaners, and furniture, since workers and plants producing those articles are needed for more urgent purposes. Raw materials and labor must be provided for industries that supply producers of military goods with machines and tools. In unessential lines, however, an effort will be made to prevent replacement and expansion of industrial equipment.

Order in the Chaos

By what means can the government obtain the necessary military goods? How can it restrict civilian demand and ensure the priority of essential over unessential needs? These questions lead us to a number of measures which will be discussed in Chapters 7, 8, and 9. War finance is the first answer, but it has been found to be a partial answer only. More specific interventions in the economic mechanism are required, such as schemes of priorities of orders, rationing of producers' and consumers' goods, and price control. It is not sufficient to restrict the purchasing power of civilians. They may spend what they retain in a way detrimental to public health and morale. It is not sufficient to tax war profits. To some extent they must be prevented from coming into existence; for they are likely to go hand in hand with rising prices, and prices have to be kept from rising to avoid strikes and other manifestations of popular discontent accompanying inequitable distribution of scarce supplies. In order to gear the national economy to highest output under a program which is new and uncustomary to all of its members, the government must not shy away from sweeping changes as well as detailed measures of control, education, and compulsion.

It will make little sense to subject civilian demand to severe restrictions while the purchasing policies of the government are left free to spread the germ of disorder. Purchasing agencies must be coördinated. Otherwise, they will counteract each other, bid up prices, and add unnecessarily to the confusion.

Conditions prevailing in this country at the beginning of the World War have been summarized by the chairman of the *War Industries Board*.

> For the purposes of supply our Army was organized to make purchases according to the use to which the commodity would be put. The Ordnance Department bought guns and ammunition; the Quartermaster, clothing, blankets, food, and trucks; the Signal Corps, telephone apparatus, field glasses, etc.; the Engineers, building materials, railroad supplies, and implements; and so on. Each service had subunits charged with responsibility for particular groups of supplies. More than one service frequently bought quantities of the same commodity. . . . Before the war was over, the Army found it necessary to reorganize its purchasing system, gradually drawing it together under one control and revising its classifications. Outside of the War Department, the Navy, and later the Emergency Fleet and the Railroad Administration were making government purchases. In addition to all, the principal Allies had purchasing missions in this country. All of these factors contributed to the difficulty of laying down a program of requirements.[8]

---

[8] B. M. Baruch: *American Industry in the War*, A Report of the War Industries Board, Washington, D. C., 1921, 31.

This lack of coördination of the numerous procuring agencies did a great deal of damage. Orders were piled upon certain producers who had previously supplied the materials needed by the various bureaus, while simultaneously other factories had to dismiss workers because of lack of orders. Congestion soon began to appear in the northeastern manufacturing district of the country.[9] Hence, it became obvious that measures had to be taken to set up a clearing system for government orders. A clearance committee was organized as an administrative unit of the *General Munitions Board,* which became later the *War Industries Board.* This committee prepared a list of relatively scarce materials, and government agencies were requested not to place orders for any of these materials without first having them cleared by the committee. Moreover, buying of the Allied governments was centralized. From August, 1917, on, all of their orders had to be handled through or with the consent of the *Allied Purchasing Commission* consisting of three American officials.

In the spring of 1918, however, a further coördination of official purchases was found necessary. The *Requirements Division* was organized within the *War Industries Board* with the task of collecting information on the prospective needs of the various government purchasing units and the *Allied Purchasing Commission.* All orders ready to be placed were to be sent to the Board for clearance. The Board developed a flexible system of dealing with these orders:

The commodity sections, on whom the burden of clearing rested, would act on these requests in one of six ways. (1) Clear without comment, in which case the purchaser was permitted to go into the market and order as he saw fit; (2) clear with restriction as to the area in which the order might be placed;

---

[9] For similar experience in Great Britain, see the *War Memoirs* of D. Lloyd George, 1914–1915, Boston, 1933, 123 and 233.

(3) clear with restriction as to the electric power system on which the order would draw; (4) clear subject to restrictions as to certain named plants or with restrictions inhibiting the creation of new facilities for the execution of the order; (5) clear with an actual allocation of the order to a particular named source of supply; (6) clear with advice as to suitable source of supply.[10]

Thus, the commodity sections of the War Industries Board became the clearing houses for the orders of the numerous government purchasing units. Here we observe a typical change in the organization of government buying. It occurred in all major belligerent countries. Government orders tended to be canalized through agencies dealing with demands on a particular *industry* rather than with requirements of a particular *division of government.*

Before turning to a record of further government measures designed to bring order into the chaos of demands, let us look at the factors that govern industry's capacity to satisfy these demands.

SUGGESTED REFERENCES

Ayres, L. P.: *The War with Germany,* A Statistical Summary, Washington, D. C., 1919.
Baruch, B. M.: *American Industry in the War,* A Report of the War Industries Board, Washington, D. C., 1921, Part I, chapters 1–3.

---

[10] Baruch, *op. cit.,* 36 and 37.

CHAPTER 6

Factors Limiting National Output

In the preceding chapter we surveyed the upsurge of military demand and the resistance of civilian demand to war-required economic sacrifices. Now we come to the question: how can these demands, or at least their essential parts, be satisfied? The task falls squarely on the nation's productive forces. Minor powers in a belligerent alliance can dodge it by relying on supplies from the leading industrial nations, but this, of course, means still larger requirements from the industrial machine of the latter. Is industry well enough prepared to satisfy these demands in wartime?

We shall see that there are a number of obstacles in the way of a sufficient expansion of industrial output. These obstacles may easily be serious enough to keep the wartime output of industry at a level lower than that prevailing before the war. It is almost certain that in their presence the warring nation cannot produce as much as it would in peacetime under full utilization of its human and material resources.

THE SOLDIER-WORKER RATIO

The first obstacle is the military mobilization of man power. Earlier we recorded a few instances from the last war showing the effects of indiscriminate mobilization on industrial life.[1] Everybody will agree that "overmobilization" has to be avoided. This, however, is more easily said than done. We are left with the task of determining the *right degree* of mobilization, the optimum ratio of soldiers and workers. The general staff of a country has to solve this problem on the basis of military and economic considerations. It will do well to base the solution on thorough research, for procedure by trial and error involves delays and losses in both the military and the economic field. Yet a certain amount of experimenting cannot be avoided, since the development of the war and its requirements can rarely be foreseen in sufficient detail.

Some estimates have been made of the soldier-worker ratio. They are based on World War experience. Possony arrived at a ratio of one soldier to thirteen workmen in a predominantly defensive type of warfare, of 1:17 to 1:20 in aggressive warfare.[2] In this estimate the workers are assumed to provide for the army *and* for themselves. Secretary of War D. F. Davis asserted in 1925 that this country would require the services of seventeen workers at home to equip and maintain one soldier on the fighting front.[3] Other estimates are more conservative. In 1918, Secretary of Labor Wilson estimated that it took from six to ten workers in the rear to maintain one American soldier in the trenches.[4] Another estimate reported in *The New York Times* of October 15, 1939, and attributed to Allied technicians in the present war puts the ratio of combatants and civilians necessary to supply them at 1:5 to 1:7 for the Allies, 1:10 to 1:12 for Germany. The over-all ratio of soldiers to workers appears somewhat variable. It depends on a great number of factors.

---

[1] See above, pp. 70–71.
[2] S. T. Possony: *To-Morrow's War*, London, 1938, 94.
[3] *Army and Navy Journal*, December 5, 1925, 330.
[4] *U. S. Employment Service Bulletin*, July 31, 1918, 6.

98   FACTORS LIMITING NATIONAL OUTPUT

The determination of the soldier-worker ratio and its application to military and industrial mobilization plans, however, solves only part of the problem. Suppose the correct ratio were found in a particular case; from which industries and occupations shall the soldiers be taken? What groups of workers shall be exempt from military service? Obviously, this part of the problem is quite as complex, and its solution quite as important, as the determination of the over-all ratio between combatants and workers. It is interesting to follow the various and not always very successful experiments undertaken in Great Britain between 1914 and 1918.

BADGING AND DEBADGING

At first there was overmobilization and frictional unemployment. The recruiting officers went around and enlisted all men who did not object to joining the military forces. "The patriotic impulse was not cautious. It did not select its men, saying to the skilled man 'Stay' and to the unskilled 'Come.' It knew nothing of key industries or pivotal workers. It chose, if not all, the best in all ranks and grades of industry." [5] While some important factories found themselves deprived of their labor forces, others were unable to keep their men occupied. The government had to improvise relief committees and work rooms for the unemployed. By October, 1914, however, unemployment decreased. England was left with the problem of combating overmobilization.

Already in September Vickers, the big armament firm, had suggested the issuance of badges to protect men employed in vital production from the recruiting sergeant. Beginning with 1915 the government started out on such a

---
[5] H. Wolfe: *Labour Supply and Regulation*, Oxford: Oxford University Press, 1923, 15.

FACTORS LIMITING NATIONAL OUTPUT

scheme. Both War Office and Admiralty began to issue badges.

The principles followed by the two agencies were different and tentative. The Admiralty badges were issued to the Royal Dockyards and to the contractors on the Admiralty list. All men working in these establishments were eligible for protection against recruitment. The badges were not numbered. The system followed by the War Office was less generous. Its badges were confined to "technical workers" employed by the Royal Factories and recognized armament producers. Under this scheme, neither unskilled labor nor any labor not *directly* engaged in the making of guns, carriages, small arms, and ammunition was eligible. The War Office badges were numbered. Under both schemes the final decision as to whether or not a worker was indispensable was put into the hands of the employer.[6]

Soon the War Office found it necessary to extend protection to skilled workers in other essential branches of production but it refrained from including miners, steel workers, or workers in food production.

In July, 1915, this dualistic system was abolished. Badging became the dominion of the newly established Ministry of Munitions. This agency largely followed the principles evolved by the War Office; but it extended the scope of the badging scheme considerably. The old badges had to be withdrawn and replaced, in cases that qualified under the new definitions of vital work, by the new national war service badges. Since data on the distribution of man power were found insufficient, a labor census was undertaken in the midst of a general revolution of working conditions. And new problems were encountered. The demarcation line between skilled and unskilled labor was found to be very uncertain in many cases. "Moreover, skill could not

---

[6] *Ibid.*, 24 and 25.

be the only criterion. The skilled man depended upon his unskilled helper for his product, and in some of the key occupations unskilled strength was from the national point of view as vital as skill." [7]

The badging system proved, however, to be very efficient. The list of protected occupations was growing, and soon the problem was no longer one of protecting men from the recruiting officer but of protecting the latter from the Ministry of Munitions' badging department. The military forces needed more men, and voluntary conscription proved insufficient in providing them. In January, 1916, England resorted to compulsory conscription. Of course, exemptions of indispensable workers from service had to be continued, but the criteria of indispensability had to be refined. At that time began the period of "debadging" or the "combing-out" of industries for recruits.

The refinement of the criteria of indispensability took place in two directions: age and physical fitness of the individual worker were taken into account. Obviously, it did not make sense to permit enrollment of workers in military service if these workers did not meet the physical standards of the service. Therefore, an attempt was made to restrict exemptions from military service to skilled workers above certain age limits and below certain standards of physical fitness. On the other hand, provision was made for the withdrawal of badges from workers in protected occupations who were fit for military service. The amount of "debadging" was, however, not very large. Up to August, 1916, only 40,000 of the more than two million badges issued had been withdrawn. From August, 1917, to the Armistice, another 70,000 men were posted to the colors.

The smallness of these figures finds its explanation in the fact that the number of "superfluous" workers was narrowed

---

[7] *Ibid.*, 31.

down by the simultaneous efforts to increase the military forces and to guarantee the production of supplies needed by them and the Allies. During the later years of the war, the British government finally obtained the powers necessary to effectuate at will transfers of men from factory to camp or *vice versa*. It also perfected its concept of "essential work." The trade-union leadership, on the other hand, attempted to provide the government with emergency squads of skilled workers (War Munitions Volunteers); but the effect was not spectacular.

The shortness of America's participation in the war and the relatively small number of men called to the colors rendered the problem of exemptions from military service less acute. It was dealt with by the *War Labor Policies Board*.[8] This board developed a system of furloughing skilled labor in essential industries.

LABOR'S RIGHTS AND THE EXIGENCIES OF WAR

We have seen that measures can be taken to remove the obstacles to output which originate in overmobilization. These are, however, not all the obstacles that have to be overcome. In countries where the state is not empowered to conscript labor, serious obstacles are bound to arise from the established rights of labor.

In all democratic countries, labor organizations have struggled for recognition of certain workers' rights. Their successes have been embodied in agreements with employers or even in legislative statutes. Maximum hours of work have been fixed by collective agreements and state laws. Unions of skilled workers have successfully striven to prevent employers from "diluting" the labor force, that is, from

---

[8] *Reports of the Department of Labor*, 1919, Washington, D. C., 1920, 135–139.

replacing skilled workers by unskilled ones, from training more than a certain number of apprentices, and from altering the proportion of male and female workers. On the other hand, the right of the worker to choose and to abandon a job has found recognition. These and other regulations can be considered the appanage of a democratic state. They are intended to improve the well-being of the working class, and some have certainly fulfilled the expectations placed upon them. It is true that some of the rights of labor render technical change and increase of output more difficult; but in times of peace it may rightly be queried whether such sacrifices of output and technical adaptability are not more than compensated for by the increase in physical and economic security of the working man, his enjoyment of leisure time, and the avoidance of certain forms of exploitation. In time of war, however, leisure and economic security lose much of their social value. The deployment of the highest productive effort possible becomes a national goal overshadowing all others. The rights of labor may obstruct the way to this goal.

During the first world war the leading labor organizations of all countries endorsed the national war policy in principle. This did not prevent them, however, from continuing the fight for the rights of labor. Numerous strikes were called. They were directed against various concomitants and institutions of the war economy. In Great Britain, the country of the strongest labor organizations, the enthusiastic support lent by the unions to the cause of war was soon superseded by a more critical attitude. Strikes, after having declined in number and importance from 1914 to 1916, flared up anew in spite of agreements with the government (for instance, the "Treasury Agreement" of March, 1915 [9]) and antistrike laws.

---

[9] *Cf.* Wolfe, *op. cit.*, 361–363.

FACTORS LIMITING NATIONAL OUTPUT

Number of Working Days Lost by Strikes
in England During the War of 1914–1918 [10]
(in thousands)

1913	9,804
1914	10,746
1915	2,953
1916	2,446
1917	5,647
1918	5,875
1919	34,969

In Germany the number of working days lost by strikes increased tremendously after 1915, rising from 41,000 in that year to 1,860,000 in 1917 and 5,218,000 in 1918.[11] In France, a similar development was observed.

What were the main grievances of labor? On the one hand we find the rise in the cost of living entailed by war and insufficiently prevented by government control.[12] On the other hand, we find that workers objected to the extension of overtime work, the dilution of labor, and the discretionary powers placed in the hands of the employers by the badging schemes. Finally, in England, they objected to the part of the *Munitions of War Act* which introduced a *leaving certificate* for people employed in munitions work. In order to find a new job, a munitions worker had to obtain consent from his employer or the "munitions tribunal" to leave his present position. In an attempt to reduce the labor turnover this sytem created conditions that labor designated as slavery. In some cases, indeed, the employer used his power to refuse leaving certificates in order to force extraordinary working conditions on his employees. Continued opposition to this system finally compelled the government to abolish it in 1917. This did not mean, however, that all restrictions on the mobility of labor were removed.

---

[10] *Statistical Abstract for the United Kingdom*, 1913–1915/28, 95.

[11] L. Grebler in L. Grebler and W. Winkler: *The Cost of the World War to Germany and to Austria-Hungary*, New Haven, 1940, 33.

[12] See below pp. 161 and 175.

The government now forbade munitions workers to change to work of another nature.[13]

Dilution

We have seen the attempts made in England to prevent the skilled-labor force from deserting essential industries. Some of these industries required even larger numbers of skilled workers than before the war; for they had to expand their output. But many skilled workers left their jobs. From where could replacements be obtained? From the ranks of unskilled labor, the labor forces of nonessential industries, from commercial occupations and domestic service, from social classes whose members had not worked for their living in normal times, and finally from the ranks of school children and household workers. Since the military forces required all dispensable men, women formed the main reservoir for replacements. More than one and a half million women entered industry,[14] coming mainly from unpaid household duties. It is true that most of them entered industry as unskilled workers; but many women as well as many of the formerly unskilled men worked their way up to skilled jobs. Simultaneously, the scarcity of skilled workers led to changes in production processes. Wherever skilled labor could be replaced by unskilled labor or by automatic machinery, there was a strong incentive to do so.

In Britain, the government took an active hand in furthering the process of labor dilution. The *Munitions of War Act* of July, 1915, stipulated that in the munitions factories (in the wide sense of the word) to be put under the control of government "any rule, practice, or custom not having the force of law which tends to restrict production or em-

---

[13] G. D. H. Cole: *Trade Unionism and Munitions*, Oxford, 1923, 81, 116 ff., 151 ff.

[14] *Cf.* Wolfe, *op. cit.*, 169. See also p. 14 above.

ployment shall be suspended."[15] This act outlawed, for the "controlled establishments," all collective agreements stipulating that a certain job could be done by a skilled worker only, that certain proportions between the number of skilled and unskilled or male and female workers should be maintained, that nonunion workers should not be admitted, or that a maximum number of hours of work should not be exceeded. Promises were given by members of the government that the restoration of such practices would not be prevented after the war.[16]

Opposition to dilution did not come from the side of labor alone. The employers too objected. They were afraid that the introduction of large numbers of semiskilled and unskilled workers into jobs previously filled by the skilled might result in a decline of output. Therefore, the British government found it necessary to set up a staff of "dilution officers."

The business of these officers was of a delicate and technical character. It was their duty to visit all engineering works and others engaged in the production of munitions to satisfy themselves, first, that the fullest use was being made of the skilled men employed; and, secondly, that upon work suitable for semiskilled or lesser skilled work-people the appropriate grades of male and female labour were being used.[17]

A great deal of patience and persistence was necessary to persuade employers constantly harassed by demands to speed up their deliveries that some of their best men were superfluous, or to convince workers that women had to be admitted to skilled jobs. Yet the dilution policy effectively increased the percentage of women workers in a number of industries. Between July, 1914, and July, 1918, the percentage of women in the total labor force rose from 9.4 to

---
[15] Ibid., 315.
[16] Cole, op. cit., 241 ff.
[17] Wolfe, op. cit., 162.

24.6 in the metal industries, from 20.1 to 39.0 in the chemical industries, and from 2.6 to 46.7 in government factories.[18]

The problem of dilution was not restricted to Great Britain. It appeared in all belligerent countries. In the United States, in July, 1918, a "Woman in Industry Service" and a "Training and Dilution Service" were created in the Department of Labor. These services as well as other agencies of Federal and State governments dealt with the introduction of women into industry and the dilution of skilled labor. Little is known, however, about the results of these endeavors, since they were short-lived and the Department of Labor lacked sufficient funds to carry out a statistical survey.[19]

While dilution and a lengthening of the hours of work took place in munition industries, there was a relaxation in the protection of female and child labor in Britain as well as in other European countries. Women were admitted to strenuous and dangerous occupations, such as coal mining, building, or powder making; twelve-year-old children were allowed to enter industry. In all belligerent countries the trend was in the direction of a more exhausting utilization of available labor forces in the making of war products. In nonessential industries, however, it was sometimes found convenient to reduce hours of work in order to conserve materials. In 1915, Germany forbade night work in bakeries and limited the work in spinning, weaving, and hosiery mills to ten hours a day and five days a week.[20]

In some countries the working population was also di-

---

[18] *Ibid.*, 170.

[19] First Annual Report of the Director of the Woman in Industry Service, *Reports of the Department of Labor, 1919*, Washington, D. C., 1920, 1131–1159. See also: G. S. Watkins: *Labor Problems and Labor Administration in the United States During the World War*, University of Illinois Studies in the Social Sciences, Vol. VIII, nos. 3 and 4, Urbana, 1919, 157 ff.

[20] Anna Rochester in an article reproduced in (Clark, J. M., Hamilton, W. H., and Moulton, H. G.; editors): *Readings in the Economics of War*, 525.

FACTORS LIMITING NATIONAL OUTPUT 107

luted in a national sense. In Germany, for instance, military and civilian prisoners as well as hired or deported Polish and Belgian civilians furnished about 400,000 workers at the turn of 1916–1917. This seems a considerable number, but it is small in comparison to the drain that the military mobilization had made on the working population.[21] In France, at the end of 1917, more than 200,000 military prisoners were at work. During the war another 200,000 foreign workers entered France from various European countries and 140,000 from French colonies.[22] In England, the trade unions successfully opposed the importation of colored labor from abroad. However, 75,000 Belgians, Danes, Portuguese, and Dutch, 7,000 people from dominions, and about 9,000 enemy aliens were put to work.[23]

We see that the war economy requires restrictions of certain rights of labor. Some of these rights, for instance the freedom of contract, the right of collective bargaining, and the protection against exploitative methods, are valuable elements of the social structure in a democratic society. A democratic nation cannot expect labor to yield these rights without guaranteeing their restitution upon the return of peace. It cannot accept war as an excuse for a general and definite abrogation of the rights of labor, which may be desired by certain groups of employers. Nothing could be more detrimental to the morale and productivity of the working class and hence to the national war effort than such a policy. Therefore, the government's labor policy should be directed by men who hold the confidence of the country's working class and who realize the requirements of the war economy. They should obtain the necessary concessions from labor by means of persuasion and secure the coöpera-

---
[21] Grebler and Winkler, *op. cit.*, 30 and 31.
[22] A. Fontaine: *L'Industrie Française pendant la Guerre*, Paris, 1925, 68 and 83.
[23] Wolfe, *op. cit.*, 80, 81, and 216.

tion of the important labor organizations for this purpose.

Let us now return to the first world war and study its effects on the productivity of labor.

Declining Productivity

While dilution, longer working hours, restrictions on the mobility of labor, and other measures were used in the attempt to facilitate the deployment of the highest productive effort, they could not but result in certain losses of efficiency. The transfer of workers from nonessential to essential industries proved extremely difficult. Workers had to be moved over long distances and trained to new kinds of work; new housing accommodations had to be provided at the new places of work. Where one or the other of these requirements was not fulfilled, the new workers furnished an unsatisfactory product. The same thing was bound to happen when workers were forced against their will to stay with unpopular employers. It should be mentioned, however, that the losses of productivity due to extraordinary frequency of changes in personnel (labor turnover) were more obvious. The problem of an excessive labor turnover during the war was particularly accentuated in this country.[24]

Upon entering the war industries many of the new workers, male and female, adapted themselves quickly to their tasks and did excellent work; but many others failed. Longer working hours did not affect the output per hour of the stronger workers; but many were unable to stand the strain, weakened as they were by food shortages and other wartime hardships. Their daily or weekly output increased by less than the increase in working time, or actually decreased. The quality of the work deteriorated; the number

---

[24] Watkins, *op. cit.*, 59 and 60.

FACTORS LIMITING NATIONAL OUTPUT 109

of accidents rose. Hence productivity of the individual worker and of factories as a whole declined in the belligerent countries.

Declining productivity appeared throughout the German economy during the first world war. In coal mining the average yield per worker per shift declined by about thirty per cent from 1913 to October, 1918.[25] Comparable decreases in productivity took place in railroad work and a number of leading industries. The decline of productivity in British coal mining was less pronounced. It amounted to only six per cent between 1913 and 1918.[26] This country too experienced a drop in productivity in the field of manufacturing during the years 1917 and 1918. After having risen during the period of neutrality (1914 to 1916) from 108 to 119, the index of output per person in manufacturing industries (1899 = 100) dropped to 110 in 1917 and to 105 in 1918. From 1914 to 1918 there was a continuous rise in the number of persons engaged in manufacturing. But the volume of their product increased only up to 1916, remained about constant from 1916 to 1917, and showed an actual decline from 1917 to 1918.[27]

There were of course many reasons for the decline in productivity besides the weakening and disorganization of the labor force. Plants producing war materials were pushed beyond normal capacity by overtime work and night shifts. Machinery wore out at a quicker rate since it was used continuously and handled without adequate care by newcomers to the job. Replacement of machines and parts was prevented by transfer of machine shops to munitions work. Moreover, losses of time and output were incurred in adjusting plants to mass production. The economies of

---

[25] Grebler and Winkler, *op. cit.*, 33 and 34.
[26] R. A. S. Redmayne: *The British Coal-Mining Industry During the War,* Oxford, 1923, 222.
[27] Leo Wolman in *Recent Economic Changes in the United States,* New York, 1929, Vol. II, 454.

the latter could frequently not be realized before the war was over.

In mining, the exploitation of poor or hardly accessible minerals was resumed and tended to lower average productivity. In Germany, for instance, the number of iron-ore mines increased from 1913 to 1917 by twenty-two per cent; but the output of iron ore *fell* by the same percentage. The number of copper mines was trebled; but the output remained nearly constant.[28] Similarly, obsolete manufacturing plants were revamped and exploited. Their output was of course low as compared with that of up-to-date establishments.

It would be erroneous to believe that industry can change from peace to war production overnight. A big automobile factory cannot be changed by magic into an airplane plant. Of course readily effective plans, acquaintance with the technical problems of mass production, and efficient organization may in certain cases make relatively quick transformations possible. But we should keep some of the experiences of the World War in mind. In this country, the typical period of adaptation was six to nine months for the production of shells, at least nine months for artillery, and still longer for tanks. Even where no fundamental changes in the production program were involved factories took a very long time to arrive at mass production of new models. The gun factory of Cammel-Laird in Nottingham, England, received orders for a new type of cannon in June, 1917. Three hundred new machines had to be installed, and the first cannon left the factory in September, 1918. The airplane firm de Havilland built a sample of a new plane in June, 1917. Large-scale production of this plane did not materialize until the end of 1918.[29] The time spent on plant adaptation may perhaps be shortened; it cannot be

---

[28] For the basic figures see Grebler and Winkler, *op. cit.,* 103.
[29] Various sources quoted in *Industrielle Mobilmachung,* 13–16.

eliminated altogether. We must not forget that it takes a modern American automobile factory about four months to perform the customary and well-prepared "tooling up" for a new car model.

Experience in the Present War: War Economy Versus Muddling Through

The first world war provided a large amount of experience with respect to factors hindering the national output and ways of combating these obstacles. Of the countries opposing each other in the present war, Germany has shown all the signs of a systematic study and application of this body of experience, while England has done comparatively little.

Under national-socialist rule, the German economic system had been geared to war conditions long before the outbreak of the war. After destroying the independent labor organizations the government organized labor in a vast state union, the *Arbeitsfront*. Under this regime, rights and prerogatives of labor could easily be taken away when they conflicted with the deployment of highest productivity, and the government did not hesitate to make use of its powers. Even before the outbreak of the war, labor was reshuffled, diluted, and moved to new working places or occupations. Workers were conscripted for special tasks (for example, the construction of the *Westwall* fortifications). Labor passports were introduced. They recorded skill, experience, and health of the worker and facilitated his classification under military and economic categories. Measures were taken to reduce labor turnover and to bind workers to their working places. Women entered industry in large numbers. And above all, the feverish armament activity brought about the almost complete disappearance of unemployment among employable workers. Based as it was on a great deal of compulsion and disregard for individual rights, this system was nevertheless admirably suited to war conditions.

When war broke out, unemployment did not increase. On the contrary it was reduced by military conscription. According to the *Frankfurter Zeitung* of December 31, 1939, the number of unemployed in Greater Germany (excluding Bohemia and Moravia) was only 126,000 at the end of November, 1939, as compared with 461,000 a year before. Only 18,000 of those were considered fully employable.

Since the distribution of workers over the production of military and civilian goods had already assumed a warlike character before the war, the redistribution of the labor force was not much of a problem. To the extent that it was found necessary, knowledge was at hand concerning the importance of various jobs for the war economy and of labor resources for additional war needs. Hence the redistribution could be effected swiftly and smoothly. While during the first world war the German government did not receive powers for industrial conscription of civilians until the end of 1916, the present regime assumed such powers years before it entered the war.[30]

The German government attempted immediately after the outbreak of hostilities to increase productivity by a further lengthening of the working day and the canceling of workers' rights to vacations. In conformity with the "war economy ordinance" of September 4, 1939, the previous eight-hour-day standard was abolished in favor of a normal ten-hour day. In war industries the working day was lengthened to twelve hours, and individuals with special functions even worked on fourteen- and sixteen-hour shifts. The only legal safeguards left were that workers should have uninterrupted rest periods of eleven hours in each twenty-

---

[30] F. Wunderlich: "Labor in Wartime," in *War in Our Time*, New York, 1939, 253 and 257.

FACTORS LIMITING NATIONAL OUTPUT 113

four, that each work period of six hours should be followed by a rest period of half an hour, and that maximum working hours for women and youths over the age of sixteen should be limited to fifty-six weekly. But this system was suddenly abandoned at the end of 1939. Probably it shot beyond the mark; productivity decreased as a consequence of the strain put on workers. Another explanation for the change may have been the desire to absorb an increasing number of workers in the war industries who had been discharged by manufacturers of civilian goods. At any rate, the eight-hour day was restored as the standard. Special permission was required for extensions of the working day to ten hours; and such permissions were to be restricted to the war industries and to cases where it was found impossible to maintain the eight-hour standard by hiring additional workers. Simultaneously, paid vacations, overtime pay, and the previous restrictions on Sunday and holiday work were restored.

It is also worth mentioning that standardization and mass production of war materials of all kinds have been pushed very far in Germany. Considerable economies of effort could be realized by the country's factories in this way.

England's record has been far less satisfactory. True, she entered the war with a scheme of compulsory military conscription in operation. It is also true that there was a schedule of protected occupations before the war and that, on the whole, overmobilization has been avoided. Nevertheless, the shortcomings of organization in the field of labor were very marked under the rule of the Chamberlain government. It was not so much a lack of powers vested in the government as inability to use them that brought serious criticism.

After the outbreak of war, a number of industries began dismissing workers. In the lead were wallpaper making, dressmaking, printing, publishing, laundry service, tobacco; but also such essential war industries as motor vehicle, cycle, and aircraft making showed an excess of thirty-seven per cent of unemployment over the norm for the month of December, 1939.[31] During the first two months of the war the number of unemployed in Britain increased by 200,000. The total remained well over a million until April, 1940. In November, 1939, there were about ten times as many unemployed among forty-five million inhabitants of Great Britain as there were among eighty million Germans. The schedule of reserved occupations has prevented certain classes from being called to the colors. Yet it was soon found that many of the men who were kept out of the army were not used for work of national importance.[32]

The necessity for bringing unskilled men into the positions of the skilled and introducing women into industry was keenly realized. Yet, at the same time, there was an apparent lack of jobs for women. In April, 1940, the unemployment among women exceeded that observed in August, 1939, by 57,000. Many of the unions remained hostile to the employment of women. *The Economist* reported on February 24, 1940:

The number of firms already training women for war work is negligible. The unions have not yet moved, publicly at any rate, from their stand that it is only legitimate to agree to the dilution of skilled with semi-skilled workers when the actual need arises—regardless of the fact . . . that it takes something like six months to turn out semi-skilled workers for new jobs.[33]

And while the unions obstructed the training of unskilled labor for munitions jobs and the government showed a lack of initiative in overcoming this resistance, training facilities

---

[31] *The Economist*, London, February 3, 1940, 192.
[32] D. H. Popper and J. C. deWilde: "Wartime Economy of Britain and France," *Foreign Policy Reports*, July 15, 1940, 112.
[33] The Economist, London, February 24, 1940, 332.

FACTORS LIMITING NATIONAL OUTPUT 115

were found to be entirely insufficient. To quote again from *The Economist:*

According to a recent statement in the German Press, the Nazi Labour Front has 16,000 full-time instructors and every factory has its quota of trainees. In Great Britain, so far from having 16,000 *instructors,* we have less than half that number of *pupils* at the Training Centres. Yet a contrast of this kind is apparently not of a nature to shatter the monumental calm of the Ministry of Labour.[34]

Hence, at the time of the great German offensive against the Low Countries and France, England was far from having her labor force organized for war production. Her pace in advancing toward this goal was very slow. Lately, the Churchill government with the trade-union leader Bevin in charge of the Ministry of Labour obtained unlimited powers to require "persons to place themselves, their services and their property at the disposal of His Majesty as appear to him to be necessary or expedient."[35] In other words, the British government was vested with the right to conscript labor as well as capital. Much will depend on the use that will be made of these rights. During the first nine months of the present war, it has not been legal restriction but lack of executive ability that has kept Britain from realizing her war potential.

What Can Be Done to Bring Wartime Output to a High Level?

We have seen a number of reasons for wartime output to decline or to stagnate. Yet in the previous chapter we have found that extraordinary demands appear for the

---

[34] *Ibid.,* May 11, 1940, 849.
[35] Emergency Powers (Defense) Act of May 22, 1940, quoted from *The Economist,* May 25, 1940, 924.

products of industry. What can be done to reduce the dangerous gap between needs and supplies?

Five essential steps in this process are as follows: (1) Measures must be taken to avoid unemployment. Efficient employment exchanges must direct unemployed workers to jobs in the essential industries. (2) Overmobilization must be avoided. On the basis of careful studies, a schedule of protected occupations and age groups has to be set up in order to bring the right man to the right job. (3) Labor rights resulting in obstacles to an expansion of production have to be suspended. Labor groups must be diluted by unskilled workers, women, and youngsters wherever this appears necessary. Simultaneously, limitations of working hours have to be suspended. But care must be taken not to exaggerate any of these policies; for this will result in decreasing returns. New workers must be trained; if they are moved to new places, housing accommodations must be provided. The extension of the working day must not be pushed so far as to lead to exhaustion, deterioration of product, frequent accidents, and other disruptions of the production process. Similar precautions must be observed with measures intended to increase the intensity of work. "Loafing on the job," frequent layoffs, and especially strikes must be avoided and arbitration agencies be created if they do not yet exist. Furthermore, a certain degree of conscription of labor may be helpful in satisfying the requirements of the essential industries. Above all, coöperation of labor and its organizations in this program must be obtained. (4) Measures must be taken to standardize products, to create an exchange of information and experience between plants producing similar products or different parts of a certain product. Such measures make it possible to apply mass-production techniques to war materials. They will help to increase output. Standardization of motors, trucks, tanks, guns, and airplanes will greatly facilitate the

FACTORS LIMITING NATIONAL OUTPUT 117

job of the army in the field. (5) The management of plants has to be advised and controlled in its effort to secure highest efficiency of production in a quantitative and qualitative sense.[36]

But over and above these measures of detail, there are the general requirements that must be met by the country's economic general staff: to plan in advance as thoroughly as possible; to replace the erroneous notion of "business as usual" by the concept of an economy of war based on comprehensive, proportionate, and speedy action.

In this chapter, we have taken a rather narrow view of the problems concerning the nation's output in war times. In reality, output depends also on a number of circumstances that we have not yet taken into account: the financing of war, the organization of raw material supplies and transportation, the distribution of consumers' goods, and the control of prices and incomes. The two following chapters will be devoted to these problems.

SUGGESTED REFERENCES

Cherne, L. M.: *Adjusting Your Business to War,* New York, 1940, chapters II and VII.
Clark, J. M.: *The Costs of the World War to the American People,* New Haven, 1931, chapter X.
(Clark, J. M., Hamilton, W. H., and Moulton, H. G.; editors): *Readings in the Economics of War,* Chicago, 1918, part XII.
Cole, G. D. H.: *Trade Unionism and Munitions,* Oxford, 1923.
Tobin, H. J., and Bidwell, P. W.: *Mobilizing Civilian America,* New York, 1940, chapters VI and VII.
War Department, Office of the Secretary: *A Report of the Activities of the War Department in the Field of Industrial Relations During the War,* Washington, D. C., 1919.
Watkins, G. S.: *Labor Problems and Labor Administration in the United States During the World War,* University of Illinois

---

[36] In connection with points (4) and (5) it is of interest to study the work of the Conservation Division of the War Industries Board during the World War. See B. M. Baruch: *American Industry in the War,* Washington, D. C., 1921, part I, chapter 5.

Studies in the Social Sciences, Vol. VIII, nos. 3 and 4, Urbana, 1919.
Wolfe, H.: *Labour Supply and Regulation*, Oxford, 1923.
Wunderlich, F.: "Labor in Wartime," in *War in Our Time*, New York, 1939, chapter XII.

CHAPTER 7

War Finance

Wars are fought with men and goods. But the men do not simply leave their homes and go to the front, equipped with rifle, cartridges, and a blanket. Food, clothing, and arms are not supplied to them as gifts of individual citizens. It is the government that organizes a modern war. It mobilizes the men, provides them with fighting equipment and necessities of life, transports them to the battlefield, pays indemnities to the families left at home, and gives some pocket money to the soldiers. The goods the soldiers consume, their arms, food, and so on, the trains and ships that carry them are bought or hired by the government. To fulfill these tasks, the government needs money, and the money must be obtained from somebody. This is the first problem of war finance.

From whom can the government obtain money? Either from individuals or corporations at home or from foreign creditors or donors. Obviously, what the government needs are not the paper-pounds or bronze-francs themselves but the purchasing power they represent, the titles they give to shares of national production. Therefore, those who give the money have to sacrifice the goods they could have bought with it. The real sacrifice of the citizens or foreign supporters consists of the cars, suits, and chickens they cannot buy, the buildings they cannot erect, the machines they cannot construct after the government has taken away part of their purchasing power. Such sacrifice cannot be avoided, unless the nation has considerable unemployed resources at its disposal on which to draw. The second problem of war finance becomes obvious: it is to make sure that these sacrifices are made and to distribute them over the various classes of people in some justifiable manner.[1]

The Scope of Financial Needs

The financing of war would not present serious difficulties if the government needed only one or two per cent of the national product for war purposes. But the requirements of a major modern war are of another order. In 1918, the British government needed about fifty per cent of the national income to cover its ordinary and wartime expenditures,[2] the American government about thirty-five per cent.[3] This is a much larger share than goes through the hands of government in peace times. In Great Britain and Germany, expenditures for war purposes alone seem to have reached about thirty-two per cent, in France, twenty-one per cent, of the national income on the average of the war years from 1914 to 1919.[4] In other words, the income transfers that the government has to undertake in a major war are enormous. We have no reason to believe that the figures of the World War cannot be exceeded during the present war. *The Economist* of January 27, 1940, 148, estimates that not less than sixty per cent of the German national income was being spent by the state at the beginning of the present war.

In order to realize the magnitude of the costs of the first

---

[1] For excellent discussions of the problems of public finance in a war economy, see the book by Pigou and the article by Viner cited at the end of this chapter.
[2] *The Economist*, London, May 13, 1939, 360.
[3] See *Statistical Abstract of the United States*, 1938, 170 and 206.
[4] To obtain these percentages the net cost in "1913" dollars of Table II in the Appendix was divided by six times the national incomes of 1913 as given by H. E. Fisk: *The Inter-Ally Debts*, New York-Paris, 1924, 265.

world war, a look at Table II of the Appendix may be helpful. It must be understood, however, that the figure of approximately eighty billion prewar dollars which this estimate reaches is certainly too low. The data refer to the direct costs of the war to the national treasuries of the belligerent powers. Costs to neutrals are not included, nor are the costs incurred by the belligerents in terms of loss of life, destruction of vitality, of buildings, railroads, lands, objects of art, and so forth. The figures given in this table present estimates, and for some countries very rough estimates only.

Distribution of the War Burden

The real burden of war consists of the social effort made to prepare it, to keep it going, and to cure its devastations. From the point of view of economic theory the real burden of war may be considered as the sum of four factors: (1) increase of productive effort; (2) curtailment of individual consumption (both affecting the health of the people); (3) declining production of new capital goods ultimately serving the creation of consumers' goods, and depletion of the existing stock of capital goods; (4) destruction of human lives and declining reproduction of the human race. Who carries this burden—the present or the future generation, the belligerent nation or its foreign supporters, the rich or the poor? In part, this depends on the way war is financed. And how are wars financed? By taxes, loans, or currency inflation. How then does the distribution of the war burden over generations, peoples, and individuals depend on the method of war finance?

Let us consider first the distribution of war burdens over generations and peoples. Ordinarily, the brunt of the war burden is borne by the generation that lives through the war; we may call it the "present generation." It furnishes the lives that are extinguished on the battlefields, and at home under the impact of epidemics and air raids. The present generation also furnishes the productive effort and sacrifices the bulk of the goods that war consumes.

Little can be done by the people living before the war (the "previous generation"). It is true that this generation maintains an unproductive organization, the army, in anticipation of war. Some war materials may be produced in advance and stored, in particular such formidable weapons as battleships and land fortifications, whose time of production is very long. War chests of precious metals may be accumulated, like the famous war chest kept by the Prussian state in the Julius tower of Spandau up to the war of 1914. Today, some part of the nations' gold reserves may be considered as war chests, maintained in the expectation of wartime purchases abroad. But the quick obsolescence of modern arms, the high cost of carrying over a long number of years stocks of goods or gold adequate for a major war, limit the extent to which the previous generation can share the war burden.

People living after the war (the "future generation") will carry some of the war burden. The future generation will have to maintain invalids, to build up devastated areas, factories, and farms. Its inheritance will be drastically curtailed through the war. The future generation will also be reduced in number, because the birth rate has dropped strongly during the war and adults have been killed. In times of high unemployment, there may be people who believe that this would not mean a loss to the future generation. But such an interpretation is highly questionable. Unemployment may harass a smaller population just as well as a larger one.

There are, however, things which the future generation cannot do. It can furnish neither the guns, shells, nor other goods which the present generation uses up in war;

nor can it furnish the men. These burdens can never be shifted to the future generation.

Can the Cost of War Be Imposed on Allied or Neutral Countries?

So far we have considered different generations of the same nation. Let us now turn to the same generation in different nations, one the belligerent, the other its military allies or neutral supporters. Can the belligerent generation shift part of the burden over to others?

It can, as many examples in history show. In the eighteenth century, England paid subsidies to Frederick the Great of Prussia to have him fight France and thus facilitate England's conquest of North America. During the struggle with France from 1793 to 1816, England disbursed more than fifty-seven million pounds of war subsidies and loans to foreign potentates.[5] As Table II shows, Germany's allies during the first world war had a good deal of their efforts paid for by Germany, and the Allied and Associated powers shifted part of their war burden to the United States and to England. These shifts of the burden were not always designed to be permanent. They were in the case of England's subsidy payments to Frederick; they were not during the World War. In that instance, help was loaned, but later the debtor defaulted on the loan and the lender found himself in the honored but undesired position of a donor. The loans shown in Table II were all defaulted upon.

What would have happened had America's former allies been able to continue after 1931 with their payments on the loans contracted in this country? Could we still say

---

[5] J. H. Clapham: "Loans and Subsidies in Time of War, 1793–1914," *Economic Journal*, Vol. 27, 1917, 495.

that part of their war burden would have been shifted over to Americans? If international war loans are honored, namely amortized with payment of interest, there is a shifting of burdens involving two generations in two countries. The present belligerent generation shifts the burden to the present generation in the supporting country; the future generation of the belligerent carries a burden for the future generation of the supporters. Two different streams of services flow, the first during the war, carrying arms or purchasing power from the supporter to the belligerent, the second mainly after the war, carrying goods or purchasing power from the former belligerent to its former supporter. In the belligerent country, taken alone, the present generation has thus found a particular way of shifting the war burden to its descendants *via* the foreign creditors. The supporting nation, on the other hand, has undertaken some kind of successful investment, with the outlay made by its present, the returns received by its future generations.

Summarizing our discussion up to this point we may say: (1) Taking the present belligerent generation as a whole, we find that its war burden may be somewhat lightened if the previous generation undertook to accumulate a war chest in form of armaments, goods, or purchasing power for foreign commodities. (2) The present generation may pass on some of the war burden by consuming—or not creating —national wealth in form of raw materials, buildings, roads, and factories and thus curtailing the future generation's inheritance. (3) Furthermore, the future generation will be burdened by all the outlays it will have to make in connection with the past war, as the maintenance of veterans and payments for foreign debts. The future generation of vanquished countries may be called upon to pay tribute to the victorious nation. (4) Finally, some part of the war burden may be imposed upon the present generation of supporting countries, if subsidies can be obtained from it, either openly or indirectly through the device of fictitious loans.

So far we have been talking about entire generations as if each constituted just one homogeneous social group. Now we are ready to give up this simplification. We know that each generation consists of millions of individuals and, what matters here, individuals that differ in many respects, in their incomes and occupations, for example. If we want to see how the financial burden of war is distributed over these many and different individuals, we must turn our attention to the three methods of internal war finance: taxes, loans, and currency inflation.

Let us apply the following criteria to each of these methods of war finance: (1) *Efficacy.* To what extent is the method effective in diverting purchasing power from civilians to the government?[6] (2) *Speed.* To what extent is the method able to satisfy the urgent financial needs of the war government? (3) *Transparency.* Does the method provide a transparent allocation of the financial war burden? (4) *Distributive effect.* In which way does the method affect the distribution of income and wealth during and after the war?

Taxation, the "Heroic Way"

Let us consider *direct taxes* first. They are levied upon specific individuals or corporations. How much each individual has to pay to the treasury depends on certain aspects of his income or wealth. Our income taxes are examples. With taxes of this kind it is possible to make individuals contribute according to their capacity to pay or other rational principles. Ordinarily, direct taxes cannot be shifted. They fall squarely on the payer and are collected

---

[6] The question may also be put in this way: Whenever a dollar appears in the state purse, is a civilian dollar canceled?

by agents of the government who transmit the proceeds to the government's treasury. In comparison to the financial contribution made, the sacrifice of consumers' well-being is smaller than under indirect taxes.[7] For these reasons, direct taxes are an ideal instrument for allocating the national war burden to individuals living during the war. They make possible an obvious, unambiguous, and honest distribution of burdens.

Indirect taxes, such as import duties and excise taxes, are a less transparent method of public finance. The burdens are shifted, partly or wholly, "frontward" from producers to wholesalers, wholesalers to retailers, retailers to consumers—or "backward," to employees and suppliers of raw materials. The extent to which indirect taxes hit the individual consumer depends on how much he is buying of the taxed commodity, how much shifting of the tax has taken place. The burdens are there, but their distribution over the various classes of people is largely unknown to the government as well as to the people themselves. Generally speaking, the bulk of direct taxes is paid by the well-to-do, whereas indirect ones are paid by both rich and poor, depending on the nature of the taxed article. While direct taxes can be made progressive, indirect taxes are regressive (that is, they are a proportionately greater burden on small incomes). Nevertheless, both kinds of taxes have one thing in common. Individuals of the present generation give purchasing power to the government, and their gift is a definite one.[8] The taxpayer does not receive a promise of the

---

[7] See H. Hotelling: "The General Welfare in Relation to Problems of Taxation and of Railway and Utility Rates," *Econometrica,* Vol. 6, no. 3, July, 1938; and M. F. W. Joseph: "The Excess Burden of Indirect Taxation," *Review of Economic Studies,* Vol. 6, no. 3, June, 1939.

[8] The economic meaning of war taxes appears most obvious if we go back to times when they were paid in kind. During the Civil War, Southern farmers had to give up ten per cent of their stocks of grains, potatoes, sugar, cotton, and so forth, and ten per cent of the hogs they slaughtered to feed the Confederate army.

government to repay what has been obtained from him by taxes. He sees his purchasing power definitely reduced, and consequently he has to cut down his spending. For that reason taxation appears as the most logical way of inducing the present generation to make sacrifices for war, to face the war burden. And the more *direct* taxation is, the more transparent is the allocation of the burden.

There are, however, certain shortcomings to taxation. Usually a considerable time, perhaps even more than a year, elapses before the revenue from a tax measure is collected. A new administrative apparatus may have to be set up or an old one remodeled. Unfortunately, delays of that kind are particularly pronounced in the case of direct taxes. During a war, there is not much time to be lost. Revenue is needed immediately. Therefore, at least for a certain period of transition, taxation may not bring in sufficient revenue. It is interesting to note in this connection that in some countries, France, for example, the first months of the War of 1914 to 1918 brought not only economic disorganization but also a decline in the revenue from existing taxes and import duties.[9]

On the other hand, certain usual objections against strong and progressive taxation do not apply in war times. One of them is that taxes may impair business confidence. Considering this argument, *The Economist* [10] arrived at the following radical conclusion:

> "Business confidence," when analysed, means a state of public psychology, in which money will be freely spent, both on consumption goods and, more especially, on extensions to capital equipment. But this is just what has to be avoided in wartime. It can almost be said that, in war, the less "business confidence" there is the better.

---

[9] G. Olphe-Galliard: *Histoire Economique et Financière de la Guerre,* Paris, 1923, 423.
[10] May 13, 1939, 360.

The Economist concludes correctly that high war taxes should not be ruled out because of the degree to which they curtail the general level of profits.

We must realize, however, that heavier taxation has no virtue as a method of war finance as long as unemployment in the industries essential to war is not conquered; for if there is such unemployment, *no sacrifice is necessary* to increase production. The nation does not need to "tighten the belt" in order to put idle resources to use; it simply has to arrange for their employment. Credit expansion and the printing of paper money are perfectly satisfactory means of paying for the employment of men who would otherwise be idle. Only under conditions of full employment in the essential industries do the economic and social advantages of taxation prevail. Among the "essential industries" referred to in this connection we have not only the various munitions industries in the wide sense of the word but also the industries producing essential consumers' goods. If there is unemployment in the former but full employment in the latter, an expansion of armament production will lead to a rise in prices of consumers' goods, for the newly hired workers will spend more money on consumers' goods than they did while they were unemployed. Other consumers will then have to make sacrifices in the form of tax payments or higher prices for consumption articles. This consequence can be avoided, however, if plant, equipment, and labor can be transferred from nonessential industries to the making of essential consumers' goods. If that is possible, the capacity of the industries producing essential consumers' goods will be enlarged. The additional demand of the new armament workers may then be satisfied without sacrifices of other consumers.

We notice here that the price-raising effect of a currency expansion depends among other things on the degree to which plant, equipment, and labor can be shifted among various uses. If resources can easily be transferred from one industry to another, currency expansion may go on without raising the prices of essential products until the last building, the last machine, and the last man are employed. If, however, the degree of mobility is low, "bottlenecks" are bound to appear, and prices of some essentials may begin to rise long before unemployment vanishes throughout the entire national economy. Policies designed to raise the mobility of labor (plant and equipment facilities as well) to its technical maximum extend the range of "free" armament production by placing additional resources at the disposition of the essential industries.

The Temptation of Loan Finance and Inflation

With *internal loans* we face quite a different situation. The citizen who buys a war bond of the government apparently bears a share of the burden equal to the amount of money he invests in the bond. And it would also seem that he has correspondingly to restrict his investments in other lines and his consumption expenditures. If this were so, would not financing the war out of loans appear the ideal way? The citizens would make sacrifices according to their own decisions, without any tax collector at the door. The voluntary nature of the sacrifice is indeed a strong argument in favor of loan finance. It implies that the money will be obtained from those who feel most inclined to contribute and who—for one reason or another—consider least important the loss of purchasing power for other things. Yet internal loans are not the ideal way.

First of all, the government has to pay interest on the war bonds and unless it repudiates its indebtedness it has to pay the principal back somehow. Of course, the government may default, either wholly or partially by means of postwar inflation.[11] But then it would have a hard time finding partners for this game, should it desire to issue another series of "bonds." If the government honors its obligations, it has to find the money for interest and amortization payments. This money ordinarily comes out of taxes. Apparently, then, the bondholder's burden is gradually shifted to the taxpayer. It is indeed, and the bondholder's job is to advance money to the taxpayer to carry the war burden. For this service the bondholder receives interest. If bondholders and taxpayers were the same people, or, more specifically, if each individual bondholder paid as much in additional taxes as was necessary to service his bond, then there would be no shifting of the burden. The whole procedure would be only a strange roundabout way of taxation. But how does it work out if bondholders and taxpayers are not the same people?

Suppose for a moment that, in this country, the North bought all the war bonds, while the South paid the taxes to service them. Then, in the course of time, the North would gradually shift the burden to the South. The government would have obtained the money to be spent on war goods from the Northerners, but it would reimburse them by taking money away from the Southerners. Now everybody will say this is a curious and unrealistic example, and it surely is. Still it is no long way from this to a more realistic example. Bonds are generally bought by the richer classes of the population. The average bondholder is likely to be a wealthier individual than the average taxpayer (direct and indirect).[12] If this is so, then the rich and

---

[11] See below, p. 298.
[12] The following data substantiate this statement. In 1937, individuals with net incomes of $5,000 and over (including partnership estates and trusts) held about *ninety* per cent of the aggregate privately held Federal, state, local, and territorial debt in the United States, while they contributed certainly not more than *fifty-six* per cent—probably much less—to the aggregate receipts of Federal, state, and local taxation—direct and indirect.

the poor play parts very similar to those just ascribed to the "North" and the "South"; some portion of the war burden is shifted from rich to poor. While it is not possible for the present generation as a whole to shift the war burden to the future by way of an internal loan,[13] the *present* generation of *bondholders* may shift part of its burden to the *future* generation of *taxpayers*.

Certainly, the tax system might be arranged in such a way as to hit every bondholder, over and above his normal contribution to government expenditures, according to the amount due him in interest and amortization. But would such a system not eliminate the incentive to subscribers that lies in the possibility of passing the burden on to others? Practically speaking, it would lead to the same result as repudiation of the loan, except that a few government officials would have to be maintained for the collecting of the tax and the servicing of the bonds.

The indefiniteness in the allocation of war burdens which loans entail is increased by another circumstance. Subscribers to war loans have generally been allowed to obtain bank credits against collateral pledging of their government bonds. When this is possible, the subscribers are not compelled to reduce their spending at all. The banks create new money for them, and they can proceed as if they had not given any purchasing power to the government. As a re-

---

The share of the public debt has been computed on the basis of estimates published by H. L. Lutz *(The Fiscal and Economic Aspects of the Taxation of Public Securities,* a report to the Comptroller of the State of New York, 1939, 52, 216, and 219); the share of taxation has been computed by applying the 1937 tax rates estimated by M. Newcomer (Twentieth Century Fund: *Studies in Current Tax Problems,* New York, 1937, 4 and 32) to the income distribution (1935–1936) established by the National Resources Committee *(Consumer Incomes in the United States,* Washington, D. C., 1938, 6). The estimated tax rates used have been those for Illinois families (Series V; A, B, C, G, H, I, J).

[13] An internal loan might, however, amount to such a shift if subscriptions were made at the expense of new investments and reinvestments. This would deplete, or prevent increments of the nation's stock of real capital. There would be no shifting if subscriptions were made at the expense of individual consumption.

sult, the government and bond subscribers together now have more money than the subscribers alone possessed before. Instead of one there are now two titles to a certain quantity of goods. The name we usually give to such a procedure is currency inflation. Under conditions of high-level employment, as may be expected to exist in war times, monetary inflation results in competition between the holders of money for goods and resources, the aggregate value of which is smaller than the amount of money that strives to purchase them. Prices of goods rise, some more, some less, until the (unchanged) volume of goods sells for an amount of money equal to the larger volume of purchasing power. Government and citizens engage in a catch-as-catch-can competition for raw materials, labor, and consumption articles. Suppose the government finally gets the goods it wants, who are the individuals who have carried the burden? Nobody knows exactly, but brief reflection leads us to believe that the classes of citizens whose incomes lagged most behind the rise of prices have been the dupes. And which are these classes? All those living on contractual payments, receivers of annuities, rents, interest, salaries, and—perhaps to a lesser extent—wages. Receivers of profits from industry, trade, and speculation on the other hand are likely to maintain or even to increase their share of the national product.

Currency inflation is the most haphazard, the least equitable way of war finance. This holds true whether the method of inflation is by government-sponsored printing of money or by the expansion of bank credit. Since under prevailing practices war bond issues lend themselves to inflationary practices, loan finance breeds inflation. We should not forget, however, that inflationary methods are justified in times of considerable unemployment which may conceivably prevail in the early days of the war. They are justifiable as long as there are unemployed resources in the

WAR FINANCE 133

essential industries. In this case, monetary expansion will not necessarily lead to a rise of the price level. Nor should we overlook the fact that both bond issues and the printing of money promise quick returns and a much less complicated administrative machinery than do certain taxes.

All the above analysis of the shortcomings of financing a war by bond issues applies equally to short-term evidences of indebtedness, such as treasury certificates.

On the basis of our preceding discussion we cannot consider bonds as the ideal way of war finance. We should prefer some reasonable system of outright taxation. Only in the early days of the war should borrowing from banks and from the public be emphasized, and only then in order to bring in revenue quickly enough. Currency inflation should only be applied as long as unemployment persists in the essential industries; but then it ought to be applied.

Have belligerent nations accepted this reasoning and financed their wars by taxes rather than by loans and currency inflation?

War Finance in the Past

For several reasons, governments have preferred to base their war finance on loans. In the past, it was frequently said that the respective country's tax system was too undeveloped or inefficient to collect revenue of the necessary amount and with the necessary speed. This was one of the considerations leading to Secretary Gallatin's policy of loan finance during the War of 1812, and its repetition by Secretary Chase during the Civil War. For the years 1862 to 1865 the North financed on the average only eleven and a half per cent of its war expenditures by taxes, the rest by loans.[14]

---

[14] *Cf.* E. R. A. Seligman: *Essays in Taxation,* New York, 1921, 688, and C. J. Bullock: "Financing the War," *Quarterly Journal of Economics,* Vol. 31, May, 1917, 359 ff.

A second reason for reliance on loan finance is the belief that the war will be short and victorious and that the vanquished enemy will reimburse the victor for his outlays. This idea was popular with Britain's Prime Minister William Pitt in the days of the war against the French Revolution. "Pitt endeavoured not to disgust the country by increased taxation and to pacify the House by describing the war as necessarily of short duration, because France had exhausted her resources and was 'on the verge, nay, in the gulf of bankruptcy.' "[15] Occasionally, this idea may be justified, at least for the party that proves victorious.[16]

During the first world war, the German government openly adhered to the assumption of a short, victorious, and remunerative war. The minister of finance, Helfferich, deduced that high war taxation would be an unnecessary hardship on the German people. Even a whole year after the outbreak of war, on August 20, 1915, he asserted:

"We do not wish to increase by taxation during the war the tremendous burden which our people bear, so long as there is no compelling necessity." With regard to the war-profits tax, which then was generally urged by public opinion, he said: "We believe that such a tax can only be levied after the war." [17]

Therefore, until 1917, war finance in Germany consisted mainly of loans, further loans, and printing of money.

Though most outspoken in favor of loans, the German government was not the only one to rely mainly on this method. With the exception of the United States and Great Britain, not a single one of the nations directly involved in the first world war was able to cover the peacetime level of current expenditures plus the debt service out of tax revenue. The main financial effort was directed to-

---

[15] A. Andréadès: *History of the Bank of England*, London, 1909, 185.
[16] See below, pp. 292–293.
[17] R. R. Kuczynski: "German Taxation Policy in the World-War," *Journal of Political Economy*, Vol. 31, December, 1923, 764.

ward raising money by loans. Even in the two exceptional countries which paid some of their current war expenditures out of taxes, loan finance predominated. Great Britain financed about one fourth, the United States about one third, of their expenditures out of taxes, the rest out of loans. Table III of the Appendix indicates the percentages that taxes and loans represented of the excess of war over peacetime treasury receipts. It appears that of the major belligerents Russia, France, and Germany relied least on war taxes, most on loans. For all belligerents taken together we arrive at the imposing figure of eighty per cent as the contribution of loans to war expenditures. Most of these loans were preceded by, and served the redemption of, short-term borrowing undertaken by the governments to cover the expenditures of the moment.

This borrowing represented the path of least resistance. Still, continuous borrowing may and did meet increasing obstacles. From 1917 to 1919, the American government raised the five Liberty Loans, partly to defray its own war expenditures, partly to pay those of the Allies. To obtain a total intake of about twenty-three billions, interest rates on the bonds had to be raised gradually from three and a half to four and a quarter per cent, interest income from these bonds to be made partially tax-exempt. Subscribers answered the call, first spontaneously, later under the impact of public opinion, house-to-house canvassing, and other inducements. In order to have the lower-income classes participate in subscriptions, the lowest denomination in which bonds were offered was fixed at fifty dollars. Further borrowing was facilitated by "Savings Stamps" and "Thrift Stamps." The largest number of subscribers to one individual Liberty Loan (the fourth) was twenty-one million.[18]

---

[18] E. L. Bogart: *War Costs and Their Financing*, New York, 1921, 199 ff. and 224.

War Finance in the Present War

During the present European war the "pay as you fight" idea seems to enjoy higher popularity. Germany's government has openly rejected inflation and proceeded to a strong curtailment of individual consumption by means of taxes. The income-tax rates have been raised by fifty per cent, indirect taxes on tobacco and beer by twenty per cent. In the main, however, new techniques have been followed. Increases in wage rates have been prevented, and wages thus kept on the very low level they had never been allowed to deviate from under the Nazi regime. The considerable profits that manufacturers are bound to make under such conditions are partly taxed away, partly directed into government-sponsored investments, such as plants to produce substitute materials. Simultaneously, care has been taken of savings of working- and middle-class families, which are bound to be stimulated by the rationing of consumer goods. Savings banks, insurance companies, and similar institutions into which these savings go, are called upon to invest in government paper. They provide the state with loan money. The government attempts to assure savers that their lot will be better than that of their unfortunate predecessors after the War of 1914 to 1918. During the first six months of the present war tax revenue and borrowing contributed about equally toward covering the Reich's expenditures.[19]

Obviously, the powers vested in an authoritarian government make it easy to avoid currency inflation, and to give practically forced savings a semblance of voluntariness. Whether the money put into German savings banks has to be reckoned as loan money or as tax money will for most practical purposes depend on the future.

Great Britain has raised the standard income-tax rate

---

[19] *The New York Times*, August 26, 1940.

from twenty-seven and a half to thirty-seven and a half per cent, while during the World War it had gradually risen from six to thirty per cent. The exemption limit has been lowered to bring this rate to bear on all individuals with yearly incomes above $673, with an allowance of about $200 for each child. The surtax on higher incomes and the estate duty have been somewhat raised, a sixty per cent tax on *excess profits* introduced, and the mass consumption articles—tobacco, sugar, beer, and spirits—submitted to higher tariff and excise charges. All this has been accomplished after only four weeks of war.[20] In May, 1940, under the impact of the war operations on the western front, the *excess-profits tax* was raised to a hundred per cent. The "heroic way" of early and heavy taxation has found more extensive application in this war.

Before passing to a survey of the methods of borrowing used in or proposed for England, let us glance over the properties of the *excess-profits tax*. The present British excess-profits tax stipulates that a hundred per cent (before May 22, 1940, sixty per cent) of "excess profits" have to be transferred to the treasury. Excess profits are defined as profits surpassing a certain percentage, varying between eight and ten, of the "average amount of capital employed" during the respective accounting period. The idea of such a tax is not new. It originated during the first world war as a reaction to the enormous profits made by certain businesses. If circumstances such as a quicker rise of prices than of costs, huge government orders, and so on, enabled businessmen to reap huge profits, then, many people argued, these profits should be made available to the government to finance the war. Certainly, such a tax would remove the unlimited profit in-

---

[20] Figures given in this paragraph are quoted from: *Revised Financial Statement (1939–40)*, H. M. Stationary Office, London, 1939, and from the daily press. Pound sterling amounts have been converted into dollars in the ratio of four to one. On July 23, 1940, the standard rate of the income tax was raised to forty-two and a half per cent. The surtax and the indirect taxes on beer, tobacco, and wines were also increased, and a twelve per cent sales tax on clothing was introduced.

centive, but it was already dubious whether this incentive should be allowed to play a major role in the war economy.

Excess-profits taxes made their appearance with all important belligerents—and even some neutrals—in the first world war. But they were not all of the same type. The excess-profits tax of this country, introduced in 1917, was progressive with the amount of the excess profits. The rates varied from twenty to sixty per cent after allowing profits from seven to nine per cent of "invested capital," according to prewar earnings. Many objections were raised against it, particularly against its progression and the evasive notion of "invested capital." [21] The English tax resembled its modern offspring described above. But it never amounted to more than eighty per cent of the excess profits, starting with fifty per cent in 1915 and reaching the maximum in 1917.[22]

New war loans are now proposed in England to supplement tax revenue. In fact, National Savings Certificates and Defense Bonds of small denomination have been put on the market from November, 1939, on, and a 300-million-pound war loan was issued in March, 1940, bearing three per cent interest. Only one and a quarter billion pounds of a total expenditure of two and three quarter billions are expected to be met by taxation as assessed until April, 1940. The British government seems inclined to raise the additional one billion and a half by loans from voluntary savings. In this it has found criticism and alternative suggestions from one of Britain's outstanding economists, J. M. Keynes.[23]

---

[21] Seligman, *op. cit.*, 700 ff.

[22] F. C. McVey: *The Financial History of Great Britain, 1914–1918*, New York, 1918, 77–78.

[23] Professor Keynes' views have been developed in several articles in the London *Times*, on November 14, 15, and 28, 1939; in an article on "The Income and Fiscal Potential of Great Britain," *Economic Journal*, Vol. 49, 1939, 626–639; and in a book entitled *How to Pay for the War*, New York, 1940. See also Groves, H. M., Keynes, J. M., and others: "How to Pay for Defense," a special section of *The New Republic*, July 29, 1940.

The Keynes Plan of "Deferred Pay"

Apart from voluntary loans and minor revenue proposals such as a sales tax on "nonessentials" and a higher excess-profits tax, both of which have been adopted in the meantime, Keynes advanced a system of *compulsory saving,* or as he called it later, of *deferred pay.* What is this system of deferred pay? It represents a collection of money from individuals in addition to the existing income taxes. Unlike the income tax, deferred pay takes a gradually falling proportion of income; furthermore, it is not considered a definite sacrifice on the part of the payer; it is supposed to represent saved money. There are exemption limits as with the income tax, but they are proposed to lie lower, namely, at annual incomes of $360 for unmarried persons, at $440 for married ones.[24] Of the excess of higher incomes over these limits Keynes suggests that the government retain portions rising from three and a half to eighty-five per cent. The collection is supposed to be done by employers for the low-income classes, and by the income-tax authorities for the wealthier groups. From the amount collected, income tax and surtax—if at all payable—are to be deducted. The rest is to be deposited in savings institutions which the payers may select. From these institutions the government will borrow in turn. It is easy to see that the percentage of deferred pay to the total amount retained from an individual will fall as the individual's income rises. It will be a hundred per cent for the lowest-income group, which is exempt from the payment of income tax, and about five per cent for people with yearly incomes of $400,000.[25] Now we come to an important point. The savings accounts are

---

[24] Keynes: *How to Pay for the War,* 39. The basic minimum income for the purposes of deferred pay shall not depend on the size of the family; but Keynes proposes a system of family subsidies in conjunction with the scheme of deferred pay.
[25] *Ibid.,* 42. (£1 = $4.)

to be blocked, that is, the savers shall be unable to dispose of them except in emergencies (illness, unemployment, payment of death duties) or for the settling of prewar capital commitments (to building societies, insurance companies, and so on). Two and a half per cent interest is to accrue on the principal. This interest accretion presumably will also be blocked. After the war the accounts shall be put at the disposal of their owners, preferably at a moment when the re-employment of idle resources may be facilitated through a purchasing-power expansion.

The reasons for preferring such a scheme to other methods of war finance seem numerous, particularly in a democratic society. (1) "Deferred pay" is politically an easier method than taxation. Repayment of the money collected is promised, and the promise will presumably be kept if the government is honest and the war not lost. (2) "Deferred pay" takes purchasing power from the lower-income classes, whose consumption expenditure constitutes a considerable fraction of the nation's total. Without reducing the spending power of the wage-earning population one cannot curtail over-all consumption expenditure to a very high degree.[26] Neither customary income taxes nor government loans are likely to tap this important source of purchasing power to a significant extent. (3) As an effective means of purchasing-power transfer "deferred pay" helps in avoiding inflation. (4) "Deferred pay," like income taxes, cannot be shifted. (5) "Deferred pay" opens up interesting postwar possibilities. Not only may the blocked accounts play a role in combating the first postwar slump, but they make possible the achievement of a less

---

[26] To illustrate this idea, one might point to the fact that in 1935–1936, American families with incomes below $5,000 held the following percentages of all families' expenditures in the nation: food, 92.6 per cent, clothing, 83.8 per cent, all items of expenditures, 87.7 per cent. (Source: National Resources Committee: *Consumer Expenditures in the United States,* Estimates for 1935–1936, Washington, D. C., 1939, 87.)

unequal distribution of property and income. Since, according to Keynes, deferred pay will represent a regressive levy with respect to income, the poorer classes will save, under his scheme, larger proportions of their incomes than the wealthier classes of the population and thus increase their share of the national wealth.

Whether this scheme would indeed provide a less unequal distribution of income and wealth after the war depends on the way the government would finance the repayment of the deferred pay accounts. If it followed Keynes' proposal of a (nonregressive) capital levy immediately after the war, or if it imposed nonregressive taxation, the objective would be achieved; similarly, if the government postponed the release of the blocked accounts until the appearance of a postwar slump and then undertook a monetary expansion. If, however, the government chose to finance the repayment by means of regressive postwar taxes, the Keynes objective would not be achieved.

The arguments that have been advanced against the Keynes proposal are as follows: (1) It is a "novelty." This argument easily found the ear of the Chamberlain government. So far, Keynes' scheme has not been tried out in England.

(2) Another argument appeared in the German press, which, on the whole, commented favorably on the plan: Germany does not need a system of compulsory savings, because people "save automatically," particularly as a consequence of the comprehensive rationing of consumers' goods.[27] It may be said nevertheless that Germany has a system of compulsory savings without the name. By means of her rationing policy and the restrictions of outlets for the consumers' money, Germany leaves her poorer classes with funds that cannot be used except for "voluntary" savings.

---

[27] See below, chapter 9.

In addition, the German government partly confiscates the business profits which are bound to appear under the wage-stop policy, and partly forces them into war investments by means of a limitation of dividend payments (to six per cent) and a priority scheme in the field of capital investments. The amount of government intervention in the individual's economic life is, of course, greater under a regime of expenditure regulations than under a system of income restrictions. In the first case, the individual meets a government ruling every time he wants to spend a dollar; in the second case, he is left with full freedom of choice in the expenditure of his money. While the authoritarian German government emphasizes the "constriction of the pantry," democratic Professor Keynes prefers the "constriction of the pocket."

(3) A more serious argument points to the possibility left open to individuals under the Keynes plan to draw on their "free" savings balances and thus to provide themselves with more purchasing power than the government wants to let them have. Keynes' plan apparently proceeds on the assumption that such withdrawals from free accounts will not become important. Furthermore, Keynes expects some voluntary saving to continue beside the compulsory saving. It cannot be said a priori to what extent these assumptions would be fulfilled if the plan were put in operation; but any losses of war funds resulting from dissaving or reduced voluntary saving could be offset by an increase of the "deferred pay" rates. Friends of the Keynes plan have recommended that higher rates be imposed.

Summary

To the extent that a belligerent nation is unable (1) to draw on stocks accumulated in the past, or (2) to find some other nation to pay for the war, or (3) to shift the burden to the future generation by way of depletion of the national capital, it has to carry the burden. Direct taxation is the most honest way of distributing the burden over the individual citizens. It may be coupled with schemes like Keynes' "deferred pay." Providing as they do a transparent allocation of the war sacrifices, both methods can be made to serve the requirements of rational economic policy and social justice. Should direct and indirect taxation prove insufficient, as is to be expected in the early days of the war, recourse must be had to internal loans, but inflationary consequences should be barred. Currency inflation is technically the easiest but certainly the most inequitable procedure, except in times of unemployment in the essential industries. If thoroughly applied, it is the best way of preparing a revolution in the belligerent country.

SUGGESTED REFERENCES

Adams, T. S.: "Excess Profits Tax," *Encyclopaedia of the Social Sciences*, Vol. 5, 1931.
Bogart, E. L.: *Direct and Indirect Costs of the Great World War*, New York, 1919.
————: *War Costs and Their Financing*, New York, 1921.
Cherne, L. M.: *Adjusting Your Business to War*, New York, 1940, chapter VIII.
Clark, J. M.: *The Costs of the World War to the American People*, New Haven, 1931.
Colm, G.: "War Finance," *Encyclopaedia of the Social Sciences*, Vol. 15, 1935.
————: "War Finance," *War in Our Time* (H. Speier and A. Kähler; editors), New York, 1939.
Durbin, E. F. M.: *How to Pay for the War*, London, 1939.
Fisk, H. E.: *The Inter-Ally Debts*, New York-Paris, 1924.
Groves, H. M., Keynes, J. M., and others: "How to Pay for Defense," a special section of *The New Republic*, July 29, 1940.
Hollander, J. H.: *War Borrowing*, New York, 1919.
Johnson, E. A. J.: *An Economic History of Modern England*, New York, 1939, chapter II.
Keynes, J. M.: "The Income and Fiscal Potential of Great Britain," *Economic Journal*, Vol. 49, 1939.
————: *How to Pay for the War*, New York, 1940.

Kuczynski, R. R.: "German Taxation Policy During the World-War," *Journal of Political Economy,* Vol. 31, December, 1923.

McVey, F. L.: *The Financial History of Great Britain, 1914–18,* New York, 1918.

Pigou, A. C.: *The Political Economy of War,* London, 1921, chapters IV–X.

Seligman, E. R. A.: *Essays in Taxation,* 9th edition, New York, 1921.

Stein, H.: *Government Price Policy in the United States During the World War,* Williamstown, 1939, chapter III.

United States Senate, Special Committee on Investigation of the Munitions Industry: *Preliminary Report on Wartime Taxation and Price Control,* 74th Congress, 1st Session, Report No. 944, Part 2, Washington, D. C., 1935, part I.

Viner, J.: "Who Paid for the War?" *Journal of Political Economy,* Vol. 28, January, 1920.

CHAPTER 8

Priorities and Price Control

The wartime needs of government control are not restricted to the fields of government orders, labor supply, and finance, although activities of the government in these fields, if undertaken with adequate thoroughness, imply far-reaching interventions in the economic mechanism. Taxation, borrowing, dilution of labor, coördination of military orders, and other measures which we have discussed before will affect every particular enterprise. They can do a great deal in bringing about the transformation of the peace economy into a war economy. Yet we have good reasons to believe that there is need for still more intervention.

Why Previously Considered Measures are Insufficient

(1) Taxation of nonessential commodities plus attempts to withhold labor from their production may accomplish much in curtailing the output of such goods. Still, if producers are able to buy raw materials (within the country or abroad), to ship these materials to their factories, and to hire labor at will, production of nonessential commodities may continue for many months. But time is counted in units of weeks or even days when adjustments have to be made in a war economy, and it may well be necessary to curtail nonessential activities more quickly. The appropriate means to this end is the enforcement of a system of priorities.

(2) War profits may be subjected to heavy taxation.

Thus, manufacturers may be prevented from profiteering by an eventual rise in prices. But it may seem necessary to avoid the very emergence of higher prices. If prices of military goods go up, problems of war finances are accentuated. If prices of essential consumers' goods rise, labor unrest and wage increases will be unavoidable. If methods of production do not change, a rise in wages will entail a rise in costs of production, and manufacturers will soon raise their prices further; moreover, they will be able to do so without encountering a serious check from the demand side. Thus, the whole structure of prices and costs will begin to change erratically, and the changes will cause numerous economic and social difficulties. These reasons make price control necessary.[1]

If conditions of perfect competition prevailed and if the adaptation of the economic system to its new tasks were sought for the long run only, adequate measures of taxation and subsidization would render price control unnecessary. Under these conditions, an uncontrolled price system would tend to produce the optimum allocation of productive resources. Taxes on nonessential production and subsidies to essential pursuits would, in the long run, bring about a sufficiently high output of essential military and civilian goods and curtail nonessential activities at the same time. Similarly, measures of taxation and subsidization would make it possible to avoid an increasing inequality of real incomes. In a war economy, however, the effectiveness of such measures is limited: (*a*) Economic adaptation is not sought for the long run but for the very short run. (*b*) Conditions of perfect competition do not prevail; on the contrary the monopolistic elements in the national economy

---

[1] If the government refrains from inflationary methods of war finance and if it prevents a general expansion of bank credit after full employment has been reached, a rise of the price *level* will be largely checked. Still, there remains the necessity of controlling changes in the price *structure*.

tend to be strengthened by the extreme urgency and the extraordinary volume of war demand. In peacetime, a munitions maker may find himself in competition with others; the government is in a position to sift out disadvantageous bids on orders of military equipment. In wartime, the output of every munitions maker is urgently needed. Even the least efficient of them becomes a monopolist who can dictate his terms to the government.

If under such conditions the government refrained from price control it would have to pay any price for military goods; and yet it would not have any guarantee of the speediest expansion of war production and curtailment of nonessential output. By means of a flexible system of taxes and subsidies the government can go a long way toward achieving an efficient and not too unpopular war economy; but it cannot go all the way without price control.

Similarly, wages have to be brought under government control. If prices of consumers' goods are allowed to rise, officially sponsored wage adjustments may be necessary to eliminate protracted labor disputes; and if, on the other hand, prices of goods are prevented from rising, the wage level cannot be allowed to go up lest one firm after another should encounter deficits. Finally, problems of wage control will arise from the policies of dilution and interindustrial shifting of labor.

Where prices of producers' goods and war materials tend to rise because of unduly conservative depreciation and obsolescence allowances or because of profiteering from the sellers' market, the government will find it necessary to fix maximum prices. In practice, price-fixing will largely amount to keeping prices *below* the level which they would reach, if the forces of demand and supply were left free to arrive at a balance. In other words, many of the fixed prices will be "disequilibrium prices," that is to say they will not bring about an equality of the quantities demanded and supplied but leave the former in excess of the latter. If that should occur, the right to buy cannot safely be left to everybody alike. There will not be enough commodities available. Hence, it appears necessary to discriminate, at the given price, between more and less essential needs. Available supplies have to be directed toward those uses which are most important, and partly or wholly withheld from less important uses. In other words, we meet here a further motive for the institution of a priority system. First, we saw that purchases have to be subjected to priorities in order to accelerate the concentration of producers on essential tasks. Now, we see that the priority system must serve a second end, namely, to prevent the "disequilibrium prices" fixed by the government from resulting in an undesirable distribution of scarce goods.

(3) Taxation and borrowing may restrict the free purchasing power of the consumer sufficiently to give government purchases a clear lane. Taxation may be administered so judiciously as to leave the nation's consumers with just enough of their income to buy the essential foodstuffs, fuels, and some clothing. But can we assume that taxation will guarantee an approximately equal share of scarce goods to every consumer? Inequalities in the distribution of money incomes will and must persist, and so will inequalities in individual wealth, not to speak of inequalities in personal connections with the grocer or near-by farmers. Rich persons, good customers, and persistent hoarders will find access to large supplies more easily than people less favored with money and time and more alive to social responsibility. Hence, whenever the per capita supply of essential consumers' goods falls below the prewar level, the problem of rationing appears. Glaring inequalities in the distribution of scarce supplies bear in themselves the germ of discontent. They weaken the morale of the "home front."

Price-fixing of consumers' goods alone will not solve the

problem. Suppose prices are fixed below their "equilibrium level," as they will almost certainly be where price-fixing is intended to check an upward trend of prices. The situation we encountered before when we were talking about war materials will be exactly duplicated. Since at such "disequilibrium prices" demand exceeds supply, consumers will scramble for the scarce goods. The goods will go to the shrewdest or wealthiest persons or to those who rise earliest in the morning. Hence, price-fixing of consumers' goods does not render their rationing superfluous. On the contrary, the fixed price is an additional reason for the ration book.

(4) Finally, the measures which we discussed in the three previous chapters are likely to be insufficient in eliminating wastes, inefficiencies, and sabotage occurring in certain industries. Industrial establishments or trade institutions of strategic importance such as railroads, shipping, munitions industries, and import trade may promise better returns if operated by some central administration.

Earlier [2] we noticed four essential defects of an uncontrolled system of private enterprise: (1) Neglect of collective wants and costs in the formation of prices; (2) insufficient speed of adaptation to war conditions owing to the inertia of individuals who do not realize the importance of their function to the war economy; (3) social inequities caused by war profits on the one hand, a rising cost of living and the strain of war work on the other hand; (4) monopolistic output restrictions.

In the following sections of this chapter and in Chapters 9 and 10 we shall study the stronger forms of public intervention which are designed to overcome these defects. The *system of priorities* can cure defect (2); moreover, it is a necessary instrument in an effective control of prices and

---

[2] See above, p. 77.

wages. *Price and wage control and rationing of consumers' goods* are remedies for defects (1) and (3). They supplement measures of taxation and subsidization which pursue the same goal. *Government operation of industry* is designed to achieve results which neither the politically possible pecuniary incentives nor detailed government regulations can obtain from private management. It can be used in particular to break down obstacles of the fourth type.

Meaning and Functioning of Priority Schemes

A priority system consists of two parts: (1) a basic schedule of priorities, and (2) specific priority orders and their enforcement. A basic schedule of priorities is a list of economic processes ranked in the order of their urgency from the point of view of the war economy. This list has to be established after considering and comparing all classes of jobs that are planned for a certain period of time, say a month or a year.

Such a basic schedule may be all-comprehensive, that is, it may include all major processes performed in the economic system whether in mining, manufacturing, or in agriculture, in transportation or in trade, in the production for civilian or for military demand. Or it may be specialized, dealing for instance only with production of military significance.

The schedule may be crude, merely distinguishing between a few broad classes of jobs. Such a schedule might look like this:

Class A: production and distribution of military supplies
Class B: essential exports, production and distribution of raw and semifinished materials needed in processes of Class A
Class C: all other jobs

This example of a crude schedule corresponds to the *Priority of Works Order* issued by the British government in March, 1917. It also resembles the schedule contained in our War Industries Board's *Priorities Circular No. 1* of September, 1917.[3] Instead of a crude schedule a refined one distinguishing between a large number of processes may be worked out. The *Priorities Circular No. 4* of the War Industries Board, issued in July, 1918, provides an example of such a detailed priority schedule.[4]

The meaning of the priority schedule is obvious. Whenever a conflict arises between two different processes over the allocation of economic resources, precedence will be given to the process that ranks higher on the priority schedule.

The task of the priority administration is not exhausted with the establishment and publication of a basic priority schedule. In spite of the fact that the schedule is known to producers and purchasers, conflicts are likely to arise. The language of the schedule may not be explicit enough, purchasers may be unable to classify their orders correctly, or finally producers may not observe the rules laid down in the schedule. Therefore, the administration has to issue specific priority orders. In this country, the specific orders issued by the War Industries Board during the World War took the form of *priority certificates*. Government purchasing agencies, the Allied Purchasing Commission, government contractors and subcontractors, and private buyers were invited to apply for priority certificates. None of them was compelled to do so. On the contrary, when a commodity could be obtained without delay from its producer the buyer was expected to proceed without priority assistance. The decision whether to request priority was left to the judgment of petitioners. "In requesting priority

---
[3] B. M. Baruch: *American Industry in the War*, Washington, D. C., 1921, 325.
[4] *Ibid.*, 330–334, 342–350.

the petitioner should join with the committee in applying the test: To what extent, if at all, will the granting of this application contribute, directly or indirectly, toward winning the war; and if at all, how urgent is the need?"[5]

Specific priority orders may be directed against manufacturers or traders of a certain commodity. In the practice of the War Industries Board, priority was ordinarily applied against actual producers only.

It must be realized that a great number of priority orders may be necessary to expedite the production of a certain commodity. Suppose the commodity in question is an army truck. The army will request a priority order against the truck factory. This factory in turn may request orders against producers of motors, steel, tires, coal, and electricity, against the railroads for preferred handling of consignments of any of these articles, against producers of machine tools for preferred treatment of orders for additional turning lathes needed in filling the order for trucks. Among the producers of materials and equipment there may be some who need preferential treatment of *their* orders. The tire factory may require priority for imports of crude rubber in the allocation of shipping space, the steel producer for his orders of iron ore, coke, or limestone, the railroads for coal, locomotives, and cars. Thus, to give one buyer priority on the supply of a certain article may entail a host of further specific priority orders.

Of course, the priority system need not necessarily be restricted to the production and distribution of material goods. Under a system of industrial conscription it can logically be extended to the allocation of labor. It is true that an extensive system of raw material, fuel, and transportation preferences will bring about an automatic reallocation of labor between essential and nonessential pursuits.

---

[5] *Priorities Circular No. 4.* Baruch, *op. cit.*, 337.

A factory that finds its supplies curtailed will be compelled to dismiss workers, and another one which enjoys a large volume of preferential orders may take these workers over. But this automatic process may be found to operate too slowly. Furthermore, as we have seen before, the shifting of labor from one occupation to another presents grave problems of interlocal migrations and retraining. It may therefore appear necessary to supplement the automatic reallocation of labor by industrial conscription, the formation of "shock-troops" of workers capable of being thrown from one urgent job to another, and the extension of the priority system to the field of labor supplies.[6]

Furthermore, private investment may be brought under a regime of priorities. The purpose of priority administration in this field would be to prevent the expenditure of private capital on nonessential projects and to divert funds into the channels of war industry or the war-purse of the government. Capital issues of corporations may be subjected to license, and the capital market may be manipulated in such a way as to facilitate the sale of government bonds.[7]

How Can Priority Be Enforced?

A system of priorities is the most important institution of the war economy. In contradistinction to the control of prices and wages it aims *directly* at the reallocation of economic resources by determining the distribution of their physical quantities. Therefore special attention must be given to the enforcement of priorities.

How can priority orders be enforced? Obviously, if the priority administration is vested with the legal power to issue specific orders, the problem of their enforcement does not present great difficulties. In this country, however, the

---

[6] For the first steps made in this direction in 1918, see Baruch, *op. cit.*, 89.
[7] *Cf.* A. C. Pigou: *The Political Economy of War*, London, 1921, 90–92.

War Industries Board did not possess such powers. From the legal point of view, priority orders outside the sphere of transportation were merely requests. (Frequently, these requests were made on the basis of understandings reached through negotiations with the businessmen involved.) Nevertheless, compliance with the requests was rather general. This was partly due to the coöperation which the Board found in dealing with manufacturers and their associations, partly to broad powers vested in the President of the United States or cabinet officials which enabled them to give preference to essential commodities in the field of transportation, to control the supply of fuel, and finally to commandeer the facilities of producers who did not coöperate in the government program. The possibility of an appeal to the Administration for utilization of any of these powers against a recalcitrant manufacturer gave the Board enough prestige to secure compliance with its specific orders.

A further instrument of priority enforcement may be put in the hands of the government by measures leading to a government monopoly of certain raw materials, supplies, shipping space, or railroad transportation. If the government itself owns the scarce materials or facilities, priorities in their use can be secured directly through allocation of available resources to the most essential of various pressing needs. Under these conditions a government unit becomes the supplier, and it can choose its customers according to the instructions of the priority administration. Government monopolies of raw materials played an important role in Great Britain during the first world war, as in the present one. The British government has bought up domestic and dominion wool crops, wheat, cotton, and other supplies. The British as well as other governments have requisitioned stocks of strategic supplies and thus secured an influence over their distribution.

TREATMENT OF NONESSENTIAL INDUSTRIES
UNDER THE PRIORITY SCHEME

Upon closer analysis the treatment of nonessential industries presents some interesting problems. If such an industry can be shut down altogether and its workers and facilities transferred to other uses, the solution is relatively simple; but in most cases complications will arise. It may not be necessary or feasible to discontinue all operations in a nonessential industry. Ordinary residential building may be stopped altogether; but a certain amount of repair work due to normal wear or air raids may be unavoidable. In addition, it may be necessary to build new living quarters for the population which has been evacuated from large cities or for crews of workers brought into centers of the armament industry. A similar situation may arise in the cotton textile industry. In war, cotton textiles ordinarily rank as nonessentials in comparison with woolen goods. Still their production must be continued on a certain level, because there will be an irreducible minimum of civilian demand for cotton articles. Government regulations may cut down raw material or labor supplies to such industries in proportion to the desired curtailment of their activities. An interesting question arises, however: How shall the available resources be distributed over the individual plants in this industry? Shall nonessential production be concentrated in a few plants or spread over all available producers? Shall production be concentrated in the most efficient plants; or would it be well to follow the example of the British Cotton Control Board which, during the World War, indiscriminately limited the percentage of machinery that could be utilized by all cotton spinners and weavers?[8]

Recently, this problem has aroused great interest in Ger-

---

[8] H. D. Henderson: *The Cotton Control Board,* Oxford, 1922, 16 ff.

many, where under the prevailing shortage and regimentation of raw materials a number of industries had to be classified as nonessential. Following the outbreak of the present war, the German government adopted a policy of concentrating the activity of those industries in a few very efficient plants. The advantages seemed obvious. Discarding less efficient producers and securing optimum use of the facilities of the efficient ones made it possible to produce at lower cost. Concentration facilitated the distribution of orders and the control of operations. Therefore, the government established a relatively small list of the most efficient producers *(W-Betriebe)*, who were to be given preference in the distribution of materials and labor.

The original idea of concentration was abandoned, however, after it was found that war requirements were not as great as had been anticipated. It was also recognized that the shutting down of many smaller plants would involve the loss of a certain amount of production experience and export markets. Spreading of industrial activity also reduced the problem of interlocal movements of workers. Therefore, the number of *W-Betriebe* was considerably increased toward the end of 1939; smaller and less efficient concerns were left in business to a larger extent than had been planned originally. Where a shutdown was decreed, subsidies were paid for the maintenance of productive facilities. The operating firms of all branches had to provide the funds for these subsidies. In contradistinction to practices followed in the first world war, there has not been an extensive transfer of equipment from smaller and less efficient producers to preferred firms.

It remains to be seen, however, whether the final effect of the present war on the concentration of industry in fewer and larger establishments will not be similar to that of the World War, which definitely contributed to industrial concentration. In the field of organization, German industry is certainly moving to higher forms of centralization. Government control of industrial operations, cartels with or without direct government supervision, economic ties between individual businesses and in particular between large firms and small subcontractors are bound to increase in importance. Experience in a sort of business as collectivistic as war production quite naturally strengthens the tendencies toward concentration and centralization which are constantly at work in our industrial system.

Control of Prices

Of all the economic problems of warfare none contains more technical intricacies than price control. In a peace economy, the structure of prices is formed under the influence of a multitude of factors conventionally classified under the headings of supply and demand. Prices bear relation to the urgency with which the goods are demanded. This urgency in turn depends on utility evaluations of individuals in the case of consumers' goods, on profit expectations in the case of producers' goods. On the other hand, prices bear relation to the cost of producing the goods. Thus, prices can be *explained* by the interplay of supply and demand factors.

What is the economic significance of prices? Prices fulfill an important function in the economic system, a function that Lange called the *parametric function of prices:*

. . . although the prices are a resultant of the behavior of all individuals on the market, each individual separately regards the actual market prices as given data to which he has to adjust himself. Each individual tries to exploit the market situation confronting him which he cannot control. Market prices are thus parameters determining the behavior of the individuals.[9]

---

[9] O. Lange and F. M. Taylor: *On the Economic Theory of Socialism*, Minneapolis, 1938, 70. By permission of the publisher, The University of Minnesota Press.

In other words, prices of consumers' goods influence the volume of purchases that consumers are going to make, prices of producers' goods determine the extent of purchases of raw materials and of machinery by producers.[10] Hence, prices play an important role in regulating the volume of consumption and production of individual commodities. Even in a planned economy they are necessary to the extent that freedom of choice is left to consumers and to managers of individual plants. If the war economy does not go so far as to ration every article of consumption, every raw material and facility of production and distribution, it has to be a price economy. There can scarcely be any doubt as to the advisability of the maintenance of a price system, when an economy like ours passes under the rules of war. The difficulties of the government would be insuperable, if it attempted to add the bewildering problems of a general paternalism to the other problems arising in the period of transition from peace economy to war economy.

From the necessity of maintaining a system of prices it cannot, however, be deduced that prices should be left free to go where the torrent of war demand and the cliffs of war supply happen to direct them. On the contrary, it can be shown that prices can be put to more efficient use in the framework of a war economy if they are subjected to regulation. In what ways can government price control render the price system more efficient?

First, and this is the less important case, certain prices may be kept above a fixed minimum in order to encourage the production of certain war essentials which are produced under highly competitive conditions. Suppose an expansion of production is not undertaken because of the justified or unjustified skepticism of producers with respect

---

[10] Under monopolistic conditions prices fulfill their parametric function only on the demand side of the market. Monopolistic producers do not adjust the scale of their operations to a market price. They *fix* volume of output and price.

to future returns. If in such a situation the government guarantees a *minimum* price for the commodity over a certain period of time, expansion of output may be encouraged. This was the case in this country with wheat and hogs during the first world war. Looking back on those days with the experience we have now, we must certainly say that any reluctance of farmers to embark on a large-scale expansion of wheat growing found its justification in postwar developments. Yet, *during the war,* stimulation of food production for domestic and Allied needs was a pressing problem. The government contributed to its solution by fixing minimum prices for wheat and hogs.[11] Though they frequently were below the prevailing market prices, these minimum prices contributed to the increase of output in the two fields by limiting the seasonal or speculative declines of the prices of wheat and hogs, and by thus reducing the farmers' risk.

Second, and this is by far the more important case, prices may be prevented from rising too high. We have seen that in the field of war materials demand is highly inelastic. Price is no deterrent from purchases of airplanes, ships, shells, and food for the fighting forces. There are no automatic forces that would keep producers from raising the price of such materials far above the cost of production, and there are no safeguards limiting the rise of prices to commodities of military significance. It is true that at a given moment the purchasing power in the hands of government and individuals presents restrictions to the rise of prices. But in the face of a rising price level the government will soon find ways of increasing its purchasing power by issuing new paper money; large profits will increase the purchasing power of manufacturers, traders, and speculators; wage

---

[11] P. W. Garrett: *Government Control Over Prices*, published by the War Trade Board in coöperation with the War Industries Board, Washington, D. C., 1920, 60 ff. and 88 ff. For similar British measures, see the *War Memoirs* of D. Lloyd George, 1916–1917, Boston, 1934, 208 ff.

earners will counter the rise in the cost of living by wage disputes; and the temporary limits to price increases will be removed again and again. If left unchecked, this development will lead to serious economic disturbances. Strikes, impoverishment and unrest among the classes living on fixed incomes, and distortion of all economic calculations in private and public business will result.

Another function that high prices and profits are supposed to perform in peace times, namely that of attracting capital to certain branches of industry, is partly superfluous in time of war. The industries needing more capital are well known to the government. Capital can be directed into these channels from public funds without any profit incentive, or from private funds with a profit incentive much smaller than that provided by an unlimited rise of prices. Hence, we must conclude that uncontrolled prices fulfill their parametric function unsatisfactorily under war conditions. Their rise will be too small to check war demand, too large in comparison to its effect on the reallocation of capital, and too disruptive to allow a smooth functioning of the war economy.

How Prices Rose in the First and Second World War

During the first world war *preventive* measures of government price control were conspicuous by their absence. Beginning with the fall of 1914 in Europe and the summer of 1915 in this country prices rose rapidly. Until the fall of 1918, the following relative increases over prewar levels (1913–1914) could be observed (in round figures): [12]

---

[12] The sources for these data are, in order:

W. C. Mitchell: *International Price Comparisons,* published by the Department of Commerce in coöperation with the War Industries Board, Washington, D. C., 1919, 18.

A. L. Bowley: *Prices and Wages in the United Kingdom 1914–1920,* Oxford, 1921, 70.

W. Zimmermann in Meerwarth, Günther and Zimmermann: *Die Einwirkung*

England—Sauerbeck-Statist wholesale price index for 45 staples: 140 per cent,
United States—War Industries Board wholesale price index for 150 commodities: 100 per cent,
England—official retail price index: 120 per cent,
Germany—war-food price index, retail: 150 per cent,
France—cost of living, 13 foodstuffs: 140 to 160 per cent.

The rise of the price level did not proceed at a uniform rate during the war period, nor did all prices rise in the same proportion. This is well illustrated by the following account of the period immediately preceding and following our entrance into the war:

[The War Industries Board's wholesale price index of 1,366 commodities had increased] to 144 by December, 1916. By March, 1917, the threat of war had brought this number up to 156. In one month from April 6, 1917, it jumped by 14 points. The prices of individual groups of commodities more directly related to the war rose high above these averages. By March, 1917, the average price of metals was 247 per cent of the average for 1913, and by July of the same year it had reached its peak of 333 per cent. Basic pig iron climbed from $32.25 per ton in March to $52.50 in July; steel plates from $4.33 per hundredweight to $9. Foods went from 142 per cent to 167 per cent during this period, wheat rising from $1.98 per bushel in March to $2.58 in July. Clothing went from 157 per cent to 187 per cent, and chemicals from 159 per cent to 180 per cent.[13]

During the present war, the rise of prices has been prevented to a larger extent, especially in Germany. Both the German wholesale price index and the index of the cost of living rose by only two per cent between August, 1939, and

---

des Krieges auf Bevölkerungsbewegung, Einkommen und Lebenshaltung in Deutschland, Stuttgart, 1932, 463.
  L. March: *Mouvement des Prix et des Salaires pendant la Guerre,* Paris, 1925, 244.
  [13] Baruch, *op. cit.,* 71.

April, 1940.[14] In England, however, where price control has advanced more slowly and the completeness of the German scheme has not been equaled, the index of the cost of living advanced by fifteen per cent between September 1, 1939, and April 1, 1940, while the Board of Trade's wholesale price index of March, 1940, exceeded the value of August, 1939, by thirty-two per cent.[15]

Multiplicity of Causes Producing the Boom

Before turning to a study of policies designed to prevent the wartime rise of prices, let us complete our picture of the factors that account for it. Earlier, we met the factors bearing the major part of the responsibility: the volume and inelasticity of military demands which encourage sellers to raise prices far above costs. Others factors, however, contribute to the price boom. They may be grouped under the heading of growing scarcity and increasing costliness of supplies. Production and shipping facilities are destroyed by war, railroads congested, cargoes lost or spoiled. Less efficient production facilities are put to use and less efficient labor is employed. All the factors limiting the national output (see Chapter 6 above) tend to render supplies scarce and unusually expensive. In addition, speculative hoarding of commodities may take place and result in an artificial rarefaction of supplies.

Government price control has to take account of this variety of forces leading to the price boom. Measures devised to restrict the boom must differentiate between price increases due to avoidable factors such as profiteering and hoarding and others entailed by unavoidable factors such as the loss of ships or the lack of good mines. In countries

---

[14] *Wirtschaft und Statistik,* 1939, 715 and 717; and 1940, 135 and 136.
[15] Royal Economic Society, Memorandum No. 82, *London and Cambridge Economic Service's Report on Current Economic Conditions,* May, 1940, 5 and 15.

which receive large proportions of their raw material and foodstuff supplies from abroad, price-raising factors beyond government control are bound to be particularly important. A certain part of the recent increase in the English price level is due to the fact that uncontrolled world market prices enter into the costs of production of so many commodities produced and consumed in England.

Above all, the government must realize the self-reinforcing character of the price boom. Prices of producers' goods enter into the cost account of the businesses which are using these goods. If the price of steel goes up, users of steel will have a reason to raise the prices of their products. Similarly, if prices of consumers' goods rise, wage earners will demand higher wages; thus labor costs will be increased and a further incentive to higher prices will be created.

The conclusion to be drawn from a recognition of these facts is very simple: If the wartime rise of the price level is to be minimized, control has to be established at the earliest possible moment and over as wide a field as is technically feasible. The earlier price control is established, the less momentum will the boom be allowed to gather. The more comprehensive price control is made, the less likely is it that a price boom will develop in the uncontrolled areas of the economy, infect the controlled areas, and render existing controls ineffective. Even in the field of luxuries it may appear advantageous to avoid a large increase of prices. True, social considerations do not dictate prevention of high prices for rare foodstuffs, silk stockings, or big radio sets. Since, however, higher prices tend to stimulate production of such luxuries and thus to deflect valuable resources into nonessential lines, the government may choose to extend price control to this field. A more direct approach to this problem, however, would be to curtail production of luxuries by means of priority control and simultaneously to divert purchasing power of the higher-income classes into the purse of the state through taxes and voluntary or compulsory saving.[16]

Of course, if it is technically impossible to extend price control to all fields, there are some prices which will merit more attention than others. Prices of raw materials, particularly of those needed for military purposes, and food are of higher strategic importance than, say, prices of garden seeds, or doctors' fees. The former enter the cost of production of many important goods, while the latter exert only a small influence on the cost of living. Similarly, it is more important to bring the wages of steel, shipyard, and railroad workers under control than those of employees in circuses. Therefore, if control cannot be general, it must at least be made to cover the prices of basic producers' goods, essential consumers' goods, and wages in a number of important occupations. In general, the activity of the government in the field of price control should be governed by two maxims: *as early as possible* and *as comprehensive as possible*. Have belligerent governments followed these maxims?

Price Control in the First and Second World War

Let us pass in review the essential measures taken by the American government during the years 1917 and 1918 to bring the war price boom under control.[17] The policy followed can be called "therapeutic" rather than "prophylactic." By this I mean that the disturbances were allowed to develop before steps were taken to bring them under control. The hesitation in introducing a control of prices

---

[16] See in this connection E. M. H. Lloyd: *Experiments in State Control at the War Office and the Ministry of Food*, Oxford, 1924, 291 and 292.

[17] For a critical appraisal of American experience in price control during the World War, see United States Senate, Special Committee on Investigation of the Munitions Industry: *Preliminary Report on Wartime Taxation and Price Control*, 74th Congress, 1st Session, Report No. 944, Part 2, Washington, D. C., 1935, part II.

was, however, not a peculiarity of our war economy. Other countries followed the same course, even more radically. As a matter of fact, this country, during its neutrality, had the advantage of observing the effects of the belligerent governments' reluctance to engage in price control, and the American government could avoid some of their errors after it entered the war. Britain, for instance, waited until 1917 before maximum prices for some essential foodstuffs were fixed. Only for sugar and milk were maximum prices fixed during 1916. In January, 1917, retail food prices in England were about ninety per cent above the prewar level.[18] In this country, the *Food Administration* was organized under Herbert Hoover in May, 1917, shortly after the declaration of war.

Still, the introduction of effective controls proceeded slowly. Until August, 1917, the Food Administration was on a purely voluntary basis, its work chiefly educational in character. It studied the market for foodstuffs and enounced the principle that prices charged should equal "cost plus a reasonable margin of profits."[19] The Administration undertook to enforce this rule by means of its power to issue or to refuse operating licenses for food producers and traders. But it is noteworthy that this power extended to only five per cent of the country's retailers—those with annual sales above $100,000.[20] Maximum prices for foodstuffs were not fixed; as a matter of fact, the Food Administration had no price-fixing power. This power was vested in and retained by the President and used, as far as foods were concerned, only to fix the minimum prices for wheat and hogs mentioned above. The system of control was rather loose, its guiding principles vague. What it

---

[18] S. Litman: *Prices and Price Control in Great Britain and the United States During the World War,* New York, 1920, 25, and N. B. Dearle: *An Economic Chronicle of the Great War for Great Britain and Ireland,* London, 1929, *passim.*
[19] See below, p. 169.
[20] Garrett, *op. cit.,* 44 and 135.

achieved was largely due to citizen coöperation, such as consumer reports about objectionable practices of food dealers. Nine thousand operating licenses were revoked, but a rise of prices could not be avoided. During the period of American belligerency the War Industries Board's food price index (1913–1914=100) rose from 142 in March, 1917, to 195 in October, 1918, that is, by thirty-seven per cent.[21]

The policy with respect to other than food prices was no less hesitant and ineffective in preventing considerable price increases. It was not until August, 1917, that a *Fuel Administration* was set up to look after the runaway market for bituminous coal and other fuels. By 1916 there had appeared a shortage of bituminous coal. In March, 1917, the price was about twenty-three per cent above the level of 1913; but one month later, it was ninety-five per cent above that level. By the end of the war it had risen by another thirty points.[22] Finally, in March, 1918, the *Price-Fixing Committee* was formed in order to deal with other basic industrial materials. The Fuel Administration and the Price-Fixing Committee advised the President in fixing and revising maximum prices for coal, steel, copper, lumber, and other goods. The level at which maximum prices were fixed was usually determined by government sponsored agreements between suppliers and buyers of a certain material.

It is interesting to note that the task of the Price-Fixing Committee was seen in preventing price rises of those goods which were mainly purchased by the various war offices of the government and the Allies, rather than in protecting the general public. Only gradually was the latter motive recognized as sufficient to justify the intervention of the Committee.

Bernard M. Baruch, who was chairman of the Commit-

---
[21] *Ibid.*, 27.
[22] *Ibid.*, 170.

tee, now advocates earlier introduction of maximum-price-fixing if a new emergency should arise. The government's policy should be more "prophylactic," the control agencies vested with more legal power, and the control extended to more commodities than was the case during the World War.[23] It seems that these ideas have been accepted to a certain degree by the belligerents in the present war. This time, it took the British government only a few weeks to arrive at a fixing of maximum prices for twelve foodstuffs and for coal, wool, iron and steel products. Germany entered the war with a comprehensive scheme of price stabilization in operation. In the Mobilization Plan of our War and Navy departments it is recognized as a matter of principle that in the field of price control "preventive measures to be applied at the source appear to be a sounder approach to the problem of preserving economic stability than reliance upon remedies after the disorders have appeared." [24]

Technical Problems of Price Control

It is not enough that the government assumes the control of prices. Principles for effecting this control must be evolved. There are a number of alternatives. (1) Shall the government accept the cost accounting of private business and restrict its control to profit rates or margins, or shall the cost basis itself be subjected to control? (2) Shall the government fix maximum prices, or shall it fix actual prices of commodities? (3) Shall maximum prices apply to all producers or traders without regard to their costs, or shall prices be allowed to vary from producer to producer? In fact, each of these possibilities has been applied by one or the other control administration in the past.

---

[23] B. M. Baruch: *Taking the Profits out of War*, New York (?), 1936 (?), 49 ff.
[24] *Industrial Mobilization Plan*, Revision of 1939, 76th Congress, 2d Session, Senate Document No. 134, 12.

(1) Obviously, a price supervision extended to costs of production and handling represents a higher form of control than the mere fixing of profit margins or rates. In this country, the former procedure was attempted by the War Industries Board and the Fuel Administration, while the latter seemed to satisfy the Food Administration.[25] The War Industries Board and the Fuel Administration carefully studied the costs of production to individual producers of copper, iron ore, iron and steel products, lumber, and bituminous coal. They used these data as a basis for price agreements with producers. In the field of foodstuffs, only beet sugar was subjected to cost control; the government found it necessary to encourage sugar production and simultaneously to prevent too sharp a rise in the price of sugar.[26]

Checking of cost accounts of private business naturally puts a tremendous task on government agencies, particularly if they have to deal with large numbers of small firms. The work may be simplified by restricting the control to representative firms. In England, during the first world war, the government used the national munitions factories as a yardstick for the costs in munitions making. But it was soon discovered that this yardstick was of limited applicability. Hence cost control was slowly extended to private munitions makers and became instrumental in the reduction of shell prices.[27] The control must prevent unnecessarily high depreciation and obsolescence charges

---

[25] For a detailed account of individual cases, see *Readings in the Economics of War*, 465 ff. See also United States Senate, Special Committee on Investigation of the Munitions Industry: *Preliminary Report on Wartime Taxation and Price Control*, 74th Congress, 1st Session, Senate, Report No. 944, Part 2, Washington, D. C., 1935, 85.

[26] Under the auspices of the Food Administration, domestic producers of beet and cane sugar were brought to agreements on the price of sugar. Establishment of the *U. S. Sugar Equalization Board* authorized to purchase the Cuban crop made it possible, furthermore, to bring the price of imported sugar in line with the fairly high prices granted to domestic producers. See Garrett, *op. cit.*, 78 ff.

[27] For an able discussion of British cost control during the first world war, see Lloyd, *op. cit.*, chapter XXV.

against the output during a certain period of time as well as other practices designed to veil profits.

Even if control agencies refrain from interfering with costs of production and limit their activity to the control of profits, the task is not easy. The experience of the Food Administration provides ample proof of this. Originally, the Administration ruled that "reasonable profits" meant the average *percentage* of profit made in the three years preceding the outbreak of the war in Europe. However, the level of costs and prices rose and this scheme led automatically to larger profit margins. The Administration then changed its attitude and fixed maximum *margins* of profit allowable on individual commodities, at first for sales made by wholesalers to retailers, later also for sales by retailers to consumers. Under this scheme, prices could and in fact did vary among dealers with different costs.

(2) Shall the government fix maximum prices, or shall it fix actual prices? In many instances where prices showed a strong tendency to rise, actual trade prices were fixed during the World War. In other cases of this nature fixed maximum prices soon became actual prices. In comparing the two systems, we find one great advantage on the side of maximum-price-fixing. If the fixed price is a maximum price, more efficient producers will be able to attract all the business they can handle by offering the commodity at a price below the maximum. The maximum price thus helps to guarantee full employment to the most efficient facilities in an industry. If, however, expansion of output is expected from all producers irrespective of their efficiency, the fixing of actual prices or of minimum prices may be found more expedient; for they provide producers with a guarantee that they will not have to sell their product for less.

(3) Shall maximum prices apply to all producers of a certain commodity, or shall prices be allowed to vary from pro-

ducer to producer? This problem is closely related to another one, namely, whether or not producers and traders shall be allowed a pecuniary incentive to render their operations more efficient. Since an economical utilization of resources is most desirable, this incentive should not be eliminated altogether; patriotism alone may not provide enough of an incentive to render business operations most efficient. If a maximum price is fixed for all producers in an industry irrespective of their costs and if this price is set high enough to cover the cost of the least efficient producer whose output is needed, every producer will have a pecuniary incentive to lower his costs of production and thus to increase his profit margin. If on the other hand individual maximum prices are set for every producer in such a way as to take account of his cost situation, and if the margin between maximum price and production costs is maintained continuously, a producer will have no pecuniary incentive to lower costs;[28] if he does his maximum price will be revised downward.

In this respect too the policy followed by the War Industries Board—and the Fuel Administration—was superior to that applied by the Food Administration. The Board fixed maximum prices for all producers in a certain field. It attempted to establish the maximum price at the cost of production encountered by the "bulk-line producer" after allowing for a "reasonable margin of profit." The "bulk-line producer" was found by means of a table or a diagram which indicated the contribution of all available producers to the prevailing total output of the industry, and ranked the individual producers according to their unit costs of

---

[28] Similar results are to be expected from government guarantees of "normal" profits. Such guarantees were given to the "nationalized" industries (coal mines, flour mills, and railroads) in Great Britain during the first world war. *Cf.* Lloyd, *op. cit.*, 355 ff., and R. A. S. Redmayne: *The British Coal-Mining Industry During the War*, Oxford, 1923, 94 ff.

For an extensive discussion of the problem of uniform or varying prices, see Garrett, *op. cit.*, 385 ff.

production. The bulk-line or price-determining producer was found at the point where from eighty to ninety per cent of the total output was included.[29] The lower the unit costs of the individual producer, the larger was the profit margin he could enjoy. Of course, the individual's freedom to dispose of these profits was limited by income and excess-profits taxes, but there remained enough pecuniary incentive to lower costs.

The scheme was rather crude. It apparently proceeded under the assumption that unit costs are independent of the volume of output of the individual firm. This assumption may in some cases be true to fact, at least when the range of output variations considered has for certain reasons to be fairly narrow; but in other cases the assumption may be misleading and result in a distorted picture of the industry's cost schedule.[30]

Furthermore, the scheme was generous in so far as it allowed a "reasonable profit" even to the bulk-line producer. Accordingly, producers with still higher costs were able to continue operations at a small profit or on a break-even basis. This may have been the intention of the creators of the scheme; but in that case it would have been better to place the bulk line at a higher percentage of total output. The fundamental idea, however, seems to have been that there can be no production without a profit.[31] This idea is at variance with economic theory and leads to an unnecessary generosity toward producers. It is important to realize that the bulk-line producer of the Price-Fixing Committee was not the marginal producer known in economic theory.

---

[29] F. W. Taussig: "Price-Fixing as Seen by a Price-Fixer," *Quarterly Journal of Economics*, Vol. 33, 1919, 219.

[30] See H. Stein: *Government Price Policy in the United States During the World War*, Williamstown, 1939, 104–106.

[31] See statement of President Wilson quoted in Garrett, *op. cit.*, 409.

The profit allowance made the scheme arbitrary to a large extent.

The price-fixing committee tried in a rough way to measure the pre-war profits and, with that weapon in hand, they fought in conference for the opportunist policy most favorable to the Government upon which they and the industry could agree. They . . . did not have the same relative success with all industries . . . the difficulties of negotiation made finally mandatory the approval of particular cotton-goods prices at figures more than 25 per cent above cost.[32]

The following fictitious example [33] illustrates the type of analysis used in determining bulk-line producer and bulk-line price. Suppose there were five producers of a certain commodity. Assume that their (constant) unit costs of production were 1, 2, 4, 6, and 9 cents, respectively, and that they could supply 30, 25, 20, 15, and 10 per cent, respectively, of the customary total output, at prices covering these costs. The authorities would want to fix the maximum price high enough to cover the cost of production up to an aggregate output of 90 per cent of the customary total, plus a "reasonable margin of profit" of, say, 1 cent. Cumulating the percentages of total output which the individual producers could furnish—beginning with the cheapest producer and ending with the most expensive one—they would find that the maximum price had to be fixed at 7 cents (the cost of producer number 4 plus the assumed profit allowance). This would be the bulk-line price, and producer number 4, the bulk-line producer. At this price producers number 1, 2, and 3 would realize profits per unit of output of 6, 5, and 3 cents, respectively. Number 4 would make the "reasonable profit" of 1 cent, and number 5 would sustain a loss of 2 cents per unit of output, if he remained in

---

[32] *Ibid.*, 410.
[33] For practical examples and bulk-line diagrams see Garrett, *op. cit.*, 399, and Stein, *op. cit.*, 101.

business. Notice that a "reasonable profit" of 3 cents would have enabled number 5 to break even.

Theoretical Bulk-Line Table

Producer Number	Unit Cost of Production in Dollars	Percentage of Customary Total Output Supplied	Cumulated Percentages
1	$.01	30%	30%
2	.02	25	55
3	.04	20	75
4	.06	15	90
5	.09	10	100

The Food Administration's technique was less conducive to cost reductions. As we saw before, the Administration fixed maximum profit margins on top of the costs of individual dealers. To the extent that this system was effective, it prevented dealers from increasing their profit margins by reducing costs. It even contained features which penalized cost reductions: Frequently more than one maximum margin was fixed for a certain trade, a *higher* one applicable to dealers with *high* costs and a *lower* one to those with *low* costs.[34] The idea underlying this procedure may have been to equalize profit *rates* of different dealers. It was bound, however, to lower their interest in improvements and cost reductions.

The maximum prices of the War Industries Board were fixed at levels that enabled the majority of producers to cover their costs. There may be reasons, however, for fixing prices at a lower level. For instance, it was found necessary in Great Britain to fix bread prices below costs. In 1917, the government began to sell imported cereals to flour mills below cost and in addition paid a subsidy to the mills in order to render a stabilization of the bread price possible.[35] It is obvious that the fixing of maximum prices

---

[34] Garrett, *op. cit.*, 52.
[35] The subsidy amounted to roughly fifty million pound sterling per year. W. H. Beveridge: *British Food Control*, London, 1928, 108 ff.

below the costs of all or a great number of indispensable producers entails subsidization. The expense to the treasury may, however, be justified by the economic and social effects of the low price. In discussing the advisability of the bread subsidy in England Beveridge concluded:

> Certainly the cost of the subsidy was not all pure loss to the State, which, directly or indirectly, had become the employer of nearly all its citizens, and was continually having to adjust wages according to the cost of living. The price of bread entered directly into the cost of living, and, but for the subsidy, wages would have been materially higher; in another war, an alternative to rising cost of living and so of wages might conceivably be found in a much more general application of subsidies.[36]

Control of Wages

It is impossible to "clamp a ceiling down" on prices and allow the level of wages to rise simultaneously. To a slight extent, perhaps, wages may be allowed to rise at the expense of profits, and for some occupations this may indeed be expedient. But when the rise of wages leads to too large a reduction of profits or even to a curtailment of necessary depreciation and obsolescence allowances on fixed capital, it will upset the working of business firms. Theoretically, it is possible to let the costs of business operation rise above the revenue from sales and to cover these losses by subsidies, which in turn may be financed by levies on the income of wage earners. But this procedure would represent an unnecessarily complicated and roundabout way of operating the nations' industries, a way fraught with the danger of declining output. Therefore, if the level of prices of producers' and consumers' goods is kept stable by government

---

[36] *Ibid.*, 112. Reprinted by permission of Yale University Press.

control, it is necessary to do the same for the level of wages.

Of course, if the cost of living is stabilized, one of the most important motives for demands of higher wages is automatically removed. Apart from this motive there remain relatively few and unimportant reasons that have led to wage disputes in the World War and the present war. In both wars the rising cost of living has been the greatest force behind the rise of wages. Most of the advances in wage rates were preceded by rises in the cost of living, and their effect on the level of living of the working class was promptly reduced or annihilated by a further rise in prices. In England, for instance, the general level of wages and the cost of living engaged during the World War in the following race. From July, 1914 (= 100), to July, 1915, the *Labour Gazette's* cost of living index rose by twenty-five per cent; the wage level followed with an increase of from five to ten per cent. By July, 1916, the cost of living had reached 145, the wage level 115 to 120; by July, 1917, the former was at 180, the latter between 135 and 140; and so on until the end of the war.[37] Most if not all of the rise in wages could have been avoided, if it had been possible to stabilize the cost of living at an early moment.

What are the other factors that may account for a rise in wages in wartime? They are the intense demand for labor in essential industries and the limitations of labor supply. Attempting to attract workers from other occupations, the munitions industries offer higher wages. In this way various classes of workers were able to obtain better pay during the World War. In Germany, for instance, men's wages on railroads, in munitions, metal, machine, and chemical industries increased from the spring of 1914 to the fall of 1918 by more than the increase in the cost of living, while wages in building and particularly in the textile and cloth-

---

[37] Bowley, *op. cit.*, 106.

ing industries lagged far behind living costs.[38] In this country, shipyard workers and certain classes of railroad workers were among the most favored classes. The American government, in its desire to enlist the coöperation of labor in the war program, took a favorable attitude toward wage increases.[39]

To a certain extent, wage increases due to these causes may be justifiable. The war industries need labor, and the flow of labor may legitimately be stimulated by pecuniary advantages. Furthermore, it may appear desirable to enlist the coöperation of "submerged" labor groups by increasing their wages. Finally, allowance should be made for increases in the productivity of labor. If a wage increase makes it possible to increase per capita output per day or per week, it may represent a valuable contribution to an essential objective of the war economy. But it is certainly true that an uncontrolled movement of wages is likely to have the same shortcomings which we found before in an uncontrolled rise of prices. Wages may rise too little to bring about the necessary reallocation of the nation's labor force, they may rise too much in comparison to their effect on production and allocation of labor, and their rise may be disruptive in so far as it leads to high labor turnover and to a permanent revolution of cost conditions in business. Therefore, even if stabilization of the cost of living has removed the main cause of disturbances in the field of wages, there remains a need of wage control.

During the first world war all belligerent countries saw

---

[38] Zimmermann, *op. cit.*, 467. For similar trends in England and France, see Bowley, *op. cit.*, 105 and March, *op. cit.*, 297.

[39] In the United States, per capita annual *money* earnings of workers in all industries (including agriculture) were, in 1917, thirty-two per cent, in 1918, sixty-seven per cent above the level of 1914. In contradistinction to the experience of European belligerents (and neutrals) there was no fall in the *real* earnings of the average American worker during the World War. Per capita real earnings (1914 = 100) rose to 103 in 1917 and to 106 in 1918. (P. H. Douglas: *Real Wages in the United States, 1890–1926*, New York, 1930, Table 147.)

the emergence and development of government agencies designed to act as mediators and arbitrators in wage conflicts. Furthermore, governments gained a direct influence on wages in nationalized industries. Finally, minimum-wage laws were passed for certain classes of workers, such as workers entering an industry under dilution schemes, women, and agricultural workers.[40] There was, however, no general scheme of wage control for private industry. In the present war, such a scheme is in force in Germany. With the outbreak of hostilities a general wage-stop was decreed. Serious efforts were made to prevent any rise of wages in the war industries. Obviously, the German government, having stabilized the cost of living, expected that all other functions of wage increases could be taken care of by industrial conscription and propaganda measures.

In England, however, developments during the first six months of the present war bear a dangerous resemblance to the race between the cost of living and the level of wages during the World War. From September, 1939, to March, 1940, the official cost of living index rose by thirteen and a half per cent, while wage rates paid by large firms in different industries rose by eight per cent and per capita earnings by eleven per cent. In the face of these facts, "there has been no common policy among the trade unions and no wages plan from the Government." [41]

SUGGESTED REFERENCES

Baruch, B. M.: *American Industry in the War,* a report of the War Industries Board, Washington, D. C., 1921, in particular part I.
—————: *Taking the Profits Out of War,* New York, (?), 1936 (?).
Beveridge, W. H.: *British Food Control,* London, 1928, in particular chapters IX and X.

---

[40] For the policies followed by the National War Labor Board in this country during the World War, see G. S. Watkins: *Labor Problems and Labor Administration in the United States During the World War,* Urbana, 1919, 165–166.
[41] *The Economist,* London, June 1, 1940, 972.

Bowley, A. L.: *Prices and Wages in the United Kingdom, 1914–1920*, Oxford, 1921.

Cherne, L. M.: *Adjusting Your Business to War*, New York, 1940, chapter VI.

(Clark, J. M., Hamilton, W. H., and Moulton, H. G.; editors): *Readings in the Economics of War*, Chicago, 1918, chapters LII–LVI (Prices and Price Control).

Garrett, P. W.: *Government Control over Prices*, published by the War Trade Board in coöperation with the War Industries Board, Washington, D. C., 1920.

Litman, S.: *Prices and Price Control in Great Britain and the United States During the World War*, New York, 1920.

Lloyd, E. M. H.: *Experiments in State Control at the War Office and the Ministry of Food*, Oxford, 1924, in particular part IV.

Mitchell, W. C.: *History of Prices During the War* (Summary), War Industries Board, Washington, D. C., 1919.

Pigou, A. C.: *The Political Economy of War*, London, 1921, chapters XI, XIII, and XIV.

Stein, H.: *Government Price Policy in the United States During the World War*, Williamstown, 1939.

Taussig, F. W.: "Price-Fixing as Seen by a Price-Fixer," *Quarterly Journal of Economics*, Vol. 33, 1919.

Tobin, H. J., and Bidwell, P. W.: *Mobilizing Civilian America*, New York, 1940, chapters VIII and IX.

United States Senate, Special Committee on Investigation of the Munitions Industry: *Preliminary Report on Wartime Taxation and Price Control*, 74th Congress, 1st Session, Senate, Report No. 944, Part 2, Washington, D. C., 1935, part II.

CHAPTER 9

Rationing of Consumers' Goods and Government Operation of Industry

RATIONING OF CONSUMERS' GOODS

Rationing is the most bothersome interference of the war economy with the economic life of consumers. The rationing system involves a serious limitation of their freedom in allocating expenditures to different articles. It does not abolish this freedom altogether; but it compels individuals or households to keep their consumption of rationed goods within certain fixed limits, to register with certain retailers and to obtain their supplies from them exclusively, and to use two types of money for their purchases: ordinary currency and the secondary currency of ration coupons. It is no wonder that such a system found most serious opposition during the World War in democratic countries such as England and France and that its introduction was postponed until the very last year. Yet, in a major war, rationing of consumers' goods is likely to be the smaller evil as compared with circumstances that may develop in its absence.

Rationing is designed to cope with a deficiency of supplies as compared to effective demand. It is unnecessary if supplies are large enough to provide all the quantities demanded at prices that are close to prewar levels. But its introduction is necessary when supplies do not satisfy demand and when for reasons of social policy a rise of prices cannot be allowed to establish equilibrium.[1] Under these circumstances, absence of rationing would enable persons favored with money, time, and good connections to outbid and outrun those less favorably situated and to reduce them to a level of starvation. "If there is only bread enough for bare physical needs and not for the full appetite, the unrestricted economic haggle will involve surfeit here and starvation there." [2]

The deficiency of supplies may appear on different levels. It may appear on the national level: aggregate quantities of certain goods fall short of the usual civilian consumption. In this form, deficiency of supplies may be due to decreased home production, reduced arrivals of shipments from abroad, or, in a rather unusual case under war conditions, to an increase in demand. Secondly, the deficiency may appear on a local level. There may not be a deficiency on a national scale; but maldistribution or a choked transportation system may create shortages in certain communities. Finally, the deficiency may appear on the household level. Even if the nation as a whole and the community are sufficiently supplied, the individual consumer may fail to obtain the desired quantities of commodities because of the hoarding undertaken by others.

Rationing of consumers' goods is concerned with shortages affecting the individual consumer. These shortages may be of either one or all of the three types mentioned above. Rationing has to deal with their cumulative effect. Schemes designed to increase supplies on a national scale or to improve the distribution of available supplies among the various communities will not concern us in this discussion. We must, however, bear in mind that such schemes may be

---

[1] For a discussion of relationships between price-fixing and rationing, see A. C. Pigou: *The Political Economy of War,* London, 1921, 136–140.

[2] J. A. Salter: *Allied Shipping Control,* Oxford, 1921, 18–19.

able to make rationing unnecessary, at least where the source of scarcity lies on the national or local level.

The normal reaction of consumers to shortages is a run on stores, the formation of queues, and attempts to buy as much of the scarce commodities as can be obtained. Just as a run of depositors on a supposedly insolvent bank is apt to render the bank actually insolvent, so a run of consumers on retail stores accentuates any existing supply difficulties. The experience in England during the second half of 1917 and the first months of 1918 provides a convincing illustration. There were shortages of sugar, tea, margarine, and meat. The government struggled with various plans for relieving the situation but could not find a solution. Early in 1915, the Food Controller had appealed to the nation to place itself on voluntary rations for bread, meat, and sugar; but the effect consisted mainly in making the country conscious of food shortages. Voluntary rationing did not and could not provide a solution. Compulsory rationing was first attempted with sugar, and in spite of an extraordinary degree of planless experimenting the British government succeeded by the end of 1917 in bringing the sugar situation under control before much discontent became manifest. Attempts to ration tea, margarine, and meat, however, had to wait a few more months, and the interval was long enough to produce the greatest disorder. Maximum prices had been fixed for meat and margarine; but supplies were not large enough to satisfy the demand at these prices.[3] Consequently, some people had to go without, and the general reaction to this condition was a rush for goods. Queues formed before the stores, women and children spent many hours a day waiting for their turn, only to be told, in many cases, that the supplies

---

[3] E. M. H. Lloyd: *Experiments in State Control at the War Office and the Ministry of Food,* Oxford, 1924, 175, 176, and 233.

had been exhausted. Such experience inevitably lengthened the queues on the following day. In London, toward the end of January, 1918, queues reached their climax. It was estimated that on the worst Saturday more than half a million persons had participated in the formation of food queues within the metropolitan police district of London.[4]

The queues were something of a stage army, and something of an occupation to people who had nothing better to do. The same household might be represented by different members in different queues for the same article; persons who had already had enough sometimes stood in hopes of getting more, which could either be kept in reserve against the uncertainties of next week or be sold at a profit to a less fortunate neighbour. A case was reported of a woman in Cardiff who fainted in a tea queue; while she was receiving attention it was discovered that she was carrying seven pounds of tea. But though to some extent the queues might be factitious, once they had begun they became compulsory—the only way of getting food at all.[5]

The patience of the people was rapidly exhausted. Munitions workers left the factories in order to take the places of their wives in the queues. Letters came from the front reporting the desire of husbands to return and to do their share of queueing. The trade unions and the government finally realized that no more time could be wasted. Rationing of margarine, tea, and meats was introduced in the spring of 1918, and the experience provided sufficient proof for the effectiveness of the rationing system in coping with the difficulties. No increase in total supplies took place and yet queues disappeared quickly. The rationing system quieted fears of consumers in two essential respects: it ensured that *everybody* would get *his allotted share* regularly and that *nobody* would get *more*.

---

[4] W. H. Beveridge, *British Food Control,* London, 1928, 207.
[5] *Ibid.,* 208. Reprinted by permission of Yale University Press.

The Technique of Rationing

The rationing of consumers' goods presents a number of interesting technical problems. (1) Which commodities are to be rationed? (2) Shall rations be in the form of quantities or values? (3) Shall the size of rations be the same for everybody, or shall it vary with needs? (4) Does rationing represent the strictest system of consumption control? Let us briefly consider these various problems.

1. The scope of rationing is a function of the scope of shortages. If it is necessary, nearly all ordinary articles of consumption may be subjected to rationing, foodstuffs and clothing as well as household supplies. The more regularly an article is consumed, the easier is its rationing, and the higher the degree to which consumption depends on accidental circumstances, the more difficult it is. Hence, we find war rations for articles like sugar, meat, and bread, or for soap and stockings, but not for medical supplies or railroad mileage. The extent to which rationing has gone in various countries varies considerably. During the first world war, sugar was the only article rationed in this country; in France, there was a nation-wide rationing system for sugar and bread; in England, for sugar, butter, margarine, lard and meats, jam, tea, and cheese.[6] In Germany, a much more extended rationing system was in force. In the present war, Germany has a nearly comprehensive regime of rations for foodstuffs and clothing articles. Only a few articles such as fish, fresh vegetables, fruit, and—for some months—potatoes have been available without ration cards.

Apart from variations in scope there are considerable variations in intensity among the different rationing schemes. The German World War system of rationing

---

[6] P. W. Garrett: *Government Control Over Prices*, Washington, D. C., 1920, 85. P. Pinot: *Le Contrôle du Ravitaillement de la Population Civile*, Paris, 1925, 24. Beveridge, *op. cit.*, 224 and 225.

was most severe, and its severity increased with the progress of the war, as is well illustrated by the following table: [7]

COMPARISON OF GERMAN NORMAL RATIONS DURING WORLD WAR AND ESTIMATED PREWAR PER CAPITA CONSUMPTION
[Prewar Consumption = 100]

Commodity	1916–1917	Second Half of 1918
Flour and bread	52	48
Meat and meat products	31	12
Fish	51	5
Eggs	18	13
Lard	14	7
Butter	22	28
Cheese	2	15
Rice	4	—
Legumes	14	7
Sugar	48	82
Potatoes	71	94
Vegetable fats	39	17

The table also illustrates how, during the war, the composition of the normal German diet changed in favor of a larger carbohydrate content and cheaper proteins. These rations were very low; they did not even cover calorie needs. Distribution of additional foodstuffs by factories and "war kitchens" were emergency measures designed to limit the consequences of underfeeding. Bootleg trade in foodstuffs was bound to spread.

The scale of rations prepared by the British Committee on Rationing and Distribution in December, 1917, was more satisfactory. The calorie content of the allowed quantities of bread, meat, fats, sugar, and potatoes exceeded that of the German rations by 61 per cent for the ordinary manual worker, 41 per cent for the heavy worker, and 43 per cent for other adults.[8] It is true that the average British

---
[7] Adapted from W. Zimmermann in Meerwarth, Günther and Zimmermann: *Die Einwirkung des Krieges auf Bevölkerungsbewegung, Einkommen und Lebenshaltung in Deutschland,* Stuttgart, 1932, 457.

[8] Beveridge, *op. cit.,* 388 ff.

consumer, too, had to accept a curtailment of his consumption of meat (by 22 per cent), butter (34 per cent), sugar (33 per cent), fresh milk (15 per cent), and potatoes (9 per cent) between 1914 and 1917. Over the same period, however, he increased his consumption of flour (by 12 per cent), bacon and ham (12 per cent), and margarine (78 per cent). (The figures refer to calorie values of quantities of food consumed during the two years.) The total amount of calories available to the average British consumer decreased only very slightly (by 4 per cent).[9]

Three months after the outbreak of the present war, food rations in Germany were still fairly high. The following table gives an illustration.

FOOD RATIONS IN GERMANY AT END OF 1939 [10]

Commodity	Normal Adult Ration in Per Cent of Per Capita Consumption in Working Class Families in 1937	Ration for Very Hard Workers in Per Cent of the Consumption of Heavy Manual Workers in 1936
Bread and flour	94	145
Meat	72	96
Fats	76	94
Cheese	39	26
Eggs	83	25
Sugar	86	98

It appears from these figures that very hard workers had to make the largest sacrifices of their peacetime way of living with respect to cheese and eggs, while ordinary consumers were compelled to make their largest reductions in the consumption of cheese, meats, and fats.

The variations of rationing systems in scope and intensity

---

[9] Beveridge, *op. cit.*, 313. See also the broader data on pp. 362–363 of this source.
[10] J. C. deWilde: "Germany's Wartime Economy," *Foreign Policy Reports*, June 15, 1940, 92.

are largely due to differences in the nature of shortages; but they are also related to differences in popular attitude and in organizational ability of the responsible administrations. In the field of rationing as well as in that of price control and other war measures, the maxim to be followed should be: "prophylactic" rather than "therapeutic" action. It is better for the safeguarding of public morale to introduce a rationing system a little too early and for some essentials that are not expected to show immediate and serious shortages, than to wait until the queues appear.

It would be unreasonable, however, to make a cult of rationing. Commodities of which there is plenty should not be rationed. Similarly, rationing should be discontinued when ample supplies can be secured or when consumers' demand shifts away from the rationed goods.[11] Of course, it is not necessary to pass directly from rationing to free sales. The transition may be made smoother by gradually increasing the individual rations of articles that become more abundant.

It must be noted in this connection that rationing of a certain article tends to divert purchasing power to other nonrationed goods. Particularly if the rations fall considerably short of normally consumed quantities will consumers try to get unrationed substitutes. This tendency may make it necessary to extend the rationing scheme. It is, for instance, scarcely possible to subject meat purchases in stores to rationing and leave individuals free to purchase all the meat meals they can afford in restaurants. This was soon discovered in England. The authorities then ordered that restaurants should require the presentation of ration tickets by all customers ordering a meat dish. By diverting consumers' purchases into new channels the rationing system has an inherent tendency to produce reasons for its introduction in further and further fields. The smaller the

---

[11] Beveridge, *op. cit.*, 211.

rations and the scarcer the unrationed commodities, the stronger this tendency will be.

2. Ordinarily rations are fixed in terms of quantities. Consumers are given tickets entitling them to buy a certain quantity of a certain article in a certain shop during a certain period of time. The time limitation results from the necessity to prevent too large an accumulation of purchases at a given moment. Compelling buyers to purchase a commodity from a certain retailer is not a necessary concomitant of the rationing system. It has been avoided, for instance, in the rationing of clothing in present-day Germany. But this restriction of consumers' freedom of choice seems to be advantageous in the rationing of many goods. It facilitates the allocation of supplies to the various retailers and seems to be helpful in preventing fraud.

The rations need not necessarily be definite quantities of certain goods. First of all, they may be permitted to vary in time. The quantity of bread to which a certain ration ticket entitles its owner may be increased or decreased by the authorities according to the market situation. Second, at a given moment, a ration ticket may be allowed to buy different quantities of different commodities. The clothing card at present used in Germany allows a man to buy fifty handkerchiefs *or* twenty pairs of socks *or* two raincoats a year. Every textile article is worth a certain number of points (for instance, handkerchiefs: two, socks: five, raincoats: fifty), and the adult consumer has a title to a hundred points during the year. He is free to buy any combination of goods within this limit.[12]

Third, the ration may not refer to quantities at all but to money values, and again the consumer may be left free to find a collection of articles of which the total cost remains within the prescribed limits. This idea found application in England for the rationing of meat. "Each coupon en-

---

12 *Frankfurter Zeitung*, November 15, 1939.

titled a customer to buy at the outset five-pence worth of butcher's meat; he could please himself whether he spent his fivepence and his coupon on a prime morsel or on a large lump of bone and scrapings." [13]

We see that there are a number of different ways in which the system of rations may be organized and adapted to the needs of the administration as well as to the desires of consumers. Consumers will of course prefer the system which restricts their freedom of choice least; and the government should satisfy their desire to the extent that is compatible with available supplies.

3. When rationing was finally introduced in England during the year 1917 it was accepted as a step toward a more equitable distribution of foods; but opposition against it flared up anew when it appeared that rations could not very well be made equal for everybody. Persons of different age and occupation obviously have different needs of foodstuffs. Their needs differ with respect to energy, mineral, and vitamin content. Heavy workers need a larger energy supply than ordinary manual workers; children, expectant and nursing mothers need more milk. Women have use for aprons, babies for diapers, men for collars, and there is no sense in giving everyone a title to equal quantities of these articles. Hence, individual rations have to take account of differences in needs.

Rationing systems had to conform to this necessity. The English World War rations of bread, meat, and fats were fifty per cent higher for heavy workers than for ordinary adults; in present-day Germany, unskimmed milk is reserved for children, expectant and nursing mothers, and for workers in a few selected occupations.

4. Rationing does not provide the strictest system of controlled distribution. It assures consumers of a certain amount of goods. There is a system that goes much fur-

---
[13] Beveridge, *op. cit.*, 210.

ther: the purchase permission. Under it consumers are not allowed to buy a certain article without a specific permission of the authorities. Before the present German scheme of rationing was extended to clothing, no textiles could be bought without a purchase permission. In order to obtain such a permission the consumer had to prove to the authorities that he could not do without the desired article, and officials were entitled to test the proof by inspecting the individual's wardrobe. In November, 1939, this regime was restricted to heavy overcoats, working clothes, household linen, and rugs. It has also been applied in Germany to purchases of shoes, tires, and gasoline. Such a system is well suited for commodities, the consumption of which shall be restricted to the most urgent cases. There is no doubt, however, that it is more difficult to handle and much more cumbersome to the consumer than rationing.

Government Operation of Industry

The government measures we have considered so far provide controls of private business. They interfere with the management of individual firms; but they do not transfer the operation of businesses from private to public management. Price control, taxation of profits, priorities, and rationing only reduce the freedom of choice of private management. They do not abolish it altogether.

Now we come to a measure of a higher order, the abolishment of private management. Under certain conditions, which we are going to contemplate, industry can be made more efficient if it is placed under public management. Generally speaking, this situation arises when neither detailed government regimentation nor the pecuniary incentives which can be granted to private management under war conditions are able to bring about the desired results. It must be realized that the transfer of certain plants or whole industries to government management may make it possible to dispense with a host of costly incentives and cumbersome regulations, the only purpose of which is to induce private managers to accommodate themselves to the war economy.

It is not necessary that the change in management be accompanied by a change in ownership. By this I mean that essential property rights such as that of selling the title to the property or receiving returns from its use may very well be left to private owners. What matters here is that private owners lose the right to determine the *modus of utilization* of the property. Since the state can acquire this control without acquisition of individual property rights, expropriation is not a necessary concomitant of government operation of industry. Improvement in the efficiency of industrial operations is, indeed, entirely independent of the nature of property titles lying in certain vaults. Leaving the essentially political question of expropriation aside, we shall focus our attention on the *transfer of management* from private to public agencies.

We must, however, take account of a correlation between ownership and management which is likely to appear in the field of new investments for war purposes. Some of these investments are extremely risky. A new factory of explosives, as important as it may be to war needs, is likely to find a small market for its product after the war is over. Possibly it can then be converted to new uses (for instance, the production of fertilizer); possibly capital invested in the plant can be amortized during the war years. However, the risk involved in such a venture may be large enough to discourage private investors. Under those circumstances, the government will find it necessary to finance this investment out of its tax revenue, bond sales, or special levies. Government operation of the new plant will probably ensue. A development of this kind could be observed in the

German steel industry during the years preceding the present war. The exploitation of poor iron ores in central Germany did not attract the interest of private steel companies. The government formed a state company, "Reichswerke Hermann Göring," compelled the private firms to subscribe part of its capital, and built large plants to be operated under state management.

Government operation of industry does not necessarily mean the assumption of managerial functions by officials of an ordinary government department. It may be placed into the hands of special administrative bodies working under definite rules and similar in nature to the Federal Reserve Board or the Tennessee Valley Authority. This procedure has the advantage of eliminating more effectively the possibilities of political corruption among public administrators.

Government operation of industries may appear advisable for several reasons. (1) Private management may not guarantee a sufficient output of commodities essential to the war economy. (2) Private management may be unable to overcome labor conflicts arising in essential industries. (3) It may not comply with official instructions—for instance, priority orders. (4) Private management may lead to insufficient coördination of the various units of an industry. Let us briefly consider these four reasons for the replacement of private by government management.

1. It is possible that private management of manufacturing firms furnishes perfectly satisfactory output with maximum efficiency. The history of the first world war in this as well as in other countries is filled with brilliant examples of private managers serving the war economy with spectacular efficiency. As far as already existing plants are concerned, private management has even a definite chance of operating more efficiently than a suddenly introduced public administration. In time of peace, private managers

are in a position to accumulate practical experience in their field. Public managers, if they do not have the same training, probably lack a close acquaintance with the technical and organizational conditions involved.[14] In some cases, however, private managers may be inefficient and the output of their plants less than it would be under government management. Such cases are likely to be met with when the character of operations in a plant has to be changed in order to fulfill the war production program, or when new plants have to be added.

Government management designed to speed up output is particularly likely to be introduced in industries which are producing military supplies. Even in peacetime and in countries operating the bulk of their industries on a private basis, governments usually run certain armament factories. Consequently, there is a good chance that a number of executives experienced in armament production can be found among government officials. During the war the production of arms has to be considerably increased, and new plants have to be organized. It may be expedient to put these new plants, too, under government management. This occurred on a large scale in England during the first world war. The Ministry of Munitions as well as its district organizations undertook the production of shells, explosives, and other war materials in a growing number of establishments. This scheme of government-managed production has been described by David Lloyd George, who was then Minister of Munitions: [15]

The first few months of the Ministry's existence saw the establishment of an imposing group of these national factories. By the end of December, 1915, when the Ministry had been in

---

[14] The government may, of course, recruit its staff of industrial managers from the ranks of private executives; but precautionary measures must be taken to avoid collusion between the businessmen on government jobs and the private firms with which these men were previously associated. See H. J. Tobin and P. W. Bidwell: *Mobilizing Civilian America*, New York, 1940, 30.

[15] *War Memoirs* of D. Lloyd George, 1915-1916, Boston: Little, Brown & Company, 1933, 34.

existence only seven months, there were, in addition to the Royal Factories at Woolwich, Waltham Abbey, Enfield Lock and Farnborough—which had been transferred from the War Office in the course of the autumn—and certain factories for explosives, no less than seventy-three new national factories. Of these, thirty-six were national shell factories for turning out the lighter natures of shells; thirteen were national projectile factories, mainly concerned with heavier shell; thirteen were national filling factories. There were eight new factories for making explosives, a new factory for filling trench mortar bombs, and two gauge factories which I took over to ensure an adequate supply of gauges for the new concerns which were springing up everywhere to produce munitions. Progress had been hampered in every direction by the inadequate supply of gauges.

As time went on, this array of national factories was steadily increased, both in number and in the variety of the products for the manufacture of which they were erected or adapted. By the end of the war they numbered in all 218; and covered not only every kind of munition from cannon and aëroplanes to small-arms ammunition, but sawmills, factories for boxes, tools, optical instruments and ball bearings, and establishments for sorting and storing salvage.

Besides these so-called national factories there were a large number of munitions factories left under private management. However, all of these establishments were put under special government control with respect to working conditions and profits. They were called "controlled establishments." [16]

Attention must be given to a particular cause of insufficient output under private management: the monopolistic underemployment of productive facilities. A munitions firm which enjoys a monopoly or quasi-monopoly—and many firms do under the conditions of urgent and specific war demand—will tend to operate below capacity if it can realize a larger profit in this way.[17] This obstacle to maxi-

---

[16] H. Wolfe: *Labour Supply and Regulation*, Oxford, 1923, 99 ff. and 314 ff.
[17] See J. E. Meade: *An Introduction to Economic Analysis and Policy*, New York, 1938, chapter VI.

mum output could easily be removed if the firm were placed under government control.

2. Hand in hand with the desire to increase production goes an interest in avoiding labor conflicts. In some industries or individual plants relations between employers and workers may be strained. As a consequence strikes may threaten or actually break out, and great damage to the country's military strength may result. Government mediation and arbitration can remedy such conditions to a certain extent; but the government may find that these measures are insufficient and that the risk of conflicts is too great. Considerations of this kind prompted the nationalization of telephone and telegraph services in this country during the World War.[18]

3. Private managers of factories may not comply with official instructions such as priority orders or measures designed to limit profits. They may attempt to profiteer, fail to give other producers access to technical experience and patent rights, or refuse to coöperate with the military authorities.[19] There may be conscious or unconscious sabotage of the war-economic steps taken by the various control agencies of the government. In such cases, modern war governments are usually empowered to commandeer the productive facilities of producers, with or without compensation. It is obvious that management cannot be left in the hands of persons who do not comply with the requirements of the war economy.

The establishment of public factories may also be useful to the government by enabling it to deal more advantageously with private suppliers. In the absence of a compre-

---

[18] C. W. Baker: *Government Control and Operation of Industry in Great Britain and the United States During the World War*, New York, 1921, 68.

[19] See the following reports of the Special Senate Committee on Investigation of the Munitions Industry (Nye Committee), 74th Congress, 1st Session, Senate, Report No. 944, Washington, D. C., 1935, *passim;* 74th Congress, 2d Session, Senate, Report No. 944, Washington, D. C., 1936, Part 4, *passim,* and Part 7, 1–64 and *passim.*

hensive scheme of public cost control, knowledge of the technical and cost conditions in the public factories will put a yardstick into the hands of the government. This yardstick will serve as a means of distinguishing between justified and unjustified prices charged by private producers.

4. Probably the most important reason for government operation of railroads and other public utilities is insufficient coördination of independent private units in these fields. Unified management of railroads makes possible a much more complete and efficient exploitation of existing facilities. In the place of a number of individual and competing companies using their own tracks, rolling equipment, terminals, and repair shops and excluding competitors partly or wholly from their use, the government may put a more economical organization. Under it, the operation of nonessential lines may be discontinued, their rolling equipment shifted over to essential ones, and perhaps even their rails used for more urgent purposes. (During the first world war, many miles of rails were torn out in England and shipped to France to be used there for military railroads.) Advertising and other competitive efforts of individual railroad companies can easily be discontinued. The important lines have all the traffic they can handle, while the unimportant ones would do best to restrict their operations to a minimum. Furthermore, the operation of all railroads provides the government with a strong tool for reducing superfluous transports, in particular cross-shipments of merchandise,[20] and for enforcing priority orders in all kinds of trades.

In the first (as well as in the second) world war, the British government was quick to assume the centralized management of railroads. This did not involve a great change

---

[20] For a description of an interesting British wartime system of economical coal distribution, see R. A. S. Redmayne: *The British Coal-Mining Industry During the War*, Oxford, 1923, 103 and 294.

in the leading personnel, since the general managers of the great systems were made a central managing board under the chairmanship of the president of the Board of Trade.[21] The results of the coördination were considered very satisfactory on the whole. The government paid a compensation to the railroad companies.

Under the law the government was required to render the railways full compensation for loss or injury sustained because of government operation and control. This requirement was met by a voluntary agreement between the government and the railways by which the government undertook to maintain the net income of the roads at the same level as during the normal period just preceding the war, while the railways on their part not only were expected to expedite all military traffic and to subordinate their ordinary activities wholly and unreservedly to the exigencies of military needs, but also agreed to handle all government traffic, of whatever nature or extent, free of charge.[22]

In this country, government operation of railroads assumed a different form. In December, 1917, a presidential order put the railroads under the management of a Director-General who became the actual chief executive of the nation's railroad business. He discharged 400 railway presidents and other high-salaried executive officers.[23] In this way, the direction of the nation's sprawling railroad system was strongly centralized. Criticism arose against over-centralization under government management and against government management in general. The government was accused of paying insufficient compensation to owners, of returning the roads in bad condition at the end of the period of government management in the spring of 1920, and of inefficient operation. On the other side, it was argued

---

[21] F. H. Dixon and J. H. Parmelee: *War Administration of the Railways in the United States and Great Britain*, New York, Oxford University Press, 1918, 71 and 72.
[22] *Ibid.*, 73–74.
[23] C. W. Baker, *op. cit.*, 58. For the proclamation under which the President took possession of the railroads, see Dixon and Parmelee, *op. cit.*, 149.

that compensation was royal, that the deterioration of railroad equipment was an unavoidable consequence of war conditions met with in all belligerent countries, that it was of relatively small importance in this country, and finally that the private companies could not have obtained better results.[24] W. D. Hines, an outstanding railroad executive and Director-General of Railroads in 1919 and 1920 pointed out that already at the beginning of Federal control many of the railroads showed badly maintained facilities, and that the charge made against the government of returning the roads to their owners in a "broken-down" condition had no foundation.[25] Unified management as such did not prove detrimental to the railroads; but in applying it the government may have made some errors which can be avoided in the future. In fairness to the private companies it must be said that certain laws and government measures were partly responsible for the lack of coördination of the railroad systems and the difficulties developing during the year 1917. The antitrust act and the antipooling sections of the Interstate Commerce Act blocked the centralization of railroads. In prewar days, the government attempted to force competitive rules upon an industry which, by its very nature, required centralization. Too generous a distribution of "preference tags" for the shipment of government freight was one of the factors entailing the congestion of tracks and terminals in 1917 and 1918.

The main difficulty with which a newly established management of industry by government organs has to wrestle lies in the fact that the change of management is undertaken at a very critical moment. Many of the shortcomings of past experiments could have been avoided, if government management had been introduced before the war and the

---

[24] W. D. Hines: *War History of American Railroads,* New Haven, 1928, 113–115, 185–191, and 211–219. See also pp. 274–275 below.
[25] *Ibid.,* 115–120.

new administration had had time to study and solve the various problems of organization in normal times. It is always dangerous to change the leader when defeat is threatening; still, this may be the last chance of avoiding defeat.

Summary

In Chapters 8 and 9, we have discussed a variety of measures that belligerent governments have undertaken in the past—and are likely to undertake in the future—in order to render war production and war distribution most efficient. There is the priority system designed to ensure to the essential industries preference in supplies, transportation facilities, and labor and to curtail the utilization of resources for nonessential purposes. Price control may pursue various aims: On the one hand it can encourage an expansion of output in lagging industries, on the other hand it is an important tool—in conjunction with appropriate measures of war finance—for preventing a rise of prices with its consequences: unstable cost accounting, profiteering, and popular discontent. Control of wages is one necessary concomitant of price control, rationing of consumers' goods another. The first is intended to prevent the disruption of the controlled price system by a revolution in costs; the second renders an equitable distribution of scarce supplies to consumers possible in cases where prices cannot be allowed to bring about the mutual adjustment of demand and supply. Government operation of industries finally becomes necessary when private management cannot assure maximum efficiency in the utilization of resources.

It is important to notice that several of these measures can scarcely be effective without being accompanied by one or the other of the remaining ones. There is no use in attempting to freeze the price level, if the government generously issues new money or permits the level of wages to rise considerably. Rationing of consumers' goods has no meaning when prices are allowed to rise to such an extent as to prevent the poorer classes of the population from buying their rations. The results of a schedule of priorities will be unsatisfactory, if private management fails to coöperate and the government does not take over the industries in question. Hence, the government has to be prepared to undertake these various measures more or less simultaneously. Not only economic mobilization but also the management of the war economy require comprehensive and proportionate efforts on the part of government.

SUGGESTED REFERENCES

Baker, C. W.: *Government Control and Operation of Industry in Great Britain and the United States During the World War,* New York, 1921.

Beveridge, W. H.: *British Food Control,* London, 1928, in particular chapters IX and X.

(Clark, J. M., Hamilton, W. H., and Moulton, H. G.; editors): *Readings in the Economics of War,* Chicago, 1918, chapters XXXIV–XL (Railroads).

Hines, W. D.: *War History of American Railroads,* New Haven, 1928.

Pigou, A. C.: *The Political Economy of War,* London, 1921, chapter XII.

PART THREE

INTERNATIONAL ECONOMICS OF WAR AND THE SITUATION OF NEUTRALS

CHAPTER 10

Foreign Trade and Shipping in Wartime

During a war, the field of international trade is ruled by conflicts among various interests. In part, these conflicts may have existed in time of peace; but warfare renders them more acute and adds the weapon of crude force to the arsenal of fighting instruments which trading nations bring into play in normal times. Obviously, the interests of the opposed belligerents clash, while allies attempt to coördinate their trade. In addition, belligerent interests conflict with neutral interests. Let us examine the various interests and the tools used in furthering them.

Imports and Exports of Belligerents

The purposes of belligerents with respect to foreign trade are twofold: (1) to maintain and adapt their own trade with dependencies, allies, and neutrals; (2) to interrupt the enemy's foreign trade. This section deals with the first point, namely, the import and export policies of belligerents. The trade war between enemies will be treated later in this chapter.

The interest a belligerent nation has in maintaining its import trade is easy to understand. Through imports it obtains foreign raw materials essential to its economy in war and peace. Imports of raw materials are the basis of the British cotton industry, of German steel production, and many other important activities. Industrial countries like

England and Germany depend on imports of foodstuffs to maintain their populations on a decent plane of living. And, strange as it may seem at first glance, industrially developed countries usually import considerable amounts of finished industrial articles. This can be explained by the specialized character of their industries and the advantages nations find in an international division of labor. Thus, Germany used to import woolen cloth for men's suits from England while England imported woolen knit goods and women's wearing apparel from Germany.

In war times, some of these imports are indispensable; domestic production of substitutes may be either impossible or very expensive. Other goods can more easily be done without. Whether a certain commodity belongs in the first or the second category depends on the country considered. Yet there are certain general rules that apply to all countries. Luxury articles can be dispensed with most easily, basic industrial and agricultural commodities least easily in a country fighting a war. Therefore, efforts to obtain these basic commodities from abroad must be expected to continue, even to increase, under the impact of war.

But it would be wrong to deduce from this that belligerent countries will always emphasize the importation of unfinished articles, such as raw materials, grains, basic steel products, rather than finished goods like arms, machines, canned food, and textile articles. At the beginning of a war this might be true, at least for a country with highly developed industry; in view of the difficulties of finding international means of payment, there might be a great advantage in having the manufacturing done by the country's own labor and in its own factories. (For example, to import the bauxite necessary for obtaining the aluminum used in airplane building costs less in terms of *international* means of payment than importing the finished airplanes.) But as war progresses, it increases the strain on domestic producing power. Military mobilization of industrial man power leaves fewer, and above all less qualified, men in the factories. The factories themselves become less efficient because of deteriorating equipment and disorganization. If then there appears any possibility of solving the problem of international buying power, the country will try to shift its imports from raw and bulky goods like wheat, copper ore, iron, and steel to manufactured and less bulky articles like flour, copper metal, and machinery. This is exactly what happened in the course of the first world war in Britain and France. An additional reason for the gradual change in the character of British and French imports was the lack of tonnage due to submarine warfare. The obstacle of international means of payment was overcome in their case by the granting of American credits.[1]

The European Allies would have been unable to finance the more expensive imports of manufactured articles, if American credits had not provided them with international means of payment. As the war progressed the commodity exports of the European Allies fell short of their imports to an increasing extent. While in 1913 the exports of the United Kingdom paid for sixty-eight per cent of her imports, in 1918 they paid for only thirty-eight per cent.[2]

The following table illustrates the divergent movements of British imports of raw and bulky articles on the one hand, and on the other, manufactured and less bulky commodities. It also shows the spectacular decline in the imports of such luxury articles as carpets and rugs.

---

[1] Of the twelve billion dollars spent by the Allied nations in the United States during the period from 1917 to 1920, nine and a half billion (seventy-nine per cent) were covered by American credits. H. E. Fisk: *The Inter-Ally Debts*, New York, 1924, 176–177.

[2] *Statistical Abstract for the United Kingdom*, 1913/1915–1928, London, 1930, 334 and 364.

IMPORTS INTO THE UNITED KINGDOM
(in per cent of 1913) [3]

	1913	1915	1916	1917	1918
Wheat (quantity)	100	84	95	86	55
Wheatmeal and flour (quantity)	100	88	83	119	220
Copper ore (quantity)	100	57	59	34	27
Copper metal (quantity)	100	167	103	134	194
Iron and steel (value)	100	69	72	68	61
Machinery (value)	100	114	109	122	147
Carpets and rugs (quantity)	100	25	16	7	1

With respect to their export policy, belligerents face the following dilemma. On the one hand, they want to conserve their resources and products for home use, military or civilian. That implies a reduction of exports. On the other hand, there are various reasons for continuing exports. (1) Exports bring in means of payment for badly needed imports; foreign credits and sales of assets to foreigners may not be sufficient to finance such imports. (2) The conquest of the enemy's export markets may be advisable from a military and a business viewpoint: it would directly impair his influence on the national economies of neutral countries and thus help to alienate the neutrals from his cause; indirectly, it would impede his imports of goods essential to warfare. (3) Loss of a foreign market to a neutral—or allied—competitor may be irreparable; a policy of complete export stoppage may imply the loss of important trade connections.

The belligerent country has to find some sort of compromise between these conflicting interests. It must prevent exports of essential war materials with the exception of necessary shipments to allied powers. Simultaneously, it must undertake export offensives where they are thought necessary to defend trade or to gain new markets. In its present war with Germany, England has prohibited exports of many

---

[3] *Ibid.*, 324, 328, and 332.

materials. At the same time, she tried to seize the German export markets in southeastern Europe and to maintain her exports to South America and the United States. Exports of whisky and other articles of little importance for the war economy have been given preference. During the short period of her belligerency, France took care to maintain her exports of luxury articles such as perfumes, champagne, and the products of her *haute couture*. Since, however, the productive facilities of a belligerent country are under the pressure of war demands, it is not likely that exports will pay for all of the imports. The total of the commodity and service items in its balance of payments will probably show an import surplus.

A belligerent government will discourage or prohibit exports of capital and facilitate capital imports. Capital imports (foreign credits) ease the problem of financing imports of foreign commodities. Exports of domestic capital as well as withdrawals of foreign funds invested in the belligerent country act contrariwise.

Regulation of Foreign Trade and Shipping in Belligerent Countries

Experience shows that the adaptation of foreign trade to war conditions cannot be left to private initiative alone. The private merchant is unable to determine the degree to which the imports or exports planned by him are essential to the war economy. He follows his own interest and the interests of his customers and suppliers; but he cannot realize the role his transactions play in the allocation of national resources and the general war policy. Hence, he may order nonessential imports, or contract for exports of essential materials; he may place his orders for imports with foreign suppliers whose services are requested by an allied power, or he may help to supply a neutral who is engaged in a flourishing transit business with the enemy. Nor can the private shipowner determine where his services are most needed. He will try to get the best-paid cargo, whether it consists of munitions steel or household furniture; he will avoid dangerous sea lanes or lay up his ship when the risk of its loss—as expressed by insurance premiums—appears too great; he will not mind carrying a cargo around the world, though this may keep his ship from more urgently needed short-distance hauls.

The upsurge of war demand also appears in the field of shipping. Troops may have to be transported overseas. Subsequently, they have to be supplied with arms, food, and fuel. The navy needs auxiliary cruisers and supply vessels; the war industries request imports of raw materials; the military authorities order cargoes of fighting equipment from allied countries. Of course, some demands will decline; there will be less oversea passenger traffic and no trade with enemy countries; but these factors are likely to provide little relief.

Simultaneously, war restricts the available tonnage. Enemy raiders ambush merchant vessels and prevent them from leaving neutral ports; other ships are held up by the congestion of port facilities or the delays involved in a convoy system. Enemy ships—apart from those that are taken as prizes—are no longer available, and neutral vessels may be kept away from the nation's ports by maritime warfare and precautionary measures of neutral governments. Construction of new ships is a slow process for technical reasons. In addition, many shipyards are requisitioned for naval construction and thus unavailable for the building of merchant vessels. Hence, in the face of rising demand for tonnage a belligerent nation may experience a decline of available facilities. From August, 1914, until October, 1918, the British Empire alone suffered a net loss of more than three million gross tons of merchant shipping, most of it during

1917, the year in which unlimited German submarine warfare was unleashed. This loss amounted to fifteen per cent of the tonnage under the British flag in the summer of 1914.[4] Wholesale chartering of neutral vessels and the tremendous expansion of American shipbuilding enabled the Allies to compensate for part of the tremendous losses of ships.

Private shipping knew only one solution for the dilemma of excessive demand: to raise freight rates. In time of peace, this measure is a useful tool for eliminating the less urgent demands from the market and leading the available tonnage to those freight operations which can stand the highest transport charges. In war, however, this instrument is pitifully inadequate. Demand for essential military and civilian goods is extensive and inelastic, and additional vessels cannot be made overnight even if freight rates should rise a hundredfold. While a rise of freight rates cannot establish an equilibrium of demand and supply in the shipping market, it can contribute to the rise of prices. Thus, it aggravates the price situation in belligerent countries. During the first world war, uncontrolled freight rates rose by several hundred per cent.[5] Governments learned quickly that they could expect nothing but difficulties if they relied on an automatic adjustment in the freight market.

Various measures can be applied by a government to assure the functioning of essential exports, imports, and shipping services. The most important of these measures represent an extension of the priority system into the field of foreign trade. Imports are subjected to license, and a government bureau is set up to sift out nonessential import projects. No imports are permitted and no shipping space is made available for purposes that are not considered essential. Exports may similarly be licensed.

---

[4] J. A. Salter: *Allied Shipping Control*, Oxford, 1921, 8 and 363.
[5] *Ibid.*, 45, 48, and 69.

Government control of exchanges between the domestic and foreign currencies is an important instrument for the enforcement of import priorities. By means of exchange control foreign exchange can be made available to essential imports and refused to nonessential ones. Export licenses, on the other hand, may be granted under the condition that receipts of foreign money resulting from the export operation be offered to a national pool of foreign currencies—at the central bank or elsewhere. Of course, the priority system of imports and exports has to go hand in hand with a corresponding scheme of tonnage priorities. There is no sense in permitting an importer to buy rubber abroad for immediate importation when there is no ship available for carrying it over the sea.

Licensing of imports and exports was applied by Great Britain during the first as well as the second world war. (In this country the *War Trade Board* was set up in October, 1917, to perform the same task.[6]) The chartering of ships was also subjected to licenses. Some measures of exchange control were introduced in Great Britain and France during the first month of the present war, while Germany entered the war with a comprehensive system of exchange control in operation. The British system provides for compulsory sales of gold and specified foreign currency assets held or acquired by residents of the United Kingdom to the government.[7]

The tendency of the British government during the first world war to centralize imports in its own hands has already been indicated.[8] In the course of the war, this tendency led to an almost complete government monopoly of imports; imports of foodstuffs and metals by the Ministries of Food and Munitions reached seventy per cent of all Brit-

---

[6] *Report of the War Trade Board*, Washington, D. C., 1920, 5.
[7] *The Economist*, London, September 9, 1939, 493–494 and December 9, 1939, 377–378. See also above, p. 66, and below, pp. 213–214.
[8] See above, p. 154.

ish imports, and those of textiles, leather, timber, tobacco, paper and pulp, twenty-five per cent.[9] Thus ninety-five per cent of Britain's import trade was operated by government institutions. A similar trend has appeared in the present war. *The Economist* [10] reported: "At the present time, probably more than three-quarters of the imports into this country are either directly purchased or at least controlled by [the Ministries of Food and Supply], and as the supply programme develops, the proportion will reach 100 per cent." In the field of exports the British government did not go quite so far. Exports were licensed, restricted, or encouraged; but they were not normally carried out on government account.

This policy represents one step beyond priority control. It tends toward a government monopoly of foreign trade. Instead of checking private import demands the government undertakes imports on its own initiative. Similarly, Britain did not stop at the priority system of shipping control. In the first—as well as in the second—world war this system soon gave way to the requisitioning of ships by the government. What route a ship had to go, what cargo it had to take was determined by government officials. The government fixed freight rates at levels which were soon exceeded by the constantly rising rates in the free market.[11]

Obviously, this governmental system could not exist side by side with uncontrolled shipping. A shipper who had the choice between running his vessel for the government at low government pay or for the highest bidder in the free market would of course have given preference to the latter. Furthermore, if private and government shipping were operated simultaneously, there would be obstacles to the most economical utilization of shipping space. The ex-

---

[9] Salter, *op. cit.*, 90 ff.
[10] May 25, 1940, 938.
[11] Salter, *op. cit.*, 43 and 349. See also *The Economist*, May 25, 1940, 937–938, and June 1, 1940, 978–979.

perimental period of British shipping control during the World War furnished instructive examples.

> Colliers . . . were required to take coal to the Mediterranean, but when they had discharged their cargo at Malta or Alexandria, there was no Governent cargo requiring return transport. Private return cargoes were, however, at the same time waiting for freight, cotton seed from Alexandria; or ore, wheat, or linseed from India, just through the Canal. If therefore Government cargoes had been carried solely by ships on continuous Government service and private cargoes by ships continuously in private employment, requisitioned ships would have gone to the Mediterranean with Government cargoes and returned empty, while private ships were going to the Mediterranean empty, to return with private cargoes—an obvious waste.[12]

After having tried various compromise solutions, as the "temporary release" of ships from government service, the British government, in 1917, ended by requisitioning all British ships. Thus, the World War produced—and the present war revived—government monopoly of foreign trade and government operation of shipping in Great Britain. The fundamental importance of foreign trade to the British economy made this complete control inevitable. The situation in this country did not necessitate such far-reaching measures.

For a country involved in major war operations a government monopoly over foreign trade appears indeed most appropriate. It permits the highest degree of flexibility in import and export policies and the conduct of trade according to specific strategic plans. Once these plans are fixed, the quantities and desirable sources of needed supplies determined, and the character and destination of exports outlined, the foreign-trade monopoly can adjust its bids for imports and the prices of exports in such a way as to execute

---

[12] Salter, *op. cit.*, 61 and 62. Reprinted by permission of Yale University Press.

these plans with a minimum of delay. Indirect methods of foreign-trade control such as tariffs, manipulations of exchange rates, and import and export licenses are likely to be slower in bringing about the desired results, if they are at all effective under war conditions. These indirect controls of foreign trade must rely on the eagerness of individual traders to maximize their profits. In wartime, however, the profit incentive may be dangerously misleading because of the failure of prices to reflect all of the social valuations involved in particular transactions.[13] Important considerations of strategic nature may dictate the execution of transactions at a financial loss. Since sound private trade will tend to neglect these important considerations it is better to have government institutions plan the whole of foreign trade and to transfer the experienced trader from the executive's chair in private business to the staff of experts on the government monopoly.[14]

In the field of international capital transactions, exchange control provides the necessary tool for restriction or complete stoppage of legal capital exports. It enables the government to refuse permission for transferring funds abroad. Thus it helps to prevent a drain of gold and foreign-currency reserves. The government can tighten or relax the restrictions imposed by exchange control according to the pressure on the country's balance of payments and general political considerations.

While, in the present war, the British government has prohibited exports of capital belonging to residents of the United Kingdom, it has deemed it wise to permit nonresidents to withdraw balances from England. The main motives for this differential treatment have been the desire to maintain good will in neutral countries, particularly in

---

[13] See above, pp. 31–32.
[14] See in this connection T. Balogh: "Foreign Exchange and Export Trade Policy," *Economic Journal*, Vol. L, March, 1940.

the United States, and to avoid too large a degree of distrust in the soundness of London as a banking and investment center. In order to discourage such withdrawals, the government has placed them under an economic penalty. A special currency of "free sterling" has been created. Outwardly a pound of "free sterling" does not differ from a pound of "official sterling"; but they do differ in their foreign-exchange value and the rules governing their use. Only nonresidents are allowed to buy or sell "free sterling." The Bank of England refuses to buy from them any sterling balances at the official sterling exchange rate (at present about $\$4 = \pounds 1$); but nonresidents are free to sell their pounds to other nonresidents. Commodity imports from Britain can be paid for in "free sterling." Yet for an increasing number of commodities, the government has requested exporters to ask for payment in "official sterling." Hence the demand for "free sterling" has been restricted and its value depressed—occasionally to as low a rate as $\$3 = \pounds 1$. Withdrawals of capital from London are of course the less attractive, the lower the value of "free sterling" is in terms of dollars or other non-British currencies.[15] By embarking on a scheme of special-use currencies with different valuations Britain has taken a leaf out of Germany's book. However, Britain has so far only one type of "discount sterling," while Germany had more than five types of "discount mark" at the beginning of 1939.[16]

The tendency toward centralization of foreign trade and

---

[15] *The Economist*, London, February 24, 1940, 337–338; March 2, 1940, 381–382; April 6, 1940, 608–609.

[16] F. A. Southard: *Foreign Exchange Practice and Policy*, New York, 1940, 192–196.

Since this paragraph was written, British exchange regulations have been modified. According to *The New York Times* of June 8, 1940, the British government further restricted the "free sterling" market by (*a*) requesting payment in "official sterling" for all British exports to the United States and Switzerland and (*b*) prohibiting sales of United Kingdom securities owned by persons residing outside the Empire. Thus both the demand for and the supply of "free sterling" have been strongly curtailed.

exchange operations in the hands of the belligerent government is likely to be paralleled by the development of bilateral trade transactions. The apparent mutual independence of particular commodity transactions, which characterizes the individualistic system of foreign trade, disappears when all transactions are executed by one nation-wide foreign-trade monopoly. If the government undertakes to supply an ally or a neutral with an essential raw material, it will probably insist on certain services in return, for instance shipments of certain other commodities.

[During the World War] American authorities practically determined the amount of steel which should be allotted to Japan. Steel was supplied to Japan only on stipulated conditions, namely, that the Japanese should furnish America with merchant ships. Similarly, Great Britain permitted the export of palm kernels only upon condition that a specified amount of glycerine should be supplied to her. Wool, coal, and other commodities were apportioned to various countries. Ships were secured to haul the coal to Brazil in order that Brazilian manganese, sorely needed in the United States, might be transported to the coast.[17]

American shipments of foodstuffs to Cuba were made dependent upon Cuban exports of sugar.

In order to relieve the pressure on shipping a considerable program of shipbuilding may be necessary. Both the American and the British governments embarked on shipbuilding campaigns during the World War. Government shipyards were set up for the building of merchant vessels, and types of ships were limited to a few standard models. Toward the end of the war the number of "standard ships" under construction in Britain represented seventy-six per cent of the total shipbuilding.[18]

---

[17] W. S. Culbertson: *Commercial Policy in War Time and After*, New York, D. Appleton-Century Company, 1919, 252 and 253.
[18] Salter, *op. cit.*, 82.

Interallied Coördination

If the war is fought in alliance with other powers, numerous problems of coördination arise. In order to obtain more favorable conditions for buying supplies, allied governments may find it necessary to pool their purchases and establish joint purchasing missions. In the early part of the present war, Britain and France maintained a joint purchasing organization in this country. Furthermore, it may be advantageous for allies to pool their merchant marines. In the course of the World War, such a system gradually developed under the leadership of Great Britain. In 1916, an *Inter-Allied Chartering Committee* was set up for the chartering of neutral tonnage. It was designed to avoid the competitive bidding-up of the freight rates charged by neutral ships. Late in 1917, a more general organization known as the *Allied Maritime Transport Council* emerged. The objectives of the Council were:

(a) to make the most economical use of tonnage under the control of the Allies; (b) to allot that tonnage as between the different needs of the Allies in such a way as to add most to the general war effort; and (c) to adjust the programmes of requirements of the different Allies in such a way as to bring them within the scope of the possible carrying power of the tonnage available.[19]

This Council did not develop into an international board with complete executive power, partly because Great Britain and the United States as the main shipowners and shipbuilders were not willing to let the other Allies control their facilities. Only with respect to the neutral tonnage brought together by the Inter-Allied Chartering Committee did the Council have executive functions.[20] Apart from

---
[19] *Ibid.*, 292. Reprinted by permission of Yale University Press.
[20] At the time of the Armistice this pool contained one fourth of the neutral tonnage chartered by the Allies, or nine per cent of the active neutral tonnage then flying neutral flags. See also below, p. 236.

that, its activity was restricted to the collection and exchange of information; it gave recommendations to the Allied governments. In the main it served as an auxiliary organization to the British Ministry of Shipping, which was called upon to help in many places: to ship coal to France or Italy, to bring relief food to Belgium, American troops to France, Canadian wheat to Britain.[21]

International Law of Maritime Warfare and its Fate

With respect to the enemy's foreign trade, a belligerent's point of view is relatively simple. In order to deprive the enemy of the advantages created by an international division of labor it appears desirable: (1) to wreck his imports and thus create a shortage of military and civilian supplies; (2) to stop his exports and thus prevent him from financing imports. The trade most vulnerable to enemy attacks is that moving over the open sea. Therefore, the major part of the trade struggle between belligerents consists in maritime warfare.

Maritime warfare does not concern belligerents alone. Neutral ships travel on the seas, performing services for traders in neutral countries or carrying export goods from and import goods to belligerent nations. Belligerent powers may be indifferent to neutral trade. But we shall soon see that in many instances the trade with neutrals may be of vital interest to a belligerent nation and, similarly, that trade with belligerents may represent profitable business to neutral merchants. Every belligerent tries to monopolize the trade with neutrals and to exclude the enemy from it, while every neutral wishes to pursue his trade with

---

[21] For plans concerning a common economic policy of the Allies during and after the World War see the recommendations made by the economic conference of the Allies in Paris, in June, 1916. They are reproduced in Culbertson, *op. cit.*, 368–373.

as little interference by the belligerents as possible. Thus, conflicts between neutrals and belligerents add to those between belligerents themselves. They make international trade in wartime a free-for-all fight. Ordinarily, conflicts are settled in the fashion characteristic of such a fight, the economic and military strength of the parties deciding the outcome. Among the belligerents, the nation having the strongest sea and air power is in the best position to safeguard its interests; among the neutrals, the stronger ones defend their positions and are treated more or less courteously, while the weaker ones find themselves exploited and treated like slaves.

Attempts have been made to fix the rules of the game and to give some protection to the weaker sea powers, belligerent or neutral. On exceptional occasions, particularly during more extended periods of international peace, the stronger maritime powers have agreed to limitations of their freedom of action. International conventions have resulted, the aggregate of which is referred to as the "international law of maritime warfare." These conventions establish rules of blockade and contraband and deal with the treatment of prizes. We shall now consider the most important regulations concerning contraband, which were established in 1909 at an international naval conference in London.

The plenipotentiaries of ten major sea powers, including the United States, Great Britain, and Germany, signed the "Declaration of London." The Declaration distinguished between three classes of cargoes: absolute contraband, conditional contraband, and free goods. Arms, ammunitions, explosives, military clothing, and other equipment of a distinctly military character were listed as absolute contraband. Foodstuffs, fuels, clothing articles, railway materials, gold, silver, and other articles were classified as conditional contraband. Metal ores, rubber, cotton, wool, hides, fertilizers, and other raw materials along with such luxuries as

FOREIGN TRADE AND SHIPPING IN WARTIME 219

feathers, clocks, and chinaware were put on the free list. They could not be declared contraband of war.[22]

Concerning the treatment at sea of cargoes falling into these various categories, the Declaration said: [23]

> Absolute contraband is liable to capture if it is shown to be destined to territory belonging to or occupied by the enemy, or to the armed forces of the enemy. It is immaterial whether the carriage of the goods is direct or entails transhipment or a subsequent transport by land.

And:

> Where a vessel is carrying absolute contraband, her papers are conclusive proof as to the voyage on which she is engaged, unless she is found clearly out of the course indicated by her papers, and unable to give adequate reasons to justify such deviation.

Belligerent rights were thus clearly stated. Any ship, belligerent or neutral, carrying absolute contraband to the enemy could be seized and her cargo confiscated, *provided* the ship's papers or other evidence allowed the establishment of such destination. On conditional contraband the main stipulations of the Declaration read: [24]

> Conditional contraband is liable to capture if it is shown to be destined for the use of the armed forces or of a government department of the enemy State, . . .
>
> Conditional contraband is not liable to capture, except when found on board a vessel bound for territory belonging to or occupied by the enemy, or for the armed forces of the enemy, and when it is not to be discharged in an intervening neutral port.
>
> The ship's papers are conclusive proof. . . .

---
[22] N. Bentwich: *The Declaration of London*, London, 1911, 59, 65, 66, 76, and 77.
[23] *Ibid.*, 62 and 65.
[24] *Ibid.*, 69 and 74.

Thus, seizure of cargoes of conditional contraband was allowed only (1) when the goods were destined for the enemy's military, *and* (2) when they were being shipped to an enemy port. Seizure was prohibited when it could be proved that the goods were destined for civilian consumption in the enemy country. But even when such destination was not obvious, the ship's plan to discharge the cargo in a neutral port made seizure illegal.

All the goods on the free list, industrial raw materials and feathers alike, were given a free pass. A belligerent warship could not stop merchant vessels carrying such goods except in the immediate neighborhood of enemy ports under "effective blockade." [25]

This Declaration, though accepted by the plenipotentiaries of all the major powers and considered binding international law at the outbreak of the first world war,[26] was soon distorted and violated. In the first place, it did not take account of the fact that modern wars are "total wars." Destruction of the enemy's industry and undermining of the health and morale of his population have become, if not outspoken aims of war, at least accidents for which the belligerents decline responsibility. Germany tells England: We destroy a cargo of frozen meat on the way from Sydney to London. This must not necessarily be taken as an act directed against your civilian population. If they do not get enough meat, why don't you decrease the food rations of your soldiers and give the meat you have to the civilians? And so for other conditional contraband and free goods. During the first world war, the powers gradually redistributed the goods over the three classes. The

---

[25] *Ibid.*, 137–140.
[26] The British House of Lords rejected the Declaration and thus prevented its ratification. In answer to an inquiry of the American government, however, Germany and her allies declared their willingness to adhere to the rules of the Declaration, if the Allied powers would do the same; the British government accepted "generally" the rules of the Declaration. See C. C. Tansill: *America Goes to War*, Boston, 1938, 136–138.

free list was gradually emptied, rubber, ores, and other raw materials being redefined as absolute contraband. Similarly, the conditional contraband list was emptied in favor of the "absolute" list. On the free lists of today we find only a few luxury goods, while conditional contraband is treated practically as "absolute." [27]

A second reason for this development is the fact that the Declaration of London put too much confidence in the disinterested law abidance of belligerents and their neutral supporters. Why label a shipment of cotton goods to Germany as "destined for army consumption"? The neutral exporter wants to get these goods into Germany. If a label "overcoats for night watchmen" serves this purpose better, why not use it? In particular, the idea that goods might be consigned to a fake receiver in a neutral country adjacent to the belligerent and passed on by him across the land frontier seems not to have occurred to the minds of all who signed the Declaration. But this practice was developed on a large scale, especially by Germany. During the first years of the World War, Scandinavia and Holland exported considerable quantities of copper, cotton, iron ore, and foodstuffs to Germany over German-controlled land and water lanes. The origin of many of these goods was overseas; they had passed the British blockade as destined for Sweden, Holland, and so forth. Even goods from Allied sources thus found their way into Germany, the neutrals acting as transit agents. Rear-Admiral Consett, British naval attaché in Scandinavia during the war, writes: [28]

> Consignments of meat products, we learn, were addressed to lightermen and dock labourers, to a baker, to the keeper of a small private hotel and to a maker of musical instruments.

---

[27] For British contraband proclamations during the first world war, see H. Ritchie: *The "Navicert" System During the World War*, Washington, D. C., 1938, 59–83.
[28] M. W. W. P. Consett: *The Triumph of Unarmed Forces (1914–1918)*, London, Williams & Norgate, 1923, 53.

222 FOREIGN TRADE AND SHIPPING IN WARTIME

Several thousands of tons of such goods were documented for a neutral port and addressed to firms which did not exist there. At one time, when it was found necessary to hold up certain cargoes of cotton on their way to Sweden, it was discovered that though the quais and the warehouses of Gottenberg were congested with cotton, there was none available for the use of spinners in Sweden. Nor did ships' papers convey any suggestion as to the ultimate destination of goods.

The Declaration of London did not prevent neutrals from acting as transit agents for a belligerent. Nor did it prohibit them from being manufacturing agents. Denmark exported Danish meats, butter, and hides to Germany. The cattle that furnished these things had grazed on pastures fertilized by phosphates imported from French Tunis and Algiers. They had been fed with high-grade fodder brought to Denmark from British colonies. A similar situation prevailed for other Scandinavian export products.[29] Neutral traders and producers drew considerable profits from these transactions, for Germany paid well. Simultaneously the population in the Scandinavian countries suffered from a shortage of goods.

The British government soon discovered that these practices offset its blockade of German trade. German sea raiders, on the other hand, showed little regard for international law. Therefore, Britain too broke her international obligations. A series of "orders in council" was passed, the most important of them being the Reprisals Order of March, 1915.[30] It announced: All German imports and exports are liable to seizure; no shipments to or from neutral harbors may pass if the goods are of German origin or destination. All ships have to call at an Allied port; if the goods they carry appear *suspiciously* of enemy origin or destination, they may be confiscated. These, in-

---

[29] See below, pp. 230–233.
[30] Ritchie, *op. cit.*, 49–58.

cidentally, are also the rules followed by England in the present war.

This order was against the spirit, if not against the letter, of the Declaration of London. Through it the British navy and its intelligence service freed themselves from all restrictions imposed by international law. As a consequence, the neutrals protested against British interference with their trade, and the strongest protests came from the United States. Britain, said the notes from our government, attempts to damage American trade with Germany and the neutrals adjacent to Germany. Pointing to the British trade statistics, the notes accused England of trying to monopolize this trade. These statistics did indeed show a considerable increase of British exports, for instance of cocoa, to Scandinavia, Holland, and Italy, and the presumption was obvious that these goods reached Germany in the end. On July 22, 1915, the British Ambassador in Washington sent the following telegram to Lord Grey: [31]

> Mr. Lansing draws serious attention to increase in export from United Kingdom to Northern European ports since the war which have formed the subject of unfavourable reports from the United States consul-general in London. Germans here are said to make use of these facts to create ill-feeling by circulating allegations that England is preventing American overseas trade with neutral countries in Europe with a view to capture this trade for herself, and that we [the British] are ourselves exporting the very goods which we have seized from Americans.

In this country feelings against the British contraband policy ran high.[32] Britain, on the other hand, turning to

---

[31] Quoted from Consett, *op. cit.*, 48. Consett, a strong critic of the British government's laxity in dealing with the Scandinavian business of British exporters, exclaims: "Our miserable and inglorious trade prolonged the war." (271)

[32] In July, 1916, "President Wilson wrote Colonel House of his irritation with the British, and that he was seriously considering asking Congress to authorize him to prohibit loans and restrict exportations to the Allies." United States Senate, 74th Congress, 2d Session, Report No. 944, Part 5, Washington, D. C., 1936, 16.

American trade statistics, pointed out in very polite notes that American commerce with the neutrals adjacent to Germany had a still better record. In fact, from 1914 to 1915, American exports to Norway, Sweden, Denmark, and Holland increased by about the same amount ($142,000,000) by which those to Germany and Austria-Hungary decreased ($157,000,000).[33] Notes went back and forth. During the period of neutrality, the American government never did accept the practices based on the Reprisals Order; the British government never did stop these practices.[34]

During the present war, the banning of American ships from belligerent coasts or "combat areas" has reduced, though not eliminated, the chances of friction with England over the searching of our vessels on the high seas.[35] Not every neutral, however, is in a position to avoid friction with the belligerents by such a policy of abstinence. Even to this country, relatively independent as it is of European supplies and export markets, the curtailment of trade connections and the necessary reallocation of American ships to new routes has brought serious problems.[36] A small neutral country like Sweden, dependent on Germany and Great Britain for essential imports and exports and for the right to maintain her shipping services, cannot simply sever her connections with the battling continent.

In the following chapter a more detailed analysis of the effects of a major modern war on the economy of neutral nations will be presented.

---

[33] *Report of the War Trade Board, op. cit.,* 11.

[34] See below, p. 243 for British World War measures designed to control American exports.

[35] Early in 1940, the strife flared up anew in connection with the British searching of American mail to European neutrals and to Germany.

[36] During the Napoleonic Wars the United States followed a still more complete policy of abstinence. In 1807, American ships were prohibited to leave for ports of any foreign power. For a description of the events leading to this decision and its economic consequences, see E. L. Bogart: *The Economic History of the United States,* New York, 1909, 106–109, and *passim.*

SUGGESTED REFERENCES

Clapp, E. J.: *Economic Aspects of the War,* New Haven, 1915.
(Clark, J. M., Hamilton, W. H., and Moulton, H. G.; editors): *Readings in the Economics of War,* Chicago, 1918, chapters XLI–XLIV.
Consett, M. W. W. P.: *The Triumph of Unarmed Forces (1914–1918),* London, 1923.
Garrett, P. W.: *Government Control Over Prices,* Washington, D. C., 1920, Book I, part II, article 6.
Pigou, A. C.: *The Political Economy of War,* London, 1921, chapter XVI.
Report of the War Trade Board, Washington, D. C., 1920.
Salter, J. A.: *Allied Shipping Control,* Oxford, 1921.
Tansill, C. C.: *America Goes to War,* Boston, 1920.

CHAPTER 11

The War Economy of Neutral Countries

Neutrality means nonparticipation in warfare between belligerent powers. A neutral country is not supposed to undertake any military operations against any of the belligerents, while belligerents are not expected to fight against neutral states. At first glance, the situation appears clear and simple. We might believe that neutrals could peacefully watch the fighting between the belligerents and go on living as if there were no war. There is, however, scarcely any country in the world for which such a belief would be justifiable in times of a major war. The status of neutrality is not only defined by the absence of military operations; belligerent powers also expect the neutrals not to "favor" the enemy in an economic sense. Whether a trade operation between the neutral and the enemy represents an undue favor to the enemy is, however, largely a matter of interpretation by the belligerent power. We have seen in the previous chapter how the few rules which were established by international convention have melted away in the heat of the struggle.

The reaction of a belligerent to a neutral's economic policy is a question of power. During the first years of the World War, Germany protested against our huge sales of arms to the Allied powers. She could not prevent them nor could she retaliate; still, she did not declare war upon this country. If Denmark had decided to send all of her meat and dairy products to England, Germany would surely have answered by crossing the Danish border.

Precarious Neutrality

The life and death struggle of world powers cannot be localized. Suppose that a small neutral nation is situated between two belligerent powers. If it provides comparatively easy access to the warring countries, both belligerents may try to invade it. If the two belligerent camps differ with respect to their political ethics, it is likely that the invasion will come from the less scrupulous side. The neutral country may sympathize with the more respectable belligerent while trying to appease the potential aggressor. In this way the absurd situation may develop that the neutral refuses economic and military concessions to his friends and grants them to his future enemies. And yet no concession may be great enough to forestall ultimate invasion. When invasion takes place the neutral may realize that it was actually facilitated by his appeasement policy. The recent history of Belgium and Holland illustrates this case. At great expense, a neutral country in such an unfavorable situation may build up military defenses and even undertake military mobilization. Yet it cannot remain unaffected by the war. Its fate knows only two alternatives: invasion in spite of the military precautions, or continuation of these measures of preparedness with the effect that the country's economic system gradually assumes the character of a war economy.

Let us think of a neutral nation in a more favorable geographic situation, but blessed with raw materials or productive facilities essential to one or both of the belligerents. In this case the danger of military invasion is perhaps not so great; but in the absence of military invasion "economic invasion" is the more likely. Each belligerent will try to prevent the enemy from obtaining neutral supplies and possibly attempt to monopolize the neutral country's resources. The belligerents will first use economic weapons to achieve their goals. If the neutral depends on certain imports under their control, they will threaten stoppage or actually stop shipments of these goods to the neutral country. If they do not succeed with these economic weapons, the belligerents may fall back upon military measures. The neutral country may, however, sustain this pressure, if it finds itself in either one of the following two situations: (1) The neutral country is very powerful. In that case, the risk of its invasion is small; a belligerent power involved in a major war will not want to engage another powerful enemy. On the contrary, the neutral may force the belligerents to respect his economic interests and to discontinue any operations which are likely to imperil them, provided he is willing to use all means of pressure at his disposition. (2) The neutral country is weak in a military sense; but it is able to balance the influences emanating from the two belligerent camps, so that they largely offset each other. In order that this situation may prevail, it is necessary that the opposing pressures be of approximately equal strength. If they are not, the neutral may soon fall under the exclusive rule of the more energetic of the belligerent powers.

The United States, during the early years of the World War (and in the present war), found herself in a situation of the first type. Both the Allies and the Central Powers were afraid of antagonizing this country. It is true that Britain interrupted American trade with the Central Powers and subjected our shipments designed for adjacent neutrals to onerous search, while German submarines sank some American ships on their way to Allied ports. Even a strong neutral power cannot expect to maintain its trade communications with both belligerent camps undamaged. However, the United States might have remained neutral in the first world war, if she had desired it. Belligerent infringements of American rights did not prompt this country to enter the war. (If they had, the United States would probably have sided with Germany, since British war measures were much more detrimental to our trade than those taken by Germany.) It was American sympathy with the Allied cause, based on economic and cultural links, which made this country give up her neutral status.

In the present war American neutrality legislation has reduced the possibilities of friction with the belligerents. Under the Neutrality Act of 1939,[1] American citizens and American ships are forbidden to enter the "combat areas" proclaimed by the President. American ships must not transport war materials proper to any belligerent seaport, even if it lies outside the "combat areas." The "cash-and-carry" clause has made exports to belligerent governments or their agents illegal unless the goods are taken over by the purchaser at the American port and paid for in cash. The belligerent states (and those of their citizens who act as government agents) cannot buy American goods on credit. Furthermore, Americans are not allowed under this Act to trade in any obligations of belligerent governments or their agents, issued after the outbreak of war, nor to solicit or collect funds on behalf of belligerent governments.

So far, no American ships and few American lives have been lost in the war, and the American economy as a whole has not had to suffer from direct pressure by either of the belligerents. Indirectly, of course, the war has strongly influenced the American economy. The influence has been of a different character in the various branches of the national economy. War has reduced export markets for wheat, tobacco, and dried fruits and thus accentuated the crisis in important sections of American agriculture. On the other hand, it has stimulated the production of armaments, partly for export (airplanes), partly for domestic needs. During the first six months of the war, American

---

[1] For an abstract and interpretations of the Neutrality Act of 1939, see L. M. Cherne: *Adjusting Your Business to War*, New York, 1940, 43–60.

exports of aluminum, aircraft, raw cotton, and iron and steel products have increased substantially.

New routes have had to be assigned to many American ships because of the restrictions imposed by the Neutrality Act. This process has been carried out without great financial losses; on the contrary, American shipping has profited from the increase of foreign trade—in particular with South America—and the limitation of foreign competition due to the disappearance of German vessels and the withdrawal of many British ships from customary services. American investments in European countries have been endangered. Yet none of the belligerent powers has been able to exert a direct influence on the American economy strong enough to dictate a policy exclusively in its favor.

The small north-European countries provide examples of the second typical situation. In the first world war, they were able to balance the approximately equal pressures of Germany and England by making concessions to both. They avoided military invasion by allowing economic invasions from both belligerent sides. We are going to see that these economic invasions affected life in these neutral countries very seriously. Toward the end of the World War, when the balance of power changed definitely in favor of the Allies, the Scandinavian countries became almost wholly dependent, economically, on the Allied powers. In the present war, however, the ropedance of neutrality has not been successful because of superior German pressure. Denmark, Norway, and Holland were invaded, and Sweden was forced into giving exclusive support to Germany.

Norway's Fish Drama

Norway's situation during the World War is well illustrated by the "fish drama," the major parts of which I want to summarize.[2] Norway is one of the world's greatest fish suppliers.

In pre-war times the market for Norwegian fish were widely diverse. For tinned goods the chief markets were the United States, Great Britain, Germany, and Australia; for fresh herring, Great Britain and Germany; for other fresh fish, Germany and Sweden. About three-fifths of her so-called "klipp-fish" were exported to Spain and Portugal. For dried fish the most important market was Italy, with Germany the next largest consumer.[3]

For the catching and preparing of fish, Norway depends on imports of coal, oil, tin, salt, hemp, and other materials.

First Act. Exports of klipp-fish and dried fish to Portugal, Italy, and Spain undergo a tremendous decline after the outbreak of the World War; rising freight rates make Norwegian fish too expensive for the poor classes of these countries. Exports to Germany and Austria, however, rise by 187 per cent between 1914 and 1916.[4] German fish buyers, without regard for price, buy all the fish and fish products they can get hold of.[5] Large-scale German purchases drive fish prices up and make fish a luxury in Norway. Fishermen earn good money; while still at sea, they sell the catch to German boats.

Second Act. By the end of 1915 the British government decides to stop Norwegian fish exports to Germany. After deliberations with the Norwegian government, Britain finds

---

[2] For a detailed account, see W. Keilhau: "Norway and the World War," in E. F. Heckscher and others: *Sweden, Norway, Denmark and Iceland in the World War*, New Haven, Yale University Press, 1930, 307 ff. See also M. W. W. P. Consett, *The Triumph of Unarmed Forces (1914–1918)*, London, 1923, part II, chapter VI.

[3] Keilhau, *op. cit.*, 307.

[4] Consett, *op. cit.*, 156.

[5] "Fish during the first two years of the war was the principal article of diet in German trains and restaurants; the fish-oil was very valuable on account of the glycerine—an explosive ingredient—which it contained; fish-guano and fish-meal were also produced." *Ibid.*, 154.

a Norwegian merchant (Mr. Martens of Bergen) who secretly agrees to act as a buying agent for the British government. Great Britain advises Mr. Martens that, in return for his services, shipments of coal, salt, and hemp to Norwegian fisheries will not be interrupted. Mr. Martens starts a huge buying campaign which results in still higher prices. Not realizing the existence of the deal, Germany tries in vain to buy Mr. Martens' stocks. Still, exports to Germany continue on a large scale.

Third Act. The British government finds the measure insufficient. Threatening to stop exports of fishing supplies to Norway, it requests that all fish not consumed in Norway be sold to Great Britain. In the "Fish Agreement" of August 5, 1916, the Norwegian government consents to restrict sales to Germany to fifteen per cent of the actual catch and to make the granting of the corresponding export licenses dependent on proof that in the catching and preparing of these fish no British raw materials—nor materials which have passed British sea control—have been used. Britain agrees to buy Norwegian fish surpluses at prices which shall remain constant until the end of the war. Again the agreement is secret.

Fourth Act. From 1916 on, Norwegian fish exports to Germany and Austria drop considerably—though, in 1917, they still are twenty-two per cent above the level of 1914. Exports to Britain recover the loss suffered in 1916. The fixed prices for sales to Britain—which the Norwegian government agreed not to exceed in its domestic price-fixing—discourage fishing, for costs continue to rise. As a consequence, fish supplies to the Norwegian population are curtailed. The Norwegian government begins to subsidize fisheries. While Britain accuses Norwegian traders of circumventing the agreement, Germany realizes what has happened. German submarines torpedo Norwegian ships in territorial waters.

Fifth Act. When the Norwegian government bans

enemy submarines from territorial waters, Germany protests strongly. The recuperation of Norwegian exports appears as the real objective of the protest. Torpedoing of Norwegian ships increases; German invasion is considered imminent. It does not take place, however, probably as a consequence of German military engagements on the continent. Norway makes a few concessions in the matter of fishing, Norwegian banks extend credits to German banks, and prohibition of exports of certain copper ores to Germany, just then under consideration, is postponed.

Sixth Act. In the last days of 1916 the British government refuses to grant licenses for exports of coal to Norway. Early in 1917, the Norwegian government completes the prohibition of copper ore exports to Germany, while unrestricted submarine warfare takes a heavy toll of Norwegian shipping. Britain resumes coal shipments to Norway.

Battles similar to the one just described were fought on neutral ground over Swedish iron ore and Danish meat and dairy products. While England gained the upper hand in Norway—she was able to curtail supplies to Germany and to enroll a large portion of Norway's important merchant marine in Allied service [6]—Germany was more successful in Sweden and Denmark. Germany was able to maintain her imports of Swedish iron ore, machinery, and so forth, on a high level in spite of the fact that Sweden depended on oversea imports—over sea lanes controlled by the Allies—for the mining and shipping of ore and the operation of her factories. Similarly, Germany took over a large share of Danish exports at England's expense. In 1913, Denmark's food exports to England on the one hand, to Germany and Austria on the other, were in the ratio of two to one; in 1916 and 1917, of one to two.[7]

---

[6] See below, p. 236.
[7] Consett, *op. cit.*, 298. Denmark had to buy Germany's permission for exports to England by supplying horses to the German army. (E. F. Heckscher and others, *op. cit.*, 449.)

Let us now consider some of the techniques used by the Allied powers for the purpose of gaining economic control over neutral countries, in particular the small neutrals adjacent to Germany. These techniques were conditioned by the strategic hold which the Allies had on important raw material supplies, partly through their possessions, partly through their control of the seas. The techniques applied by Germany were generally of a different character. Lacking monopolistic control of essential raw material supplies,[8] Germany largely relied on military pressure. Our account will deal with conditions prevailing during the first world war. In many respects they have been duplicated in the present war.

"Bunker Pressure" and Tonnage Agreements

Great Britain, her possessions, and her allies controlled all important coaling stations along the world's trade routes. This monopoly was useful in various respects. Since neutral ships could hardly avoid touching at one of the Allied coaling depots on extended voyages, Allied authorities were able to check their cargoes and refuse coal to ships transporting goods of use to the enemy. Furthermore, pressure could be brought to bear on neutral vessels to make them perform services useful to the Allies.

The actual administrative arrangements . . . took various forms. Vessels suitable for North Sea and Channel work were required, for example, to complete two voyages of certain specified kinds as a condition of receiving the bunkers for those two voyages and a third, which might be any the owner wished so long as it did not profit the enemy . . . a rule was made that all vessels loading in the United Kingdom for Scandinavia should return with cargo, unless furnished with a certificate of exemption. . . . The neutral ship which had once given her

---

[8] Only with respect to potash, dyestuffs, drugs, and, to a smaller extent, coal and sugar did Germany have a strong hold on basic supplies.

undertaking and obtained her coal was carefully watched by the [British] Shipping Intelligence Section, and, if she broke her engagement, was at once reported, with the result that she was refused bunkers for a sufficient time to prevent similar breaches of obligation in the future.[9]

In this way "bunker pressure" was used for the purpose of leading the individual neutral shipowners to the Allied institutions for the chartering of neutral ships,[10] and for enlisting neutral tonnage in operations which were of interest to the Allies. It was also used for more comprehensive undertakings. The Allies had not only a pressing need for the ships that neutral owners maintained in operation; they also needed the vessels which were for various reasons laid up in neutral ports. Hence they began to acquire large blocks of neutral tonnage. The most "direct" approach would have been simply to capture and confiscate neutral vessels. This has indeed always been the policy of strong belligerent sea powers. During the Napoleonic Wars, for instance, England confiscated thousands of neutral ships (among others American ships) and in addition forced their crews into the British naval service.

In the first years of the World War the Allies preferred the more gentlemanlike course of chartering individual neutral ships. Next they entered into *tonnage agreements* with the Scandinavian neutrals, by which the latter permitted the use of a large number of their ships in Allied service.

Concessions in the blockade system, under which the countries contiguous to Germany were themselves rationed, were used as factors in the bargain, together with every form of economic or political pressure available. A particularly interesting example is the arrangement made by Great Britain to organize

---

[9] J. A. Salter: *Allied Shipping Control*, Oxford, Oxford University Press, 1921, 105.
[10] See above, p. 216.

the whole coal imports of Norway . . . in return for Norwegian shipping.[11]

In the case of Norway, the tonnage agreement was concluded between the British government and the Norwegian association of private shipowners (Norges Rederforbund). Britain requisitioned more than a hundred Norwegian ships and operated them under the British flag. Norwegian shipowners received compensation and the assurance that their ships would not be used in the war zone.[12] The Norwegian government commanded Norwegian shipowners not to lay up their ships.[13] Similar agreements were concluded with Denmark and Sweden.

Finally, in 1917 and 1918, the Allies fell back upon a more "direct" method. Some of the neutral countries, afraid of German retaliation, had shown signs of reluctance to enlarge their shipping concessions to the Allies. Therefore, Norwegian, Danish, and Dutch ships were seized and operated by the Allies with or without the consent of either private owners or neutral governments. The owners received compensation for the services performed by their ships and were frequently quite satisfied with this solution, while the neutral governments could point out to Germany that the ships had been surrendered under the impact of *force majeure.*

At the time of the Armistice, the Allies had *chartered* —for services of economic and military character—thirty-eight per cent of the active tonnage belonging to neutral countries and still flying neutral flags. In addition, neutral ships with a total tonnage of 600,000 gross tons (equivalent to fifty per cent of the chartered tonnage) were *requisitioned* and sailed under American, British, and French flags. In

---

[11] Salter, *op. cit.,* 106–107.
[12] This did not prevent the sinking of thirty-four requisitioned Norwegian ships.
[13] Keilhau, *op. cit.,* 354 ff.

all, "about half of the entire neutral tonnage of the world was in the direct service of the Allies." [14] Control of these ships was of utmost importance to the Allies; but for the neutrals it had dangerous implications. Germany treated neutral ships as enemy vessels. Under the system of unrestricted submarine warfare they were sunk at sight whenever they were found in the extended ban zones proclaimed by Germany. Norway alone lost over a million gross tons of shipping during the World War, nearly half of her prewar tonnage. Two thousand Norwegian sailors lost their lives and huge financial losses were suffered.[15] The shipowners, however, frequently made considerable profits and were able, by way of the insurance system, to pass on a great deal of the losses to other branches of the national economy.

During the present war large-scale transfers of neutral tonnage to belligerents have not taken place on a commercial basis; but numerous neutral ships have continued to serve British trade. Neutral shipping losses have been extensive. Up to June 15, 1940, 221 neutral ships of a total gross tonnage of 600,000 were sunk,[16] exceeding in number—though not in tonnage—the aggregate losses of British ships. After the invasions of Denmark, Norway, Holland, and Belgium, part of the merchant marines of these countries was put into British and a small part into German service.

Economic Supervision and Rationing of Neutrals

Comparatively little can be done in a direct way against the enemy's foreign trade crossing his own land frontiers or going over protected water lanes. But there are indirect

---

[14] Salter, *op. cit.*, 108. The figures refer to ships of more than 500 gross tons.
[15] *Norsk Naeringsliv og dets Problemer*, Oslo, 1938, 177.
[16] Not counting 30,000 tons of Norwegian, Dutch, and Belgian shipping lost after the invasion of these countries. Source: *The New York Times*, June 16, 1940.

ways of impairing this kind of trade. First, those companies in neutral countries which trade with the enemy may be blacklisted, cut off from supplies, and their trade connections may be interrupted in general. By October 15, 1939, the British government had listed 330 companies that were to be boycotted by British traders and shippers. If such a scheme is applied by both belligerent sides, it will of course result in a splitting-up of the manufacturers and traders of the neutral country into two groups, each concentrating on trade with one belligerent.

This situation is well illustrated by the following report from World War days. The report also shows that British boycott measures were not always effective.

> One of the most astute commercial men in Norway, and probably Norway's largest fish exporter, who had been engaged exclusively from the outbreak of war up to about August, 1916, in supplying Germany with fish, had on that account, in the early days of coal control, been placed on the Black List, where he remained until August, 1916. He then left the German camp and, coming over to our [the British] side, rendered us great services in connection with the purchase of Norwegian fish. Some time after his removal from the Black List he stated to a British Foreign Office official, who had come to Norway in connection with the Norwegian Fish Agreement, that in spite of his being on the Black List, with the exception of coal he had been able to obtain all the commodities he desired. Coal he had never been able to obtain.[17]

Second, a belligerent power will attempt to build up control organisms in neutral countries in order to supervise the use of imported materials and, in general, the extent and character of trade between the neutrals and the enemy. Since during the World War the small neutrals adjacent to Germany depended on the Allies for essential imports, they could not refuse the establishment of such

---

[17] Consett, *op. cit.*, 121.

control organisms. In some cases they were able to limit the extent of foreign interference by establishing control institutions of their own. In this way, numerous institutions for the supervision of neutral trade came into existence during the World War. The "Netherlands Overseas Trust," the "Danish Merchants' Guild," the *Société Suisse de Surveillance Economique* (Swiss Company for Economic Supervision), and various Swedish and Norwegian associations had to undertake guarantees that imports passing Allied control were not going to be used for enemy purposes.[18] These organizations or the neutral governments themselves had to act as sole consignees for shipments of basic materials. In many cases, however, the Allied powers were not satisfied with the control of neutrals by neutrals and established their own control bureaus, mainly in connection with Allied consulates. British consulates and Inter-Allied Trade Committees set up on neutral territory controlled the use of imported raw materials and the origin of export goods.

Neutral exporters who desired that their goods should go unmolested through Allied sea controls had to prove, irrespective of whether they were trading with Allied or neutral countries, that the goods did not contain more than an allowed small percentage of German raw materials and that there was no other German interest in their sale. The last point was interpreted rather strictly: the exporter had to show that neither he nor the consignee abroad did business with blacklisted companies. The present war period has witnessed the revival of these controls.

Such control institutions of neutral trade are valuable to a belligerent power, while for the neutral country they represent serious infringements of its sovereignty. But the

---

[18] For a list of agreements between the British government and neutral associations and governments, see H. Ritchie, *The "Navicert" System During the World War*, Washington, D. C., 1938, 37–41.

controlling belligerent is likely to go even further than that. The control of a multitude of individual commercial transactions going on in a neutral country will prove to be bothersome and inefficient. The control agencies may fail to detect all the trading that is being done with the enemy. Therefore, the belligerent power may find it advisable to supplement the detailed supervision of individual transactions by a general scheme of trade control. In particular, if it is possible to ration a neutral country's aggregate imports of basic materials, supplies can be so curtailed that re-exports to the enemy or the production of finished goods for the enemy can no longer be carried on.

During the World War the Allied powers proceeded to ration neutral imports. In fixing the rations they generally took prewar imports as the point of departure; but the rationed imports soon fell short of prewar imports. Before granting the shipment of a commodity to one of the neutral countries, the Allies investigated whether they themselves had not a more urgent need for it and whether there did not exist stocks in the neutral country which could be drawn upon. In all cases where the neutral could not guarantee the strictly domestic consumption of the imported commodity, supplies were cut off. This system was already in partial operation when the United States entered the World War; with that enlargement of the Allied front it was perfected and resulted in a drastic curtailment of neutral imports.

The complete supervision and rationing of neutral imports operated in the following way (illustrated by the case of an export from the United States to a Scandinavian country, after America's entry into the war): [19]

1. The neutral importer secured an import permit from the domestic trade organization which was entitled to receive supplies.

---

[19] *Report of the War Trade Board, op. cit.*, 19 and *passim*.

2. The Inter-Allied Trade Committee supervising the trade organizations in the neutral country reported the issuance of the permit to the Allied Blockade Committee in London and to the War Trade Board in Washington.

3. The American exporter applied to the War Trade Board for an export license. In this application the number of the import permit had to be indicated.

4. The War Trade Board passed upon the character of the consignor and established whether American conservation policy permitted exportation of the commodity. If approved, the application for an export license was referred to the Allied Blockade Committee.

5. The Allied Blockade Committee compared recent imports of this commodity into the neutral country with the ration. If the ration was not exceeded, the Committee would be agreeable. Furthermore, the Committee passed upon the character of the consignee and the ultimate purchaser in the neutral country.

6. The representative of the American War Trade Board in London cabled the recommendation of the Committee to Washington. The War Trade Board had to make the final decision. Frequently a further exchange of views between Board and Committee was necessary. Finally, the export license was granted or refused.

As we have seen before in the Norwegian "fish drama," the control of neutrals went even further than the rationing of their imports, the prohibition of re-exports to Germany, and the boycotting of businesses trading with Germany. In order to obtain supplies from the Allies the adjacent neutrals had to prohibit exports of certain *domestic* products to Germany (for instance, Norwegian metal ores, Dutch cattle, and Danish hides), and to keep certain other exports within fixed limits. Toward the end of the World War, Danish exports of dairy products were placed under the following restrictions: (1) Denmark had to send thirty per cent of her exportable surplus of butter, bacon, milk, and cheese and twenty-five per cent of her surplus of eggs to Sweden and Norway. (2) Denmark was not allowed to export more than fifty per cent of the remainder to the Central Powers, but under no circumstances more than was bought by Britain. (3) An upper limit for Danish exports of dairy products to the Central Powers was fixed at 24,200 tons per year.[20]

If the neutrals were not forced to stop all of their exports to Germany, it was partly because of German counterpressure, partly because the Allies realized that ensuing stoppage of certain German exports to the neutral countries might be useful to Germany (apart from being detrimental to the neutral countries). Germany had indeed undertaken to supply Switzerland, Sweden, and Holland with coal, steel, machinery, and other products for which she herself had an urgent need. The Allies were not interested in replacing these supplies by drawing on their own resources.

How could the Allies control neutral imports before the United States entered the war? This country was one of the chief suppliers of the neutrals adjacent to Germany. Obviously, rationing of these neutrals would have failed, if Britain had not extended her control to the exports of neutral America to neutral countries of Europe. This extension of control indeed took place. At first, American ships were held up on their way to the contiguous neutrals. Their cargoes were submitted to thorough inspection and their passage was frequently forbidden. American exporters and shippers suffered great losses, and sharp protests were made by the American government.[21] Early in 1915, a number of agreements were concluded by which Great Britain permitted exportation of rubber, hides, wool, man-

---

[20] *Ibid.*, 22. In 1917, Danish exports of milk, butter, cheese, and eggs to the Central Powers amounted to 47,000 tons. (Consett, *op. cit.*, 302.)
[21] See above, pp. 223–224.

ganese, and other materials from her empire to the United States on the assurance that neither they nor any articles manufactured from them would be sold to enemy countries or to neutrals from whom the British government had not obtained sufficient guarantees against re-exportation. On the American side, these agreements were concluded by private companies, Standard Oil and Vacuum Oil, the American Rubber Manufacturers, the American Metal Importers, and others.[22]

These agreements covered only a fraction of American exports. For the rest, the method of detention and arbitrary obstruction found application until, in the spring of 1916, a smoother procedure was worked out: the so-called "Navicert" system.[23] The navicert was a sort of commercial passport in the form of a letter issued by the British Embassy in Washington in which assurance was given that British contraband control would not obstruct the shipment for which the navicert had been requested. For goods which did not require export licenses in Britain, the British Embassy was entitled to grant or to refuse a navicert. For goods which could only be exported from the United Kingdom under licenses the Embassy had to submit the application of the American exporter to the British government. There, the case was studied by the departments dealing with contraband and blockade. If these did not object to the shipment, the Embassy in Washington was informed that it might issue the navicert. Then, the American exporter could ship the goods to the neutral country with the prospect of benevolent and speedy treatment by the British naval patrols. In deciding whether to issue or to refuse a navicert the British authorities considered the character of consignor and consignee and compared previous imports of the neutral country with its allotted ration.

---

[22] Ritchie, *op. cit.*, 38.
[23] For a detailed description of the system, see Ritchie, *op. cit.*, 4–27. "Navicert" is a contraction of the term "naval certificate."

The navicert system was a more efficient way of controlling American exports to the neutral neighbors of Germany. British control ports were cleared of the large number of vessels under inspection. American exporters and shipping companies experienced a minimum of delay and were therefore less likely to ask the Government in Washington for an intervention. Above all, the navicert system spread and solidified British control of neutral trade, north-European imports as well as American exports. Britain could decide in certain cases whether she wanted to satisfy the import needs of the adjacent neutrals by her own exports or whether American exporters should be allowed to do so. British consuls in this country made sure by inspecting, occasionally even by X-raying, that the cargoes covered by navicerts corresponded to description. By the end of 1916, nearly all American shipments to the European neutrals were effected under navicerts.

In the present war, the system of rationing neutral imports and issuing navicerts has again found application. Shortly before the invasion of Holland and Belgium, the American oil companies were advised by the British Embassy in Washington that navicerts for shipments of lubricating oil to these two countries would be refused in view of the considerable stocks accumulated there. However, the invasions of several neutral countries by Germany and the declining influence of Great Britain upon the remaining European neutrals upset the system of British control.

Neutral War Economy

How a neutral country will fare under war conditions cannot be told in general terms. The location of the country with respect to the scene of war, its military strength, and the nature of its economic system determine the way in which it is affected by warfare. The nation as a whole may prosper by doing business with the belligerents, as was the case in the United States in 1915 and 1916, or it may suffer from these transactions as did the small European neutrals adjacent to Germany. Let us concentrate upon the effects of war on the national economies of the small neutrals close to the war zones and in intimate economic contact with the belligerents. In these countries we observe the emergence of a war economy very similar to that of the belligerents but different in one important respect: The war economy of the small neutrals is far less autonomous than that of the belligerents; the freedom of action of the small neutral countries is limited by their economic dependence on the large powers.

From the preceding sections of this chapter it has become clear that one of the outstanding economic problems of a neutral country is how to maintain its foreign supplies of basic agricultural or industrial materials. Several factors tend to render these supplies scarce: (1) Decrease of production takes place in some supplier countries as a consequence of warfare. (2) Shipping is requisitioned by the belligerents and impaired by naval warfare. (3) The belligerents attempt to direct essential supplies to their own uses. (4) The belligerents ration neutral imports to avoid re-exportation to the enemy.

In order to maintain a minimum of supplies, the neutral country will be compelled to barter for them with the belligerents. It must create import organizations of official or semiofficial character which are in a position to make comprehensive deals. The government will have to institute a system of import licenses and perhaps even a government monopoly for the importation of essential commodities. The restriction of certain nonessential imports will be necessary, not so much in order to conserve international means of payment but to free tonnage for essential imports. Scarcity of international means of payment is likely to be less pronounced than in belligerent countries, for the suction of goods into the belligerent countries is probably stronger than their export pressure. While the balance of trade and service items will tend toward an import surplus in major belligerent countries, it will tend in the direction of an export surplus in neutral states. The neutrals become creditors of the belligerent nations or reduce their usual capital imports from them. Of course, difficulties may arise because balances in one belligerent country may not be usable for purchases in another. But on the whole the import problems of the neutrals will be created by the unwillingness of belligerents to supply goods or the difficulties of shipping them, rather than by the lack of foreign exchange at the disposition of the neutral country.

The next problem is the preservation of an adequate supply of foodstuffs and other goods needed in the neutral country. For two reasons purchasing agents of the belligerent powers try to buy up these supplies: (1) in order to ease the supply situation of their own country and (2) in order to prevent the enemy agents from obtaining goods. They are likely to find accomplices among the merchants of the neutral country who may prefer to sell to well-paying foreigners rather than to less potent domestic buyers. The majority of the population in the neutral countries, in particular the poorer classes, will suffer greatly from the scarcity of foodstuffs resulting from the simultaneous compression of imports and expansion of exports. Industries will have to curtail operations because of the lack of raw materials. The necessity of conserving supplies will force the neutral government to intervene, partly in order to avoid the depressive effects of "overexportation" on the domestic economy, partly to satisfy the belligerents' request for a curtailment of trade with the enemy. It will be necessary to ration imported raw materials to manufacturers, to subject certain exports to license, and to prohibit certain others entirely.

During the first and the second world war, licensing of both imports and exports, centralization of imports in the hands of governments or government-supported organizations of businessmen,[24] prohibition of certain exports and rationing of certain raw materials were forced upon the small neutrals of northern Europe. Serious shortages could, however, not always be prevented. During the first world war, conservation policies were introduced very late; in addition, the neutral countries were frequently unable to solve the problem by the means at their disposition. They could not remove the fundamental difficulties created by their powerful neighbors.

It is therefore not surprising that the small neutrals became acquainted with wartime schemes of price control and rationing of consumers' goods. In both the first and the second world war they attempted to ensure more equitable distribution of scarce supplies by means of maximum prices for essential consumption goods. Bread, meat, sugar, coal, gasoline, and other commoditites were rationed. Subsidies were paid to keep essential foods within everybody's reach. During the first world war, Holland, for instance, subsidized the consumption of grain, flour, and coal. The government purchased supplies from England and Germany at high prices and sold them to millers, bakers, or retailers at a loss which had to be covered from general state revenue.[25] By restricting the opportunities of profiteering, the neutrals were able to limit the rise of prices somewhat; but they were far from isolating their domestic econ-

---

[24] Toward the end of the first world war Holland even centralized export operations. They had to be transacted through the government-controlled Netherlands Export Company. M. J. Van der Flier: *War Finances in the Netherlands up to 1918*, Oxford, 1923, 42.

[25] *Ibid.*, 39-43.

omies entirely from the world-wide price boom. Again in Holland, the cost of the commodities ordinarily consumed by wage earners in 1911 rose by thirty-two per cent from that year to 1917. In 1918, it towered sixty-five per cent above the level of 1911. As was the case in all belligerent countries—with the exception of the United States [26]—the general level of money wages lagged behind that of prices. (The Dutch wage index—100 in 1911—reached 119 in 1917 and 133 in 1918.) Hence real wages dropped [27] and consumption of essential commodities decreased heavily, in some cases even more heavily than in the belligerent countries. According to estimates of the British Ministry of Food,[28] the *percentage drop in per capita consumption* of bread and flour, meats, and fats in 1918 compared with prewar times was as follows:

Commodity	In Belligerent England	Germany	In Neutral Holland
Bread and flour	7% [29]	37%	58%
Meats	38	78	71
Fats	12	73	47

These figures indicate that flour consumption in Holland dropped more heavily than in Germany, while English consumption increased. With respect to meats and fats the curtailment of consumption in Holland was stronger than in England, less than in Germany. These conditions and the subsistence of profiteering and smuggling in spite of state controls caused great discontent among the neutral populations.

The situation was aggravated in still another way. The scarcity of raw material supplies, the impairment of certain

---

[26] See above, p. 176.
[27] Van der Flier, *op. cit.*, 123–124. For the Scandinavian countries, see Heckscher and others, *op. cit.*, 21, 544, and 576.
[28] W. H. Beveridge: *British Food Control*, London, 1928, 316.
[29] Increase.

exports, and general insecurity caused a slackening of business activity and unemployment in many fields. In the World War, the first wave of unemployment followed the outbreak of hostilities. In 1915 and 1916 the unemployment figures dropped; but in 1917 and 1918 they rose again. The average percentage of unemployment in Denmark and Holland developed as follows: [30]

	1913	1914	1915	1916	1917	1918
Denmark	7.5	9.9	7.7	4.9	9.7	18.1
Holland	5.1	13.8	12.0	5.1	6.5	7.5

Of course, individual industries were variously affected by war conditions. The industries depending on foreign raw materials suffered heavily. In Holland, for instance, there was great unemployment in the building, cotton textile, pottery, glass, and chemical industries. The curtailment of shipping brought distress to sailors and harbor hands, and the reduction of foreign demand for luxuries threw diamond workers out of their jobs.[31]

The public finances of neutral countries cannot fail to reflect the influences of war. Heavy expenditures are caused by precautionary military measures,[32] subsidization of basic consumption articles, unemployment relief, and care of the refugees who are likely to stream into the country. Hence, the neutrals too face problems of war finance. Special defense and war-profits taxes are likely to appear, and the tax burden on the population will increase. But tax revenue may not increase sufficiently, partly because of the government's hesitation to discourage private business by new taxes, partly because of declining returns from tra-

---

[30] Van der Flier, *op. cit.*, 51, and Heckscher and others, *op. cit.*, 492.

According to Keilhau, Norway experienced "practically no unemployment" during the World War except for the first weeks following the outbreak of hostilities. (Heckscher and others, *op. cit.*, 294.)

[31] Van der Flier, *op. cit.*, 101 and 107.

[32] In 1918, Holland's military expenditures were 343 per cent above the level of 1914. *Ibid.*, 36.

ditional sources of revenue (for instance, import duties). The budget of the government will then show deficits, and borrowing will be used to fill the gap.[33] The more thoroughly war upsets the neutral economy, the more will the financial situation of the neutral approach that of a belligerent.

Up to the recent invasion of the small neutral countries of northern Europe there was little difference in the effect of the first and the second world war upon them. However, in 1939–1940, war-economic measures were taken more quickly. While in the first world war the Norwegian government did not ration sugar, coffee, flour, and other consumption goods until the end of 1917, a rationing system for these products and gasoline was started during the first weeks of the present war. Similarly, measures designed to conserve stocks of raw materials were introduced with greater speed, and efforts were made to limit the rise of prices to the unavoidable allowances for the increasing costliness of import articles.[34] The experience of the first world war has made the small neutrals conscious of the war-economic requirements of neutrality.

SUGGESTED REFERENCES

Cherne, L. M.: *Adjusting Your Business to War*, New York, 1940, chapter III.
Consett, M. W. W. P.: *The Triumph of Unarmed Forces (1914–1918)*, London, 1923.
Heckscher, E. F. and others: *Sweden, Norway, Denmark, and Iceland in the World War*, New Haven, 1930.

---

[33] Let us again take Holland as an example. In 1918, the per capita burden of direct and indirect taxation was 175 per cent above the level of 1914. In 1914, the deficit of the state budget which had to be covered by borrowing amounted to thirty-two per cent of total expenditures; in 1918, to sixty-six per cent. (Van der Flier, *op. cit.*, 94 and 142.)

[34] The Norwegian wholesale price index of imported commodities rose from August, 1939, until December of the same year by thirty per cent, that of domestic products (partly manufactured with the help of imported raw materials) by twelve per cent. (Information obtained from Mr. Arne Skaug of the Central Statistical Bureau of Norway.)

Jessup, P. C.: *Neutrality, Its History, Economics and Law*, Vol. IV (Today and Tomorrow), New York, 1936.
Report of the War Trade Board, Washington, D. C., 1920, Parts II and III.
Ritchie, H.: *The "Navicert" System During the World War*, Washington, D. C., 1938.
Turlington, E.: *Neutrality, Its History, Economics and Law*, Vol. III (The World War Period), New York, 1936.
United States Senate, Special Committee on Investigation of the Munitions Industry: *Report on Existing Legislation*, 74th Congress, 2d Session, Senate, Report No. 944, Part 5, Washington, D. C., 1936.
Van der Flier, M. J.: *War Finances in the Netherlands*, Oxford, 1923.

PART FOUR

POSTWAR ECONOMICS

CHAPTER 12

The Population After the War

War is a most efficient destroyer of human lives. In the course of the last few centuries medical science and hygiene have tremendously reduced the loss of life due to epidemics, but in warfare modern society has retained a means of destruction equaling the scourges of the past. The demographic effects of warfare are direct and indirect. Human lives are destroyed in battle, others are extinguished behind the front. Not only the belligerent but also the neutral populations are affected.

In several masterly studies Professor L. Hersch of the University of Geneva has analyzed the demographic effects of modern warfare.[1] In what follows, we are going to draw on some of the results he obtained.

VICTOR AND VANQUISHED ALIKE

The demographic effects of the World War appeared with about the same intensity in victorious and vanquished nations. In a prolonged major war, both sides are likely to suffer numerous casualties in battle. Both sides will find life at home deeply affected by the departure of many men for the front, the disruption of marriages, the failure of new marriages to be concluded, and declining birth rates. In a protracted struggle, both victor and vanquished will see

---

[1] L. Hersch: "Demographic Effects of Modern Warfare," *What Would Be the Character of a New War?* New York, Harrison Smith and Robert Haas, 1933, chapter VII. (The previous studies by this author are referred to on p. 314 of that book.)

their power of resistance against disease weakened by lack of food and extraordinary physical and mental strains. It is true, however, that these conditions may vary from nation to nation and from war to war. The shorter, the less inten-

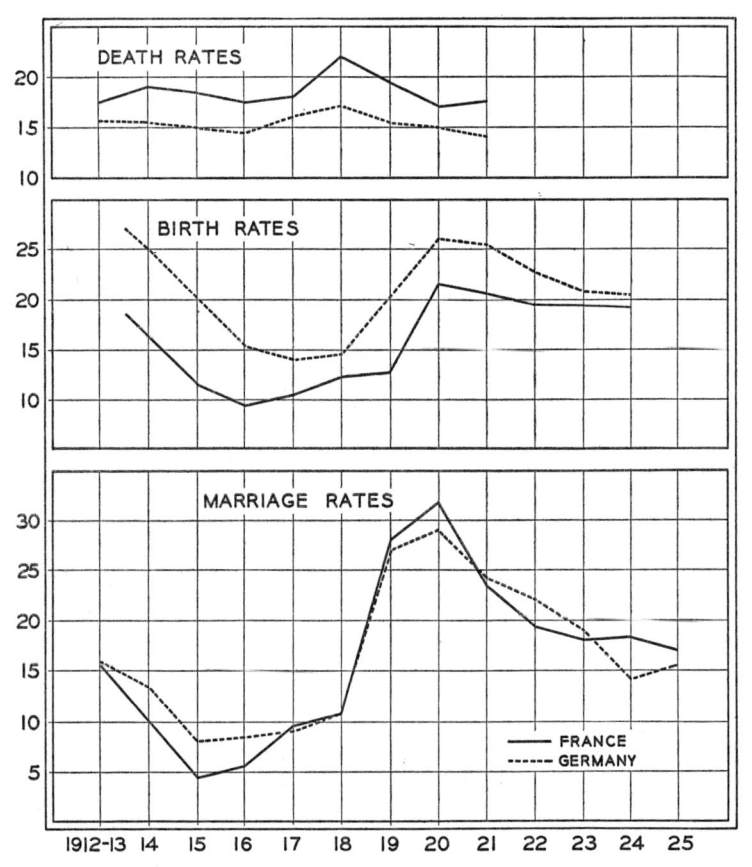

Civilian Death Rates, Birth Rates, and Marriage Rates per Thousand Inhabitants in France [2] and Germany [3]
(Data: Hersch, *op. cit.,* 279–280)

sive, and the more successful the country's participation in warfare, the less will its population be affected by the war.

---

[2] For 1914–1919, results observed in the uninvaded departments. From 1920, new territory of the Republic.

[3] From 1917, new territory of the Reich.

We may consider first the effect of war on the death rates, birth rates, and marriage rates. Investigating a number of European wars during the nineteenth century Hersch found that the effect of war on the development of the population is twofold. There is first a *destructive phase,* during which death rates rise, birth and marriage rates fall. It coincides more or less with the duration of the war. This is followed by a *restorative phase* during which the death rate returns to its normal level and birth and marriage rates show a recovery, sometimes so considerable as to reach a level higher than that prevailing before the war. We find these phases superimposed upon the long-run movements of the three demographic phenomena.

Taking the World War as an example, we may illustrate the appearance of both phases in victorious France and vanquished Germany. The diagram shows the development of birth, marriage, and civilian death rates in the two countries. For each of the three phenomena the parallelism of the two countries' curves is very pronounced. First, we notice the destructive phase. The marriage and birth rates begin their decline with the outbreak of the war. The civilian death rate does not react as quickly. It remains almost constant until 1916, when it starts on a substantial rise which lasts until the end of the war. The restorative phase is ushered in by the end of hostilities. It is true that even during the war the marriage rate shows a slight recovery in both countries, but its level remains well below that of 1912–1913. After the cessation of hostilities, both birth and marriage rate rise considerably, while the death rate drops back to its normal level. In 1920 the marriage rates are nearly twice as high as they were before the war. They exceed the highest rates ever before observed in the two countries. In France, the highest rate registered before the World War was 26.4 per thousand inhabitants (1813), in Prussia, 22.9 (1816). In 1920, however, the

French marriage rate was 31.8, and the German, 29.0. The birth rate shows a less pronounced recovery. In France, it exceeds the rate of 1913–1914 by only a small amount; in Germany it does not even reach the prewar level. The long-run tendency of the birth rate to decline, reinforced by war conditions, reduced the significance of the restorative phase to very small proportions in both countries and in Italy and England as well.

The essential features illustrated by our example can be found in the record of other belligerent countries as well. Let us therefore leave the example and turn to the general case. What causes the rise of the civilian death rate during the war, what accounts for the precipitous fall and later rise of the marriage and birth rates?

War, Father of Epidemics

"While it cannot be denied that serious epidemics have raged and do rage apart from war periods (especially in time of famine), it is nevertheless certain that the most terrible epidemics which have ravaged civilized countries—and this from the most remote antiquity—have always been associated with periods of war. So true is this that it may be said that the history of great wars is at the same time a history of great epidemics, and, vice versa, that the history of the greatest epidemics is also a history of great wars.

"Wars provoked epidemics in two ways which, more often than not, were complementary: on the one hand they imported persons affected by the epidemic into countries where it had previously been unknown (as was the case, for instance, with cholera, which was propagated in France after the Crimean War); on the other hand, diseases which existed in a sporadic form or which were even endemic, but which were ordinarily of a mild type, were transformed by the war into extensive and terrible epidemics (as was usually the case with typhoid fever, small-pox, measles, dysentery, etc.). In the one case, as in the other, the epidemic spread even beyond the countries at war.

"This transformation of sporadic cases into epidemics, and of relatively mild affections into serious diseases, was brought about by war on the one hand by the creation of conditions favorable to the propagation of the pathogenic agent (the microbe) and the increase of its virulence, and on the other by diminishing the individual resisting power of the population. Gatherings (of troops, prisoners, inhabitants), the frequent impossibility in war-time of early isolation of patients and their clothing from their fellows, combined with defective feeding and housing, and the over-work and worry of every kind inseparable from war, create in the army centres of infection which spread later to the civilian population. Once this latter is affected the epidemic makes the more rapid progress in that the population is usually weakened by the privations and sufferings imposed by the war.

"Thus war provokes, propagates and aggravates infectious diseases. . . ." [4]

In the nineteenth century, the number of deaths due to epidemics in the hinterland of war zones ordinarily exceeded the number of soldier-casualties. During the World War, however, prophylactic measures enabled the western European belligerents (England, France, and Germany) to keep the toll of epidemics below the number of military casualties. In the relatively backward countries, Serbia, Russia, Austria-Hungary, and Italy, the "sanitary front" broke down rather early. And as the more advanced nations became gradually weaker, they too were unable to resist the invasion of the World War's outstanding epidemic:

---
[4] L. Hersch, *op. cit.*, 283–284. Reprinted by permission of Random House, Inc.

influenza. In 1918–1919, influenza played havoc, causing the death of about 200,000 victims in the United Kingdom, 400,000 in Germany, 430,000 in Italy, and 600,000 in the United States. Moreover, influenza did not stop at the frontiers of the belligerent countries. It spread to the neutral nations which, as we have seen before, were economically weakened by the great social catastrophe. Thousands succumbed to it in Spain, Holland, Sweden and Switzerland. Still, the more civilized nations were comparatively well off. "In the space of a few months, up to the end of 1918, *seven million* human beings were carried off by influenza in British India, and a *million and a half* in the native states of India."[5] According to Hersch's estimate, the world total of influenza victims was in the neighborhood of fifteen million.

If we want to arrive at the total number of civilian deaths caused by the war, millions have to be added who fell victims of typhoid fever in eastern Europe, the plague and cholera in Asia and Africa, and numerous ordinary diseases in all parts of the world. The total number of civilian deaths caused by the World War (that is, that above the normal level for these years) has been estimated by Hersch at more than *twenty-eight million,* or more than double the number of military deaths (see Table IV of the Appendix). Civilian and military deaths together amounted to over *forty-one million.* Men of military age, women, old people and children, inhabitants of belligerent and neutral countries paid this bill.

The "Hollow Classes"

War delivers its first blow against the living. Its second blow hits the generation to come. We have seen the effects of the World War on marriage and birth rates in Germany

---
[5] *Ibid.,* 287.

and France. Looking now for the causes, we find them close at hand.

The drop in the marriage rates is due to the mobilization of many marriageable men. It is true that in some countries an increase of marriages has been observed during the first weeks of a war. In Germany, for instance, the marriage rate for the fourth quarter of 1939 amounts to fifteen and six tenths per thousand inhabitants. It exceeds by about fifty per cent the rates observed in the same quarter for each of the three preceding years.[6] Many young couples may decide to marry before they are to be separated for an indefinite time. But this is a short-lived stimulus. The longer the war lasts, the greater must be the number of marriages that fail to be concluded.

The restorative phase of the marriage rate is explained first by the large number of postponed marriages. In all cases where marriage was postponed because of separation, the insecurity of life, or for other reasons, marriage is likely to take place if and when the prospective husband returns from the military forces. Second, the number of marriageable persons is increased by the disruption of marriages through the war. Married men have been killed; their wives have become widows. Or wives have died at home of epidemics, and their husbands return as widowers. Usually a great number of war widows and widowers remarry. These two factors in large part explain the tremendous post-war rise in the marriage rate.

The variations of the birth rate find their explanation mostly in the same factors. Couples are separated during the war, and the birth rate is bound to drop. Usually, a rise in the proportion of illegitimate births is taking place, but their total is likely to decline as well. It is worth noticing, in this connection, that at present the German government lends material and moral support to the procreation of chil-

---
[6] Cf. *Wirtschaft und Statistik*, first May issue of 1940, 124.

dren not only by married couples but also by unmarried ones. In the registration of illegitimate births, the father is designated as "Kriegsvater." The mother receives government support irrespective of whether marriage has been concluded. In a letter to an unmarried mother, Rudolf Hess, deputy leader of the Nazi party, said: "How much poorer would the world be, if Leonardo da Vinci, instead of being born 'illegitimately,' had never seen the light of day. What would the Prussian army have been without the 'illegitimately born' [General] Yorck!" [7] It remains to be seen whether Germany will be able to avoid the wartime drop of the birth rate in this way.

The conclusion of peace, the return of the men, and the consummation of marriages are followed by the restorative phase of the birth rate. The word "restorative," however, can scarcely be taken in an absolute sense.

In the present epoch, which is characterized in all Western countries by a constant and marked fall in the birth-rate, the extraordinary fall brought about by the war reduces the rate during the destructive phase to levels hitherto unknown, whilst the rise in the birth-rate during the "restorative" phase only retards and attenuates the normal fall instead of effectually raising the birth-rate above the pre-war level.[8]

The destructive phase of the birth rate creates a quasi-permanent scar on a nation's body. The classes born during the war are smaller than they would have been otherwise, and, immigration excluded, they will remain so until they have reached the end of their lives. The age distribution of a country's population shows these "hollow classes" [9] over decades. A number of diagrams ("age pyra-

---

[7] *Frankfurter Zeitung*, December 24, 1939. (Author's translation.)

[8] Hersch, *op. cit.*, 296. The "high" level of the French birth rate after the war, as shown by the diagram on p. 256, may partly find its explanation in the large immigration of Italians, Spaniards, and Poles into France. Natives of these countries have a higher birth rate than the French.

[9] *"Les classes creuses,"* as the French have called them.

mids") in the Appendix illustrate how recent population censuses reveal the "hollow classes" created by the first world war.[10]

The age pyramids of Germany and France in 1937 and 1936, respectively, show the hollow classes in the age groups from fifteen to twenty-four years. Italy, who did not enter the war until 1915, shows them in the fifteen- to nineteen-years bracket (1936); in Soviet Russia, where the last census data available are those of 1926, the classes reduced by the war are mainly in the five- to nine-years bracket. In England and Wales, the "hollow classes" were scarcely noticeable in 1937 because of the relatively low degree of military mobilization and the consequently feeble reaction of the birth rate during the World War. The age distribution of the United States, finally, does not show any numerical deficiency of the classes born during the war. This is due to the shortness of our participation in the war and the comparative smallness of our expeditionary forces. Notice, however, the marked notch in the age pyramid of neutral Switzerland (1938) in the twenty- to twenty-four-years bracket. Switzerland, surrounded by belligerent countries, mobilized an army and manned her frontiers. In neutral countries farther away from the great battlefields of the war the decline of birth rates was smaller. In Norway, for instance, it was practically imperceptible.

The "hollow classes" are reminders of past wars. Their smallness creates various economic problems, as we are going to see. These abnormally small groups are, however, not only passive reminders. They will, when they are of marriageable age, that is, of twenty-five to thirty years, procreate a relatively small number of children. Thus, there will be new "hollow classes" in the future, created by a sort of echo

---

[10] *Statistical Yearbook of the League of Nations, 1938/39*, 24–30. In this source an arrangement of the data in age groups of five-year intervals is used. One-year intervals would have brought out the hollow classes more spectacularly.

effect *(Eilert Sundt's Law)*. They will doubtless be much less pronounced than the primary "hollow classes," but the smaller these were, the more perceptible will be the deficiency of their offspring.

The echo effect of the "hollow classes" will of course be very pronounced if the country enters another war at the time when they have reached military age. The fall of the birth rate in the second war will then affect a population already decimated by the first war, and the "hollow classes" of the future will become particularly small. It so happens that the second world war began twenty-five years after the first one started. The "hollow classes" resulting from the latter are now of marriageable age. Moreover, they include the age groups that are most completely mobilized. If this war should last for a number of years, the age pyramids of the future will show tremendous gaps.

Economic Consequences

The war's effect on a country's population has its repercussions in the postwar economic life of the nation.

War has been called the "rejuvenator" of a nation. Chauvinists are fond of its destructive effects, which will, they believe, free the nations of weak and detrimental elements. Their belief is, however, far from the truth. It may be true that epidemics ravage the ranks of the sick and old especially, but the bullets and shells hit the cream of the nation, the young men that have been found strong and skilled enough to enlist in the military forces. War is no rejuvenating cure. It destroys a nation's young men, it destroys valuable lives through sickness that might otherwise have been cured, and it destroys civilization. Men who have been in the trenches for a number of years and who have become accustomed there to the life of savages, living in continuous danger and satisfying only their most primitive needs in the most primitive ways, find it extremely difficult to readjust to orderly work, family life, and other conditions of civilization. Thousands of those who returned from the armies of the World War were unable for years to find the way back to normal living conditions. Thousands never succeeded and became living wrecks. Some found their jobs taken by other people, others went on indefinitely looking for a first job. Since modern war rarely brings immediate riches to the victor, millions of discontented men may appear in victorious as well as vanquished countries. Yet the economic aftermath of war will be more accentuated in the latter. Revolutionary parties will find numerous followers among the discontented and the unemployed. It is no accident that a number of the leaders of the Nazi movement came from the ranks of the dissatisfied and unadjustable officers of Germany's World War army.

Not only the soldiers will be subject to the weakening and disorganizing effects of the war. The civilian population is likely to be underfed, ill-clothed, and badly housed when the war nears its end. Shortages of essential foodstuffs may appear even in the wealthiest countries. Deficiencies in the popular diet are likely to increase. Stocks of wearing apparel are being used up. They cannot be adequately replaced because of the mobilization of industry for war needs. Residential building is bound to be curtailed most severely in war times. What poverty and misery there was before the war will reappear with increased intensity when peace returns.

Hence, the postwar generation will be a tired lot of people, alienated from peaceful and civilized life, poor, rude, and hysterical. It takes years to heal the "rejuvenating" effects of a major modern war.

In a nation which suffered great losses of soldiers during the war, men will have better chances to find wives than women will have in finding husbands, because of the smaller proportion of males in the population. During the World War period the proportion of males to females fell in Germany from .492 to .465, in France from .490 to .470, in Great Britain from .479 to .470, and in the United States from .519 to .514.[11] As a result an increase of women's share in occupations is likely to take place.

The "hollow classes" too will present economic problems to the people living after the war. As this group advances in age its smallness causes economic disturbances. First, it will make for empty classes in kindergartens and in primary and secondary schools. Teachers will become superfluous; the demand for toys, school equipment, children's clothes will fall. Next the problem is passed on to the labor market, colleges, and to the peacetime military forces. The number of young workers entering the labor market will suddenly drop, and so will the enrollment of higher institutions of learning. The military authorities will discover that normal ways of recruiting furnish a smaller number of men. The scarcity of new workers may be considered by some as a favorable condition, if its appearance coincides with widespread unemployment. But this view is superficial. Unemployment in modern industrial societies does not result from an excessive number of people of working age. It is a defect of social organization. Wherever the "hollow classes" make their appearance, they will create disturbances. So will the appearance of the stronger classes that are going to result from the more numerous postwar births.

Finally, care of the war veterans will present an economic problem. A belligerent nation's bill of death and disability is not paid when the war ends. The postwar generation has to care for the mutilated, the wives and children of the dead,

---

[11] A. L. Bowley: *Some Economic Consequences of the Great War*, London, 1930, 54 and 57.

and the vocational rehabilitation of the uprooted. These expenses have to be met for many years after the conclusion of peace. A few quotations from our own record serve to illustrate the longevity of these costs to the nation.[12]

Patients cared for by the government have formed a large and continuous burden. . . . Hospital patients reached their greatest number in March, 1922, when they were nearly 31,000. . . . From then on the cases due to World War causes declined quite steadily, to 15,237 at the end of 1930, with 922 under observation to determine the cause of disability. This decline has been largely balanced by the admission, from 1925 on, of cases not due to war service, now numbering 12,631 among the World War veterans. This has brought the 1930 total up to 31,311 of whom 28,840 are World War veterans. There are 1,208 Spanish War veterans, 79 Civil War veterans, and 174 veterans of other service.[13]

Death compensation is paid to members of the immediate families of persons who died while in service, or afterward from causes connected with service. Parents and children are entitled to benefits only during actual dependency. In June, 1930, benefits were being paid to dependents of 90,954 veterans, the dependents numbering approximately 135,000. There were 21,754 widows, 32,746 children, and 65,205 cases with parent or parents. . . . The monthly compensation is 2½ millions, or at a rate of 30 millions per year. Parents apparently receive about $200 annually per person. . . . Compared to the French widow's pension of $67.60 a year, ours is munificent; though, even so, France with her 630,000 war widows and orphans must spend several times as much as we do for this purpose.[14]

So we find the economic aftereffects of war manifold, far-reaching, and persistent. If it were possible to evaluate the opportunity costs of these extinguished, vitiated, or unborn

---

[12] See also L. Grebler and W. Winkler: *The Cost of the World War to Germany and to Austria-Hungary*, New Haven, 1940, 100.

[13] J. M. Clark: *The Costs of the World War to the American People*, New Haven, Yale University Press, 1931, 189. In chapters XIII and XIV Clark gives an extensive analysis of the costs to this country of death and disability caused by the World War.

[14] *Ibid.*, 191.

lives in terms of money, we would probably arrive at stupendous sums for a major war. Yet, need we account for them in dollars and cents? Is the record of population statistics not eloquent enough? The peoples of the "western civilization" cannot invent a more effective instrument than war for the acceleration of their decline.

SUGGESTED REFERENCES

Bowley, A. L.: *Some Economic Consequences of the Great War,* London, 1930, chapter II.

Clark, J. M.: *The Costs of the World War to the American People,* New Haven, 1931, chapters XIII, XIV, and XVIII.

Hersch, L.: "Demographic Effects of Modern Warfare," in *What Would Be the Character of a New War?* New York, 1933, chapter VII.

Joergensen, J.: "The Effect of a Future War Upon the Spiritual and Mental Attitude of the Civil Population and the Fighting Forces," in *What Would Be the Character of a New War?* chapter VI.

CHAPTER 13

Economic Demobilization

"*La paix est plus terrible à faire que la guerre.*" (The making of peace is more terrible than the making of war.) Georges Clemenceau, France's World War prime minister, is reported to have spoken these words when he wrestled with David Lloyd George and Woodrow Wilson over the fate of the German Saar territory in the spring of 1919. This sentence may head our entire discussion of economic readjustment to peace conditions. Not only does it express the troubles the postwar government of a victorious nation may have to go through in order to present an obvious and salutary gain to the people, but it also indicates that the problems of the postwar economy are likely to be more confusing than those of the war economy. At first glance, this seems astonishing. Cannot the nation's economy simply relapse into its prewar condition? Cannot the government simply turn the mobilized men loose, stop rationing, price control, and priorities, and cancel its contracts for further munitions?

Prewar Conditions Are History

The nation cannot relapse into its prewar condition. Human society, particularly in our days, is not static; and wars, more than anything else, are suited to accelerate its dynamism. Before war broke out, the economic system was in the process of transformation. Groups of people strove for changes in social and political conditions. The war temporarily suspended part of these trends and ambitions; the return of peace resuscitates them. Moreover, the economic changes brought about by the war regime itself may be saluted by some as the forerunners of social changes. During the World War, nationalization of industries, limitation and taxation of profits, and government control of labor relations were hailed by some sections of the labor movement as the beginning of socialism. Their abolition was opposed. Finally, the end of the war generally results in new political and economic frontiers, the disappearance of old and the creation of new states, and a reallocation of natural and human resources among the peoples concerned. Hence, prewar conditions are history. Nations cannot simply expect to see them restored by the ending of the war. But what can they expect?

The conditions which a nation will face at the end of the war depend on a number of important circumstances. Does the nation emerge as victor or victim? If it is victorious, will it impose a peace that is to the true advantage of its own economy—and that of other nations? Or will it favor a peace of blind revenge, destructive to all parties and laden with the germs of a new world conflict? If it is vanquished, will the nation be able to recover from its war losses of men and goods; can it survive as an autonomous section of the world or must it bow to foreign domination and exploitation? Will the nation maintain its political and social regime after the war, or will the war bring success to revolutionary forces?

To go into a detailed discussion of these alternatives would lead us too far afield. Innumerable illustrations of one or the other could be cited from the first world war, and every country would present an interesting case to study. In large part, however, the conditions resulting from the World War are unique experiences which have now become history. Who can predict that the end of the present or of a future war will again be accompanied by leftist uprisings? Who can predict that the victorious nations will endeavor to re-establish private capitalism, a gold standard, and international exchanges of commodities and capital on an individualistic basis? Victorious powers will presumably attempt to enrich themselves and to gain a larger share of world control. But the means to these ends may differ from those used by the Allies against Germany after the first world war. Suppose Germany is victorious in the present European war. She may organize Europe along entirely new lines, welding her own national economy and those of her victims and allies into a "pan-European" economic system. Within this system the "mark standard" may replace the gold standard, while in dealings with the rest of the world the techniques of bilateral trade and clearing accounts may find application. Whereas the peace treaties following the World War multiplied the independent customs areas in Europe, a *"pax germanica"* may well lead to the abolishment of barriers in intra-European trade and the simultaneous erection of a "foreign-trade monopoly" over the whole area of Europe. Furthermore, government control of industry may become a general European institution. Not only the situation of the European nations but also that of the United States would be affected by such a solution. The economic repercussions of a German victory would differ very greatly from those of the peace of Versailles.

In some fundamental respects, however, the conditions resulting from the present or future wars will resemble those created by the first world war. Let us restrict our task to a discussion of those fundamental problems which are likely to appear at the end of *every* major modern war.

Demobilization of Men

The first of the problems common to all postwar periods is the demobilization of the armed forces. This problem appears simultaneously with final victory or defeat; but its solution may require some time. The bulk of the armies becomes superfluous when military operations stop. Some of the men may be needed to fulfill the functions of an army of occupation in foreign territory; but this will normally be a fairly small force. What will happen to the majority who are disbanded?

In the previous chapter we have shown some of the difficulties that are likely to appear at this moment. Soldiers have lost contact with civilian life. Returning full of expectations, they encounter difficulties in finding new and satisfactory employment. Accustomed to being fed and clothed by military officials, they now face the responsibility of caring for themselves and their families. Women or younger men have taken their jobs, and industry may not be quick enough in opening up new possibilities; in fact the postwar period is likely to begin with a stagnation of economic activity: the demobilization crisis. Only after the necessary readjustments have taken place, the crisis may give way to a reconstruction boom. In the meantime, however, the specter of unemployment looms large before the war veterans, and the postwar government has to face the task of removing the political dangers inherent in this situation. There can be no doubt that failure would result in serious political difficulties.

The measures that the government may take can be grouped under three headings: gradual demobilization, public works, and stimulation of peacetime industry. As far as the stimulation of peacetime industry is concerned, the main problem consists in transferring the nation's productive forces from wartime to peacetime occupations.

There will be large potential demands for civilian consumption goods; for people emerge from the war ill-fed, ill-clothed, and ill-housed. Similarly, industry will require the immediate replacement of equipment worn out during the war. These demands will help to overcome the demobilization crisis. In order to render them fully effective the government may encourage credit expansion and strengthen the purchasing power of consumers.[1] In this way it can counterbalance the depressive consequences of a curtailment of war orders.

Still, the process of economic rehabilitation is bound to consume time. The war has disrupted routines; the economic machinery has lost some of its agility and responsiveness to new demands. Therefore, the government may be compelled to resort to one of the two other measures, public works or gradual demobilization.

Gradual demobilization, of course, does not in itself present a solution. It is a mere postponement of the solution. If gradual demobilization means keeping men idle while they are still under military command, it is nothing but a disguised variety of unemployment relief; and there can be justified doubt whether this is a desirable form of relief. It is true that it may be a relatively cheap way of subsidizing idleness. Furthermore, the measure may recommend itself to a politically weakened government: the mobilized men may be used to forestall or to combat revolutionary movements. On the other hand, gradual demobilization results in a deplorable loss of productive effort, at the very moment when the world is crying for goods and services.

Public works represents a more desirable solution. It may be combined with gradual demobilization by transforming military units into brigades of workers. Public works may easily be executed under a military organization.

---

[1] See in this connection the provisions of the Keynes plan for a postwar expansion of purchasing power. Above, p. 140.

However, it is by no means necessary to combine the two, and it seems even desirable not to do so. The return of the soldiers to their homes and families, or to the creation of new homes, is essential to the re-adaptation of men to civilian life. It would seem advantageous not to obstruct this re-adaptation by an extension of the time of military service.

Are there enough tasks for public works after a war? Certainly. During the war, highways and bridges were not kept in good repair or were destroyed by enemy action; whole communities were annihilated in the zones of fighting; houses, plants, public utilities have to be rebuilt. Here are innumerable jobs for workers on reconstruction programs. The government should plan for such projects and put them into operation as soon as the war is over.

Exhaustion of the Nation's Real Capital

Not only is war waged at the expense of civilian consumption; it also encroaches on the nation's wealth. Wealth has been consumed by the insufficiency of replacements. During the war, both man power and productive equipment had to be withheld from postponable maintenance and repair work. The history of the German railroads during and after the first world war provides a striking example of the exhaustion of real capital. By 1917, only seventy-five per cent of the prewar complement of maintenance workers was available for work on the roads.[2] Production of rails had dropped to forty per cent, that of rolling equipment to sixty-seven per cent of the 1913 level.[3] The number of locomotives on German railroads increased during the war; but the number of machines ready for use showed

---

[2] A. Sarter: *Die Deutschen Eisenbahnen im Kriege*, Stuttgart, 1930, 285.
[3] L. Grebler and W. Winkler: *The Cost of the World War to Germany and to Austria-Hungary*, New Haven, 1940, 87.

a strong decline. The reason was the terrific increase in the percentage of locomotives out of repair. From 1913 to 1918, this percentage rose from nineteen to thirty-four; in 1919, it reached forty-seven. Thus, at the close of the war, scarcely more than half of Germany's locomotives were in running condition and there was practically no locomotive that did not show some defects.[4]

Similar neglects of repair work occurred in mining. When the first world war was over, a great deal of energy had to be devoted to the resumption of repairs. The yearly per capita output of coal miners continued to fall during the first years following the war, partly in consequence of this condition, partly as a result of labor disputes and a shortening of the working day.

Yearly Output of Coal per Miner
(in metric tons)[5]

Country	1913	1918	1919	1920
England	264	234	199	186
France	200	156	129	108
Germany	291	280	177	185

Manufacturing industries are not likely to be exceptions to this rule. Their equipment is also bound to deteriorate during the war. In agriculture we are confronted with soil exhaustion and deterioration of farm equipment. As an industry producing for easily postponable needs, residential building is reduced to a minimum. As a result, the nation's living quarters are bound to be seriously deficient in quantity and in quality at the end of the war. This deficiency may not be very obvious as long as the soldiers are at the front; but it will be strikingly apparent when they return to join their families or set up new homes.

The nation's wealth will suffer in still another respect.

---

[4] Sarter, op. cit., 165 and 166.
[5] F. Friedensburg: Kohle und Eisen im Weltkriege und in den Friedensschlüssen, Munich, 1934, 186.

Besides productive equipment, stocks of consumable goods will be reduced. There will be a depletion of stocks of durable consumers' goods in the hands of the people. In a peacetime economy, large stocks of merchandise are continuously kept by producers and traders; these stocks too are likely to be depleted by war consumption. The rule, however, is not without exception. Under a successful conservation policy stocks may increase in wartime. This seems to have been the case with stocks of most meats and cereals in England during the first world war.[6]

All over the nation there appears an urgent demand for repairs of the material damages caused by war. From these damages arises a great incentive to productive activity; but we must not forget that their very existence impedes production. Years will pass before the wounds which a major war inflicts upon the nation's productive equipment are healed.

Conversion of Industries to Peacetime Activities

As war demand disappears, industry has to adjust itself to the conditions created by the new peace. In part these conditions resemble those prevailing before the war: the major portion of personal incomes will again be spent on articles for individual consumption, while industry will require producers' goods for replacements and additions to capital equipment. Hence, plants converted to the production of military equipment will have to be reconverted to their original uses. The problems arising from this situation are likely to be difficult. Their solution, however, will be facilitated by the astonishing capacity of mankind to conserve technical and organizational abilities during periods of idleness or destruction. To the extent that the recon-

---

[6] W. H. Beveridge: *British Food Control*, London, 1928, 348 ff.

version of industry consists in a return to prewar conditions the task is not insuperable.

Difficulties are likely to be the greater, the more postwar conditions deviate from the prewar setup. The drawing of new frontiers may disrupt long-established economic relations. After the World War, the splitting of the Austro-Hungarian Empire into Austria, Hungary, and Czechoslovakia and the transfer of large parts of its territory to Rumania, Yugoslavia, Poland, and Italy left the industrial system of the former empire in a pitiful state. The industrial region around Vienna was separated from the agricultural areas of Hungary and the other Balkan states by political and customs frontiers. Coal mines in Czechoslovakia were cut off from iron ore in Austria; and Bohemian spinning and weaving, from the Viennese garment industry. Similar disruptions of economic life were caused by the splitting of the mining district of upper Silesia into a German and a Polish part and the transfer of the Lorrainian iron ore from iron-poor Germany to iron-rich France.

It is true that the peacemakers of Versailles and Trianon had certain plans concerning the future coöperation of the mutilated economic bodies that they had created; but the system of national capitalistic states proved to be incapable of developing such coöperation. During the two decades following the war, every state attempted to round off its national economy to an approximately self-supporting unit. At enormous sacrifices, each took the road of protectionism. Schemes designed to reorganize central Europe, such as the Federation of the Danube or the Germano-Austrian Customs Union, failed because of the rivalries of the great powers and the jealousies of the small ones. Hence, many industries found it extremely difficult if not impossible to reorganize themselves on a peacetime basis. The great depression following 1929 removed what weak support the western powers and the United States had lent to the rehabilitation of central Europe. Industrial unemployment on an unprecedented scale ravaged Germany, Austria, and Czechoslovakia; agricultural surpluses accumulated in the Balkan states; foundations were laid for new wars and revolutions.

The postwar problems of economic adaptation were not restricted to the vanquished powers of the World War. England's export industries found that their foreign markets had been lost to American or Japanese competitors. Moreover, industries had developed in formerly agricultural countries which had been cut off by the war from their previous sources of industrial supplies. Canada, Australia, and India had built up their manufacturing industries, the ABC-states of South America had multiplied their industrial production. The new industries claimed and found protection after the war, while dark clouds gathered over Wales and Lancashire. They even cast their shadow on the peace negotiations in Versailles, where England prevented France from permanently annexing the German coal fields of the Saar and Ruhr areas. Considerations of the plight of the British coal exporters—who relied to a large extent on the French market—were probably at the back of the objections which the British negotiators raised on ethnological grounds. France, on the other hand, obtained German coal supplies on reparations account, the right to exploit the Saar coal mines for fifteen years, and the iron ore of Lorraine. Yet she soon had to face the difficult problems of dispensing with surpluses of iron and even coal, which her economy could not absorb.

Problems of still another kind are likely to trouble postwar industry. By its huge demand for metals, coal, chemicals, and mechanical equipment and its restrictive effect on individual consumption, war tends to bring about an excessive development of the heavy industries at the expense of consumers' goods industries. While an economic structure of that kind may be adequate for solving the problems of reconstruction, it is bound to aggravate economic difficulties in times of stagnating investment activity and to accentuate business fluctuations in a postwar economy operated on the basis of private capitalism. On the other hand, a long-run policy designed to readjust industrial proportions in favor of the light industries may find itself opposed on the ground that preparedness for future wars requires the maintenance of excess capacity in the heavy industries. Thus, war and war expectations force the economic system into a particular kind of strait jacket.

The problems of war-born industrial excess capacity will appear the more acutely the smaller the possibilities are of converting plants to peacetime uses. For shipyards or gun factories these problems will be even more serious than for ordinary steel plants. At the end of the World War, the American government had to face problems of this kind with respect to the ships and shipbuilding plants of the Shipping Board and Emergency Fleet Corporation.

These organizations had expended, to June 30, 1921, $3,316,100,000; most of it for ships, shipyards, houses, transportation facilities, and other durable productive assets. The real economic value of these assets carried over is a doubtful quantity; certainly only a very small proportion of their cost, and in many cases a minus quantity. Some have simply lain idle, some have been sold, and some have been operated at a loss.[7]

Only about one tenth of the expenditure referred to above could be recovered.

Not only do phenomena of this kind represent losses to individual owners and the national economy as a whole. If they appear in private concerns, they may also lead to very bothersome political and legal disputes between govern-

---

[7] J. M. Clark: *The Costs of the World War to the American People,* New Haven, Yale University Press, 1931, 55.

ment and private owners about compensation for non-amortized war investments.

While we are on the subject of excess capacities created by war we must not forget the case of American agriculture. During the World War, even the most extravagant expansion of wheat growing and cattle raising could not keep up with the insatiable demand of the Allies; in 1919 and 1920, America's farmers were kept busy by the famine in central and eastern Europe; but when normal conditions returned, competition increased, and European countries raised the tariff walls protecting their domestic agriculture, a protracted crisis broke out in American agriculture. The tendency of agricultural exports to decline, which had already appeared before the World War, reappeared with increased force and brought the short-lived war prosperity of the American farmer to an abrupt end.

In general, the effect of the War on agriculture was the reverse of its effect on the country as a whole, save that in both cases it meant more hard work during the emergency. For the country as a whole it meant privation during the emergency and probably some partial recompense in the way of heightened prosperity afterward. For agriculture it meant prosperity during the emergency and heightened privation afterward. This difference in order of sequence is not an unimportant one; indeed, one present-day writer has found in such differences the whole distinction between virtue and vice, alleging that drunkenness would become virtuous if the headache came first and the feeling of elevation afterward. However that may be, the application to the present instance is somewhat marred by the fact that both sequences have ended—if the present [1931] is the end—in an accentuated depression.[8]

The agricultural depression could have been overcome, if it had been possible to raise domestic consumption of surplus products, to stimulate other types of agricultural

---

[8] *Ibid.*, 233.

production, or to shift the farm population to the nonagricultural branches of economic life. Up to 1929, the expansion of American industry indeed acted in these three directions—particularly in the third one. But the following depression and the failure of industry to restore a high level of employment quickly counteracted these trends and brought the agricultural depression to its climax. Many of our farmers lost their tenacious struggle against poverty. They were compelled to give up their way of living, their savings, the ownership of their land, and finally the occupation of the land, to become homeless, workless paupers.

The Struggle Over the Continuation of War Controls

In view of the difficulties of adapting the war economy to the new peace conditions it is understandable that forces will be at work to maintain some of the wartime government controls and to use them for new purposes. Firms that worked for the government will desire further orders; domestic industries built up during the war in order to replace suspended imports will ask for continuation of import licenses or tariff protection in their fight against revived foreign competition. Labor groups which gained government support during the war will ask for its continuation, while others will request government help in their fight for a general relaxation of working conditions and in particular for a shortening of working hours. If supplies of consumers' goods increase slowly, a postwar problem of price control will arise; consumers will request the government to prevent a rise in the cost of living. Continued scarcity and price-fixing may make it necessary to extend the rationing of consumers' goods for some time after the war. Opposition may arise to the transfer of centralized railroad and public utility systems to private monopolies.

Of course, certain forces will press for decontrol. Private industry and consumers will be tired of government interference and will welcome a relaxation of control, if it does not damage their immediate interests. Similarly, workers will request discontinuation of economic conscription, relaxation of the production tempo, and restoration of the rights which they gave up during the war.

The nature of this struggle necessarily depends on the political reactions following the war. If the postwar administration adheres to a policy of government control in industry, many of the war controls will not simply be abolished; they will rather be transformed into control mechanisms suited to peace times. If, however, the postwar government envisages a return to private capitalism, it will attempt to do away with the war controls. Moreover, the general situation of the postwar economy will influence the development. If shortages of consumers' goods persist, there will be a greater incentive to maintain rationing than if supplies become plentiful at once.

The events following the first world war provide interesting examples of this struggle. Then, the governments of the victorious powers—and consequently also those of the vanquished—set out on the road toward a re-establishment of private capitalism. It is true that socialist and partly socialist governments ruled in Germany, Austria, and even in Great Britain during some years of the postwar period; but they found themselves—sometimes to their own surprise—in the role of trustees of the basic capitalistic institutions. Nationalization of mines, heavy industries, and other economic branches was defeated; public control of industry subsisted only at the margin of the economic system. Only in Russia did events take another turn.

The removal of food control after the first world war was impeded by the persistence of acute shortages. In December, 1918, rationing of tea and many meat articles was discontinued in England, and free use of imported flour was allowed; rations for other goods were made more liberal. During the spring of 1919 the government seriously considered the abandonment of the rationing and price-control administration of the Ministry of Food. But prices of foodstuffs continued in their rise, and toward the middle of the year it became obvious that decontrol could not proceed at the rapid pace originally intended. In the Ministry of Food the government found a useful tool for combating the railroad strike in the fall of 1919. Then, the rationing system was tightened again. The Ministry's stocks of foods and its influence on food distribution minimized the effect of the strike on food supplies. The decontrol of flour and bread prices and the discontinuation of the flour subsidy had to wait until 1920. Gradually, bread and flour prices were raised to a level which rendered subsidies unnecessary. In 1921, under the impact of the first postwar depression, control of flour mills was discontinued as was government control of railroads and coal mines. Thus, wartime controls did not come to an end until two years after fighting had stopped. In Germany, shaken by revolution, counterrevolution, and inflation, they were retained even longer. Rationing of bread and milk, for example, continued in some regions until 1923; in Russia, rationing of consumers' goods has survived until our own day.

If after the present war governments follow different aims in their economic policy, the maintenance of a number of wartime controls appears probable. Among them, government management of public utilities and government control of new investment and foreign-trade relations will be most important. These levers in conjunction with the controls of a centralized fiscal and monetary system enable modern government to regulate the dynamism of economic life and prevent cyclical unemployment. But after the war and postwar disturbances are overcome, there is no necessity for maintaining a detailed quantitative regulation of economic processes by priority systems, or the rationing of consumers' goods, or the fixing of prices and wages. The continuation of such institutions would render the economic system unduly rigid and reduce its efficiency, not to mention the fact that such a regimented system would be incompatible with economic and political democracy.

Re-establishment of International Exchanges

War brings about disruption and dislocation of international commerce and finance. Relations have been disrupted between enemies, between blockaded countries and the rest of the world. Neutrals have been prevented from trading with belligerent countries which were compelled to restrict their imports of nonessential commodities, to divert resources from the production of export articles to the making of munitions, and to use ships for military purposes. As a consequence of these obstacles to trade, dislocation of international commerce has taken place. Belligerents have covered their import needs by shipments from allies or near-by neutrals, and comparatively inefficient industries have sprung up everywhere to satisfy the peculiarly distributed war demand. Price levels and price structures have undergone extensive changes in the different countries, and the exchange ratios between currencies have been upset. The whole structure of war trade has been entangled in a network of specific regulations such as import and export licenses and priority orders for shipping space. What uncertainty and arbitrariness there was before the war with respect to international economic relations has come into full bloom during the hostilities.

The chaos produced by war is possibly increased by the stipulations of the peace treaty. Colonies change hands and the prerogatives of their exploitation are transferred

ECONOMIC DEMOBILIZATION 285

from members of one nation to those of another. Regions with which the victor has traded before on an international basis are now inside his own national or customs boundaries, and the victim's relations with part of his former territory become obstructed by tariff walls. The victor may force a particular trade policy upon the victim; in Versailles, Germany had to grant unilateral exemption from customs duties to products imported from the ceded territories, as well as unilateral most-favored-nation treatment of the Allied and Associated Powers for the duration of five—in some cases three—years.[9] If the defeated country loses its political independence—formally by annexation or tacitly by the "synchronization" of its government—more fundamental transformations may be imposed upon it. The defeated country may be deprived of essential industries and thus be reduced to an economic colony of the victorious power. As a result, it may have to export raw materials and agricultural products in order to obtain the manufactured articles which it is not allowed to produce. The problems which arose from the creation of new national states and customs areas after the first world war have been mentioned earlier.

Even if the peace treaty contributes to the elimination of tariff barriers between countries, it will create problems of international readjustment; for the trade relations between the newly created economic bloc and the rest of the world now have to be arranged. In addition, the industries of the politically united regions will have to find a modus of coexistence. Competitive conditions will change; markets will have to be redistributed among the various producers; migrations of capital and labor may result.

The first major problem of international exchange that has to be solved after the end of a war is the feeding of the

---

[9] B. M. Baruch: *The Making of the Reparation and Economic Sections of the Treaty*, New York, 1920, 90 ff. and 191 ff.

peoples in conquered or hitherto blockaded areas. After the World War was over, the Allies sent large quantities of foodstuffs to the starving nations of central and eastern Europe. Such help may be extended gratuitously; in other words, the foodstuffs may be paid for with funds at the disposal of belligerent or neutral governments; or they may be made available by charitable organizations (Red Cross) in the victorious or neutral countries. Or help may be given in the form of credits to the vanquished nations. Besides foodstuffs, fuel and essential clothing articles may have to be sent to the distressed areas.

The second problem consists in the reconstruction of destroyed means of production. Frequently, a country will not be able to rebuild its ruined cities and factories without outside help; it must look for a foreign loan. With the proceeds of this loan, it will buy abroad the building materials, machines, and tools needed in reconstruction; and these goods will have to be shipped to the country in need. After the World War, not only Germany and Austria, but also the victorious European countries, rebuilt their industries partly with the help of foreign loans and goods. Many of these loans originated in the United States.

The nature of the international exchange system following a major war is strongly dependent on the policy of the victorious powers. If they aim at the establishment of international exchanges on an individualistic basis, many of the wartime schemes of government control will die out in their own countries as well as in those of the former enemies. Import and export licenses will be abolished as a general system; a comparatively free market in foreign exchange will be established; international trade and capital movements will be entrusted to the profit-seeking merchant and banker. On the whole, this was the policy followed after the World War. It would be wrong, however, to describe the regime of international exchanges following the

World War as free trade. Free trade was the ideal of a number of statesmen, and in particular during the period from 1924 to 1928, several countries—with the notable exception of the United States—reduced their tariffs. But protective tariffs, import and export prohibitions or quotas, discrimination against the products of individual countries remained well-established institutions all over the world. Under the impact of the post-1929 depression they underwent a cancerous growth. All economic units, empires, nations, communities, and families retracted into their shells and attempted to become self-sufficient under a system of state-controlled commerce.

If, on the contrary, war results in the creation of large and centrally controlled economic units, international exchanges will assume other forms. There is no reason why they should be discontinued altogether; economic incentives to international exchanges will persist as long as the world is not brought under unified political control. Since, however, large economic units are usually closer to self-sufficiency than small ones, the volume of trade passing over political frontiers will decline in proportion to the amount of intranational trade whenever a number of small national economies are merged. To give an illustration: at present none of the European nations except Russia and Rumania is self-sufficient in oil; a merger of all Europe into a single customs area will conceivably lead to an oil autarchy of that continent. Within such continental units some political trade barriers may subsist, as is well illustrated by the present obstructions to trade among the states of this country. There may remain political obstacles to the migration of labor and capital. On the whole, however, economic intercourse between the regions of a centrally controlled empire will be comparatively free from political obstruction.

International exchanges between such economic empires

will probably present new features. Foreign-trade monopolies similar to that established by Soviet Russia may regulate trade in commodities. The international market for foreign exchange may be replaced by clearing accounts; international capital movements may be transacted between governments. Bilateral trade will gain in importance, as the number of trade partners decreases. The exchange rates of the currencies circulating in the various continental empires will be determined by government policies, either indirectly through monetary control, or directly through agreement.

Comparatively small economic units subsisting for some time in a world of such economic giants will probably find themselves in a rather uncomfortable situation. Since the small countries will depend on the empires for supplies as well as for export markets, they will have to gratify the economic and political whims of the Great Powers. The nature of this dependence can be illustrated by the relations between Germany and England on one side, Denmark on the other, before the outbreak of the present war. Denmark's international and national economic policy was then made in London and Berlin, with Berlin's influence gradually eclipsing that of London.[10] In the long run, the small nations will have to choose between two ways of giving up their economic independence: they may join one of the big economic blocs, or they may form one by themselves. Recent history makes the second alternative appear rather improbable.

Summary

The postwar generation faces problems of reconstruction and of adaptation to new conditions which are perhaps even more difficult than those created by war itself. Men have

---

[10] See J. Joesten: *Rats in the Larder,* New York, 1939.

to be reintroduced into the economic life of the nations, starving populations have to be fed; the nation's stock of real capital must be replenished; industries have to be reconverted to peacetime purposes; control mechanisms have to be dissolved or transformed into tools suitable to peace conditions. Finally, international exchanges must be reorganized. The scope of these various tasks depends on the strength of the influences that the war exerted on the economic system of the nation. The ease with which the tasks can be carried out depends on the degree of harmony between the conditions created by the peace treaty and the requirements of the contemporary economic system.

This picture of postwar economics is incomplete in one important respect. So far, we have not taken the problems of postwar finance into account. The next chapter will deal with these problems.

SUGGESTED REFERENCES

Baruch, B. M.: *The Making of the Reparation and Economic Sections of the Treaty*, New York, 1920.
Beveridge, W. H.: *British Food Control*, London, 1928, chapters XIII and XIV.
Bowley, A. L.: *Some Economic Consequences of the Great War*, London, 1930, chapters IV, VII, and VIII.
Clark, J. M.: *The Costs of the World War to the American People*, New Haven, 1931, chapters IV and XV–XVII.
(Clark, J. M., Hamilton, W. H., and Moulton, H. G.; editors): *Readings in the Economics of War*, Chicago, 1918, part XVI.
Cole, G. D. H.: *Trade Unionism and Munitions*, Oxford, 1923, chapter XII.
Culbertson, W. S.: *Commercial Policy in War Time and After*, New York, 1919, chapters V, VI, and XIII.
Garrett, P. W.: *Government Control over Prices*, Washington, D. C., 1920, book I, part II, article 12.
Hirst, F. W.: *The Consequences of the War to Great Britain*, London, 1934, book III.
Johnson, E. A. J.: *An Economic History of Modern England*, New York, 1939, chapters VI and VII.
Lloyd, E. M. H.: *Experiments in State Control at the War Office and the Ministry of Food*, Oxford, 1927, chapter XXX.

Pigou, A. C.: *The Political Economy of War,* London, 1921, chapter XVIII.
Report of the War Trade Board, Washington, D. C., 1920, part IV.
Salter, J. A.: *Allied Shipping Control,* Oxford, 1921, part IV, chapters X and XI.
Schumpeter, J. A.: *Business Cycles,* New York, 1939, chapter XIV.

CHAPTER 14

Postwar Finance

How will the ending of the war affect public finances? Generally speaking, postwar governments will have to solve three financial problems: (1) termination of war finance, including both war expenditures and war revenues; (2) reconstruction finance; and (3) settlement of war debts.

TERMINATION OF WAR FINANCE

Of these problems, the termination of war finance is probably the least disturbing. Everybody, with the possible exception of a few munitions makers, will agree on the necessity of reducing military expenditures. Similarly, abolishment of wartime taxation will be popular. Still, it cannot be expected that war finance will terminate upon the armistice day. At that moment, many orders for fighting equipment may be outstanding; even if they are canceled at once the government will be obliged to compensate producers for outlays which they have already made. Hence payments in liquidation of war orders may well continue for some months and even years; so will compensation payments to owners of requisitioned equipment; and expenditures for the upkeep of the armies (which are gradually being disbanded) and for the care of war veterans.

The wartime sources of revenue may be considered indispensable for the financing of these expenditure items. Furthermore, the lagging of state revenue behind taxpayers' income receipts and of these individual receipts behind the transactions from which they originate, may make it necessary to continue wartime levies for a short while. If for instance the levying of an excess-profits tax were discontinued upon the signing of the armistice, profits made on business operations during the last war year would largely go untaxed, because they might not yet be realized and a fortiori not yet be taxable. Therefore, it is easy to understand why excess-profits taxes and other wartime revenue measures were continued for several years after the World War. In Great Britain and the United States, excess-profits taxes were finally repealed under the impact of the depression of 1920–1921, which, as we have seen before, killed various war-economic institutions.[1] Wartime taxation will gradually die out, unless there appears an interest in its continuation from the angle of the two other problems of postwar finance.

Reconstruction Finance

The importance of public reconstruction finance depends among other things on the extent of the ravages caused by the war and the ability of private enterprise to undertake reconstruction with its own forces. The smaller the amount of damage and the stronger the automatic re-employment process, the less will reconstruction strain the country's public finances.

The burden of reconstruction which a defeated nation has to carry will tend to be larger than that of the victor, since the vanquished nation will most probably be encumbered with the task of reconstructing both its own and the victor's country. It may be compelled to supply the victor with the materials, the equipment, and perhaps even the

---

[1] See above, p. 283.

labor (prisoners of war!) for reconstructions and improvements. Hence, for the vanquished the end of hostilities may not mean the end of great sacrifices. The defeated nation must expect a particularly heavy tax burden, for its government needs funds to buy the tribute goods and to maintain the families of the "exported" workers (if not the workers themselves) in addition to funds for domestic reconstruction expenditures.

From the point of view of employment opportunities the burden of reconstruction appears in a different light. If the defeated nation is compelled to furnish goods and services to the victor, it will find it easy to re-employ its demobilized men. And the more the victorious country burdens the vanquished nation with reconstruction tasks, the more difficult may it become for the victor to find employment for his own labor. Thus the heavy burden imposed upon the vanquished may turn out to be a blessing: his production machinery is stimulated. On the other hand, the gratuitous services which the victor receives may prove to be a burden: the employment opportunities for his own industry are restricted. We can visualize a trend of social change originating in this situation: the victor becomes a parasite on the body of the vanquished; his productive activity stagnates, while the vanquished develops—and is strengthened by—his productive energy, the fruits of which he has to share with the exploiter. The unwillingness of the victorious powers after the first world war to accept German tribute payments in kind and the final breakdown of the system of "reparations" can be explained by the realization of this trend and the refusal of the victors to accept its consequences.[2] Faced by these alternatives: ac-

---

[2] Only during the first postwar years, and for a while under the Dawes Plan, did the Allies, in particular France, accept large tribute payments in kind (cattle, locomotives, ships, coal). Under the pressure of domestic producers they requested with increasing strength German tribute payments in the form of gold or non-German currencies. Germany could obtain gold or foreign curren-

ceptance of benefits from the vanquished and domestic unemployment *or* refusal of benefits and better domestic employment prospects, the victors finally chose the second way.[3]

It would be erroneous to believe that the post-World War development must of necessity be repeated after the present or a future war. If the victorious country possesses and uses effective machinery for the maintenance of full employment (monetary policy, public investments, or subsidization of consumption), it may receive gifts from the vanquished and yet keep its domestic resources employed. Humanity has unlimited wants; the time will never come when no further productive tasks can be invented. Only if the economic system is faulty in the sense that it permits the simultaneous existence of needs and unemployment, will victory turn into loss, benefit into burden.

Returning to the financial aspects of reconstruction we find that heavy sacrifices may have to be made by the postwar generation, particularly in the defeated country, as soon as full employment is reached. How these sacrifices are distributed over the members of society will depend on (1) whether taxation or currency devaluation is resorted to, (2) how the postwar tax measures affect the various social classes. Essentially the situation is the same as that prevailing at a time of feverish war activity. The reader is therefore referred to the earlier discussion of war finance in Chapter 7. Taxes introduced during the war may be maintained for

---

cies only by means of exports or foreign loans. Her exports were limited by the protectionist policies of the victorious powers and were far from providing sufficient funds for tribute payments. In most of the postwar years Germany's exports did not even balance her imports. Extensive international loans to Germans, mainly from America, provided the means of "reparation" payments up to 1928, when they declined in volume. The great depression stopped the inflow of loans entirely and rendered the transfer of tributes impossible.

See H. G. Moulton and L. Pasvolsky: *War Debts and World Prosperity*, New York, 1932, 283–288, 301–362, and 386–402.

[3] If, in the preceding discussion, we replace "victor" by "creditor," and "vanquished" by "debtor," we have an approximate picture of the conditions leading to the breakdown of the inter-Ally debts.

the purpose of providing funds for reconstruction finance. The internal political situation of the country after the war will largely determine the choice between various tax measures and between taxation on the one side, currency devaluation through an overissuance of money on the other.[4] The sacrifices may be postponed if foreign loans can be obtained, and perhaps even shifted definitely to foreign creditors if these postwar loans are defaulted upon. By defaulting upon part of the loans which had enabled her to pay "reparations," Germany shifted a portion of the tribute burden to her creditors in formerly Allied or neutral countries.

Settlement of Internal War Debts

Ordinarily war will increase the public debt. The increase will be the greater, (1) the larger the real costs of warfare, (2) the smaller the contribution of taxation, money printing, and foreign assistance [5] to the defraying of these costs, and (3) the less the government succeeded in preventing a price rise of war goods and profiteering of the munitions makers.

The first world war witnessed an extraordinary increase of public debts. Great Britain's national debt, for instance, was about eleven times as large in 1919 as in 1914. The high interest rates (up to five per cent) at which the war debts had been contracted rendered them even more conspicuous. While in 1913–1914 the service of the British

---

[4] Internal noninflationary borrowing is not likely to assume major proportions during the years following the war because the propensity to save is likely to be low after the war privations and the needs of private industry for capital will tend to be large.

[5] From the *intake* point of view the problem of settling public war debts to foreigners is the same as that of settling internal debts. From the *outlay* point of view, however, the situation is different in so far as payments made to foreigners involve problems of international transfers of purchasing power. In the previous section we have touched upon these problems in connection with the World War tributes.

national debt required £24,000,000, in 1919–1920 it consumed £332,000,000; that is to say, nearly fourteen times as much.[6]

The volume of a country's internal debt does not stand in any fixed relationship to the nation's well-being. While to an *individual debtor* great indebtedness means that he will have to work strenuously and "tighten his belt" in order to satisfy his creditors, to the *government* of a nation it means only that it has to collect money from the people in order to disburse it to the people. With respect to its internal public debt the nation is debtor and creditor at the same time.[7] A high public debt may go hand in hand with prosperity as well as with poverty, and so may a low debt. This resolves the matter as long as we consider the nation as one *collective individual*.

We gain a different aspect of the situation if we take account of the fact that the people to whom the government owes money (the bondholders) may have different shares in the *benefits* and the *sacrifices* involved in the debt service.[8] The nation as a whole owes its internal debt to nobody but itself; but in collecting the funds for the debt service and in disbursing interest and amortization the government may —and ordinarily does—use different measure for the *individuals* composing the nation. Hence debt service involves transfers of income and wealth between individuals; and the larger the debt, the more important these transfers will be.[9]

This aspect of the debt problem is very serious, not only because a redistribution of income and wealth among the various classes of the population involves questions of social

---

[6] F. W. Hirst: *Consequences of the War to Great Britain*, Oxford, 1934, 234 and 251.

[7] The situation is different in the case of debts to foreigners. There the indebted nation is in the same position as an indebted individual.

[8] See above, p. 130.

[9] I assume here for a moment that the modus of distribution of benefits and sacrifices connected with the debt service is given.

justice, but also because it may affect national production. To make this point clear, let us assume that the government takes money from a poor worker and gives it to a rich manufacturer as interest for his war bond. What are the consequences? (1) There is an increase in social and economic inequality; (2) there is very probably an increase in saving and a decline in consumption, since the rich man saves a greater part of his income than the poor man.[10] This may mean more investment, and a stimulus to the industries making producers' goods. Or it may mean more hoarding, and hence a net curtailment of productive activity. Since different classes of people dispose of their funds in different ways, a redistribution of funds among them affects the structure and even the aggregate volume of the demand for goods; and therefore the structure and volume of national production.[11]

With these possible repercussions in mind let us take up the problem of war-debt settlement. In what ways can the government deal with the internal war debt? (1) It can repudiate it; (2) it can extinguish it by hyperinflation; (3) it can repay it with newly created money in times of widespread unemployment; (4) it can settle it by a special levy; and (5) it can service and gradually repay it out of tax revenue.

Which way the government will choose depends largely on political circumstances. Repudiation is a quick method of getting the debt problem out of the way; but it decidedly means hardship and injustice to the people who loaned their funds to the government. If the government thinks of ever borrowing again, it cannot treat its creditors in this way. Therefore, we can scarcely find examples of open repudia-

---

[10] See H. Mendershausen: "Differences in Family Savings Between Cities of Different Size and Location, Whites and Negroes," *The Review of Economic Statistics*, August, 1940.

[11] Other repercussions on production operate through the effects which the redistribution may have on various people's incentive to produce.

tion of internal war debts. Even in the international field, it will not take place except when a country breaks away from other parts of the international society. (Soviet Russia repudiated her debts to the World War Allies.)

Hyperinflation by means of an unlimited issuing of paper money is another quick and drastic method. As soon as a high level of employment is reached it must lead to a rise of the price level. This method also results in the disappointment and impoverishment of the creditors, not only the creditors of the government but *all* creditors, since the rise of prices decreases the real value of all the fixed sums of national money which debtors are obliged by contract to make over to their creditors. In addition, hyperinflation is unfair to all people living on contractual payments (salaries, annuities, and so forth), while it favors those receiving residual incomes (profits). Therefore, a government will use it only if other methods are politically impossible. After the first world war, Germany, Austria, and Russia extinguished the whole of their internal war debts by hyperinflation, while Italy, France, and Belgium went halfway. The resulting impoverishment of the middle classes proved politically disastrous for countries with capitalistic economies.

A limited currency expansion undertaken in times of unemployment may help to repay the debt without causing a price boom and a currency devaluation. Under conditions of widespread unemployment there is a unique chance for the government to give without taking, that is to say, to satisfy the bondholders without pressing the taxpayers. And in addition the measure will tend to reduce unemployment. But if the government has been successful in avoiding unemployment, this ideal method is not available.

A special levy on incomes or wealth represents the third way of liquidating the war debt. It amounts to the same as the repayment of the debt from tax revenue except for one important circumstance: Since the debt is extinguished with one stroke, interest will not have to be paid in the future. Thus, the problem of the war-debt service will be taken from the shoulders of government once and for all. Whether or not to choose this way is largely a matter of political expediency. A postwar government may have a definite concept of how the financial burden of the war debt should be distributed over the various classes of the population; it may be afraid that a future government will have different ideas. Hence the postwar government may attempt to settle the debt problem once and for all by imposing a special levy. From an economic and social point of view the answer to the problem: special levy or protracted debt service out of tax revenue, is determined by the way each method affects the various classes of the people. These effects in turn depend on the nature of the special levy (whether it is assessed on income or wealth or some special type of wealth, how steeply it is graduated with respect to income or wealth, and so on) and on the nature of the taxes which are envisaged as alternatives. It also depends on the degree of evasion to be expected under each of these measures. Only if these conditions are known can the problem be brought to a solution.[12]

To some extent the technique of a special levy found application in Germany after the first world war and before the final extinction of the debt by hyperinflation in 1922 and 1923. At the end of 1919, a *Reichsnotopfer* (emergency sacrifice levy) was imposed in order to amortize the debt. It was a graduated tax on fortunes. In cases where the taxpayer was not able to pay the levy from his income or out of cash received from the sale of assets to other people the government accepted securities and even real property.

---

[12] For a discussion of the possible advantages and shortcomings of a special levy, see A. C. Pigou: *The Political Economy of War*, London, 1921, chapter XVII, and by the same author: *A Study in Public Finance*, London, 1929, Part III, chapter VI.

The principle of a special once-and-for-all levy was, however, not strictly adhered to. Taxpayers were allowed to postpone their payments. Currency devaluation progressed and reduced the significance of the war debts in real terms. The levy contributed little to the solution of the debt problem.[13]

Other experiments with capital levies were carried out in Austria, Hungary, Italy, Poland, Greece, and Czechoslovakia. In most cases, the effects were unsatisfactory because of insufficient prevention of capital exports, or were nullified by failure to collect the levy at once before currency devaluation could progress further. In England and Switzerland, capital levies were requested by the socialist parties; but the proposals were defeated.

Finally the war debt may be treated as an ordinary government debt, that is to say it may be serviced and gradually repaid out of tax revenue. This procedure was followed in Great Britain and the United States after the World War. In order to decrease the volume of income transfers involved in the debt settlement the government may attempt to convert high-interest-bearing war loans into new low-interest loans. At a moment when more advantageous investments of similar security are not available to bondholders the government may offer the new loan to them in exchange for war bonds. The conversion may be compulsory or, as was the case in Great Britain, voluntary, the bondholders being given the option of receiving the value of the war bonds in cash from the treasury. In Great Britain, the government attempted from the end of the World War on to convert the war loans. Minor conversions took place in the first postwar years, and finally in 1932 the entire five per cent war loan was converted into a new three and a half per cent loan. In that depression year, bond yields

---

[13] B. S. Chlepner: "Capital Levy," *Encyclopaedia of the Social Sciences*, 1930, Vol. III, 190–192.

had dropped so low that the government could make the conversion offer to the bondholders without having to expect a sizable demand for cash repayments. Still, the burden of taxes necessary to service the public debt and to meet other types of postwar expenditure remained considerable. In 1914, even the richest British taxpayer did not have to give up more than one eighth of his income to the state in the form of income and surtax. In 1933, two thirds of the income of the richest taxpayer was needed to pay these two taxes. Apart from higher income taxes postwar England faced higher import duties and excise taxes. In 1933, the tax on beer, for instance, was more than twelve times its prewar rate.[14]

We see that any settlement of the war debts must necessarily lay burdens upon some of the individuals that compose the postwar generation, unless, in times of unemployment, the debt is repaid by means of currency expansion. The burden may consist in deceived hopes and impoverishment of creditors or in sacrifices made by taxpayers. Who will suffer most, what effects the debt settlement will have on the distribution of income and wealth, the volume and composition of the national output: all this depends on the type of debt settlement chosen. This hang-over from war times may be dealt with in a fashion which accentuates economic and social difficulties; but in liquidating it society may just as well choose a method which contributes to the improvement of economic and social conditions.

SUGGESTED REFERENCES

Bowley, A. L.: *Some Economic Consequences of the Great War,* London, 1930, chapters IV and V.
Haberler, G.: *The Theory of International Trade,* London, 1936, Part I, chapter VIII, sections 4 and 5.
Keynes, J. M.: *The Economic Consequences of the Peace,* New York, 1920.

---

[14] Hirst, *op. cit.,* 235.

Moulton, H. G. and Pasvolsky, L.: *War Debts and World Prosperity*, New York, 1932.
Pigou, A. C.: *The Political Economy of War*, London, 1921, chapter XVII.
———: *A Study in Public Finance*, London, 1929, Part III, chapter VI.
Shirras, G. F.: *Science of Public Finance*, London, 1936, Vol. 2, chapters XXXV–XXXVII.

Appendix

TABLE 1
ECONOMIC WAR POTENTIAL*

Description	Units g	United Kingdom	Rest of British Empire a	French Empire a	Belgian and Dutch Colonies	British Empire and Allied Colonies	Germany b	Poland	Denmark and Norway	Belgium, Holland, and Luxemburg	France	Italy and Albania	Germany, Italy, and Included Countries u	Sweden and Baltic States c	Balkans d	Spain	USSR	USA	World	Description
Population t	millions	47.4	24.9e	…	…	72.3	90.7	34.5	6.7	17.3	42.0	44.1	235.3	15.6	74.1	25.0	169.0	129.8	2,125.6	Population t
Population of dependencies t	"	…	449.6	70.0	77.8	597.4	…	…	…	…	…	8.6	8.6	…	…	1.0	…	16.0	…	Population of dependencies t
Tonnage of merchant vessels	million gross tons	17.8p	2.9p	…	3.3n	24.0	4.2p	.1p	5.7p	…	2.9p	3.3p	16.2	2.6p	2.6p	1.2i	1.3p	11.9p	67.8p	Tonnage of merchant vessels
Railroads: goods carried	billion ton-kilometers	28.4p	96.5h	…	.9h	125.8	84.0h	19.9h	1.4h	?	35.1h	11.1h	151.5	31.6h	9.7	?	354.8h	525.7h	1,237.0h	Railroads: goods carried
Motor vehicles in use (end of 1938) f	thousands	2,542	3,241	…	80s	5,863	1,773	34s	225s	384s	2,461	389	5,266	248s	79s	182	678	29,212	42,912	Motor vehicles in use (end of 1938) f
Production																				Production
Motor cars f	"	493h	207h	…	…	700	364p	…	…	2	223p	75h	664	8	…	?	215p	4,809h	6,362h	Motor cars f
Crude petroleum	million metric tons	…	6.8	…	7.4p	14.2	1.2	.5	…	…	…	.1	1.8	…	7.2h	…	28.9p	172.9p	279.7h	Crude petroleum
Gasoline	"	.5	2.5h	…	…	3.0	1.4	.1	…	…	2.2p	.4	4.1	…	.4h	…	6.3h	60.7h	?	Gasoline
Bituminous coal and anthracite	"	244.3h	68.9p	2.7p	1.5p	317.4	200.0p	38.1p	.8r	44.2p	46.5p	1.0	330.6	.5	4.5	7.0k	132.9p	448.4h	1,307.4h	Bituminous coal and anthracite
Lignite	"	…	7.9i	…	…	7.9	207.0p	…	…	.2	1.1	1.3p	209.6	…	17.8p	.3	?	…	237.0h	Lignite
Iron ore (metal content)	"	4.3h	5.7h	1.8h	…	11.8	4.0h	.3h	1.0p	2.9h	11.5h	.5	20.2	9.2h	.6	1.2p	14.0i	37.3h	98.0h	Iron ore (metal content)
Pig-iron and ferro-alloys	"	8.6h	3.9h	…	…	12.5	19.8p	1.0	.2	6.6h	7.9h	.9	36.4	.7	.5	.5	14.7p	37.7h	104.0h	Pig-iron and ferro-alloys
Copper ore (metal content)	thousand metric tons	…	583.3	…	150.6h	734.3	31.0h	…	…	22.6i	…	.6	54.2	21.5h	42.0p	28.0h	95.5h	763.8h	2,348h	Copper ore (metal content)
Copper (smelter product)	"	12.6k	457.2h	…	150.6h	620.4	70.6p	…	8.4i	90.3h	1.0	2.9p	173.2	19.7h	45.6p	12.0p	95.5h	820.3h	2,338h	Copper (smelter product)
Bauxite (crude ore)	"	.7m	395.9h	7.0h	591.3h	994.9	93.1h	…	…	…	688.2h	386.5h	1,167.8	…	1,110.9p	2.5m	250.0h	427.0h	?	Bauxite (crude ore)
Aluminum (smelter product)	"	23.0p	64.0p	…	…	87.0	164.0p	…	29.0p	…	45.3p	25.8p	264.1	1.9	2.5	1.3	49.0p	132.8h	581.9p	Aluminum (smelter product)
Zinc ore (metal content)	"	7.7h	517.5h	17.6h	6.1h	548.9	172.9h	58.0h	8.8h	3.0	.9h	87.0p	330.6	37.3h	77.8h	25.0i	70.0h	568.2h	1,856h	Zinc ore (metal content)
Cotton	million quintals	…	12.3h	.2	.4	12.9	…	…	…	…	…	.1p	.1	…	.9p	…	8.4p	41.1h	82.8h	Cotton
Wool (greasy)	thousand metric tons	50.0p	770.6h	42.1h	?	862.7	21.2p	5.9p	3.2p	1.5	25.0h	15.9h	72.7	6.1h	101.9p	29.9p	137.6p	207.6h	1,780.0h	Wool (greasy)
Rubber (crude)	"	…	606h	59p	439h	1,104	…	…	…	…	…	…	…	…	…	…	?	…	1,158h	Rubber (crude)
Wheat	million quintals	20.0p	255.8p	26.2p	?	302.0	78.1p	21.2p	5.3p	10.1p	94.0p	81.4p	290.6	13.5p	179.2p	43.0k	442.4p	253.3p	1,479.1p	Wheat
Rye	"	.1	3.0	.1p	?	3.2	108.8p	72.5p	2.9p	9.4p	8.0p	1.4	203.0	15.9p	22.5p	4.9	213.6k	14.0p	461.2k	Rye
Potatoes	"	52.0p	55.2h	2.2h	.5	109.9	712.8p	402.2h	21.8p	63.8p	158.8h	29.5	1,388.9	71.7p	66.0p	50.6p	697.4p	107.3h	2,215.0k	Potatoes
Butter	thousand metric tons	54.4i	606.6i	7.0h	?	668.0	606.0h	?	195.5h	168.1h	…	46.4	1,223.7	157.0h	30.5p	7.1m	187.8p	1,041.8p	3,350h	Butter
Margarine	"	211.6p	18.1i	?	…	229.7	422.5q	2.9	136.3p	132.5p	207.7h	2.5	696.7	59.5p	…	…	69.2i	179.9p	1,350.0p	Margarine
Beet sugar (refined equivalent)	million quintals	5.3i	1.4	…	…	6.7	28.0h	5.1h	2.1h	4.4h	8.7h	3.6p	51.9	3.9h	4.2p	2.3i	24.0h	15.3p	101.7h	Beet sugar (refined equivalent)
Cane sugar (refined equivalent)	"	…	50.0p	1.9	15.8p	67.7	…	…	…	…	…	…	…	…	…	.1	…	4.9$p+$	179.9i	Cane sugar (refined equivalent)
Meat	million metric tons	1.4i	2.5h	.2i	…	4.1	4.2p	.8h	.4	.7h	1.5i	.7m	8.3	.4h	.4	?	4.5‡	7.4p	?	Meat

* The figures have partly been taken over from a table published by *The Economist*, London, September 2, 1939, partly assembled from the *Statistical Yearbook of the League of Nations, 1938/39*. Many of the data are based on estimates. In order to show the maximum productive capacity of the different countries, the production figures are, in nearly every case, those of the highest annual output achieved in the period 1936 to 1938. Where several countries are grouped, the year taken is that of the highest output of the largest producer in the group. The figures in the columns "British Empire and Allied Colonies" and "Germany, Italy, and Invaded Countries" are simply sums of the figures shown in the preceding columns (counting "?" as zero). The year used is indicated by a footnote except for minor producers.

a Including mandated territories.
b Germany, Austria, and Czechoslovakia (1937 territory).
c Estonia, Finland, Latvia, Lithuania, Sweden.
d Bulgaria, Greece, Hungary, Rumania, Turkey, Yugoslavia.
e Dominions, excluding the colored population of South Africa, which is included with dependencies.
f Private and commercial vehicles.
g 1 metric quintal = 220.5 pounds; 1 metric ton = 1.1 U.S. short ton.
h 1937. i 1936. j 1934. k 1935. m 1933. p 1938.   ‡ 1930.
n Dutch and Belgian tonnage.

q 1936 Germany only; Czechoslovakia produced nearly 70,000 tons in 1934.
r Spitzbergen.
s Automobiles registered January 1, 1938. (Source: *Foreign Commerce Yearbook, 1938*, 417–418.)
t Estimates for December 31, 1937.
$+$ Excluding Philippine Islands (about ten million tons in 1936–1937).
u Germany, Italy, and Albania, Belgium, Denmark, France, the Netherlands, Norway, Poland.

THE COST OF THE FIRST WORLD WAR TO THE BELLIGERENT GOVERNMENTS

(COVERING THE 6 FISCAL YEARS 1914 TO 1919[a])

[000,000 omitted]

Nations	Date of Entering War	Normal Expenditure [b] (1)	Direct Cost [c] (2)	Loans to Allies (3)	Loans from Allies (4)	Net Cost (2)+(3) −(4) (5)	Net Cost in "1913" Dollars [d] (6)
Allied and Associated Powers							
British Empire							
Great Britain	August 1914	$4,692	$40,445	$8,770	$5,403	$43,812	$21,234
Australia	August 1914	548	1,772	...	162	1,610	751
Canada	August 1914	1,180	2,321	211	−8	2,540	1,050
India	August 1914	2,312	1,032	...	129	1,032	20
New Zealand	August 1914	586	555	...	129	426	137
Union of South Africa	August 1914	576	198	...	56	142	40
Crown Colonies, Protectorates, etc.	August 1914	684	202	...	...	202	−104
TOTAL BRITISH EMPIRE		$10,578	$46,525	$8,981	$5,742	$49,764	$23,048
Belgium	August 1914	$618	$1,386	...	$1,386	$28,160	$9,282
France	August 1914	5,020	30,740	$2,817	5,397	42	−143
Greece	August 1916	234	326	...	284	14,721	3,211
Italy	May 1915	2,942	18,632	...	3,911	564	−86
Japan	August 1914	1,476	564	...	91	598	134
Portugal	March 1916	456	689	...	413	679	−201
Rumania	August 1916	411	1,092	...	3,625	16,329	5,369
Russia	August 1914	5,903	19,662	292	435	−6	−6
Serbia	August 1914	144	435	...	397	36,186	17,139
United States	April 1917	2,864	27,060	9,523			
TOTAL ALLIES, INCLUDING BRITISH EMPIRE		$30,646	$147,111	$21,613	$21,681	$147,043	$57,747
Central Powers							
Austria-Hungary	August 1914	$5,407	$14,394	...	$1,000	$13,394	$4,727
Bulgaria	October 1915	472	798	...	476	322	274
Germany	August 1914	3,282	45,001	$2,047	571	47,048	19,894
Turkey	November 1914	932	1,267	...	...	696	333
TOTAL CENTRAL POWERS		$10,093	$61,460	$2,047	$2,047	$61,460	$24,680
GRAND TOTAL		$40,739	$208,571	$23,660	$23,728	$208,503	$82,427

[a] The cost of the war is taken to be the excess expenditure over the average expenditure of the three years (in some cases two or one) preceding entrance into the war. Dollar figures are obtained by applying prewar exchange rates to the amounts of foreign currency appearing in the accounts of the various countries.
[b] "Normal expenditure," shows what the expenditure would have been on the prewar basis.
[c] "Direct cost," shows excess of actual government expenditure over "normal expenditure." The totals, respectively, of columns 2 and 5 and of columns 3 and 4 should exactly agree, but differing accounting methods followed by the various nations have made an exact balancing impossible.
[d] Obtained by dividing the figures in column 5 by the wholesale price index number of the several countries (1913=100). Thus, some correction is made for the changes in purchasing power that occurred in the various countries during the war.
Source: H. E. Fisk: *The Inter-Ally Debts*, New York-Paris, 1924, 13 and 325.
Reprinted by permission of The Bankers Trust Company.

TABLE III

How the First World War Was Paid for
(Covering the 6 years 1914 to 1919)
[000,000 omitted]

Nations	Excess of Wartime over Peacetime Receipts	Percentage of Excess Receipts Due to Increased Tax Revenue	Percentage of Excess Receipts Due to Increased Borrowing at Home	Percentage of Excess Receipts Due to Increased Borrowing Abroad
	(1)	(2)	(3)	(4)
Allied and Associated Powers				
British Empire				
Great Britain	$49,000[a]	28.7%	57.4%	13.9%
Australia	1,802	23.5	63.5	13.0
Canada	2,533	15.9	84.5	−0.4
India	1,139	46.5	65.2	−11.7
New Zealand	605	32.7	64.8	2.5
Union of South Africa	180	44.4	93.9	−38.3
Crown Colonies, Protectorate, etc.	329	90.3	...	9.7
TOTAL BRITISH EMPIRE	$55,588	28.7	58.8	12.5
Belgium	$1,386	...	...	100.0
France	33,447	4.2	76.4	19.4
Greece	326	30.1	3.7	66.2
Italy	18,634	28.1	50.9	21.0
Japan	760	98.7	1.3	...
Portugal	769	24.7	63.5	11.8
Rumania	1,091	−6.0	68.2	37.8
Russia	19,775	3.8	76.2	20.0
Serbia	435	...	...	100.0
United States	36,743	37.3	61.6	1.1
TOTAL ALLIES, INCLUDING BRITISH EMPIRE	$168,954	22.5	63.2	14.3
Central Powers				
Austria-Hungary	$14,391	12.6	80.4	7.0
Bulgaria	799	30.7	9.7	59.6
Germany	46,970	12.3	87.7	0.0
Turkey	1,269	−1.3	56.3	45.0
TOTAL CENTRAL POWERS	$63,429	12.3	84.4	3.3
GRAND TOTAL	$232,383	19.7	69.0	11.3

[a] Dollar figures are obtained by applying prewar exchange rates to the amounts of foreign currency actually appearing in the accounts of the various countries.
"Excess of Wartime over Peacetime Receipts" indicates the excess of actual wartime expenditures over the peacetime level of expenditures as calculated on the basis of the last three (in some cases two or one) peace years.
Source: H. E. Fisk: *The Inter-Ally Debts*, New York-Paris, 1924, 330. Reprinted by permission of The Bankers Trust Company.

TABLE IV

DEATHS CAUSED DIRECTLY (MILITARY) AND INDIRECTLY (CIVILIAN) BY THE FIRST WORLD WAR*

[000 omitted]

Country	Military Deaths	Civilian Deaths	Total
France	1,320	500	1,820
United Kingdom	744	292	1,036
Italy	700	1,021	1,721
Belgium	40	92	132
Serbia and Montenegro	325	450	775
Rumania	250	430	680
Greece	100	150	250
Portugal	8	220	228
Germany	2,000	758	2,758
Austria-Hungary	1,200	2,320	3,520
Bulgaria	100	102	202
Turkey	500	250	750
Former Russian Empire	5,350	5,050[a]	10,400
Neutral Countries	...	584[h]	584
Europe, Total	12,637	12,219	24,856
America	174[b]	1,500[c]	1,674
Asia	69[d]	13,700[e]	13,769
Africa	99[f]	900[c]	1,000
Oceania	76[g]	60[c]	136
GRAND TOTAL	13,055	28,379	41,435

* Figures and notes are taken over from L. Hersch: "Demographic Effects of Modern Warfare," *What Would Be the Character of a New War?* New York, 1933, 291. Reprinted by permission of Random House, Inc.

[a] Not including the millions of deaths, after 1921, following the terrible famine, which was itself due largely to the consequences of the war.

[b] 116,000 soldiers of the United States and 58,000 of Canada and Newfoundland.

[c] Incomplete figures; we have considered almost exclusively the victims of influenza.

[d] 64,000 for the Indian Empire and 5,000 for Japan.

[e] Of this total 10,250,000 belong to British India, and 1,500,000 to the Indian Native States; incomplete for many countries.

[f] 72,000 belong to the French colonies; for the Union of South Africa, 7,000 whites and about 20,000 natives.

[g] 59,000 Australians and 17,000 New Zealanders.

[h] Denmark, Holland, Norway, Spain, Sweden, Switzerland.

UTIONS OF VARIOUS NATIONS

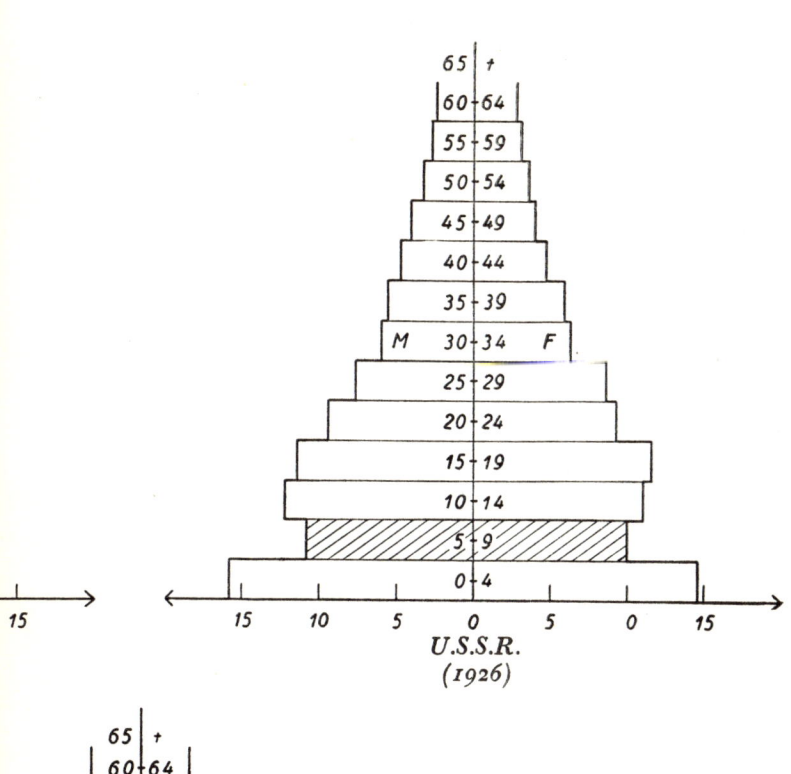

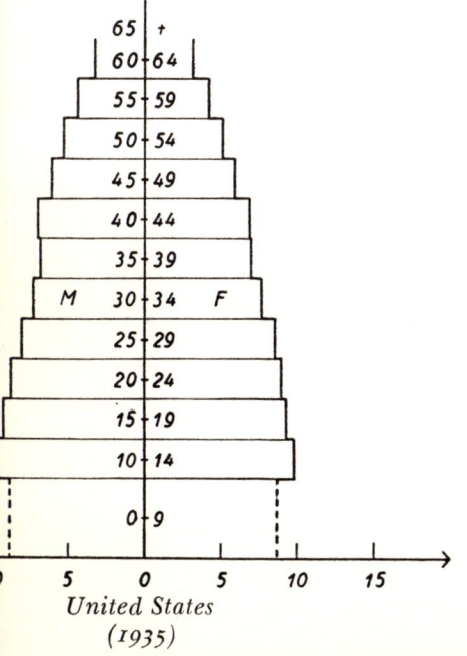

U.S.S.R.
(1926)

United States
(1935)

THE "HOLLOW CLASSES" CAUSED BY THE FIRST WORLD WAR IN RECENT AGE D

(See Text, Page 263)

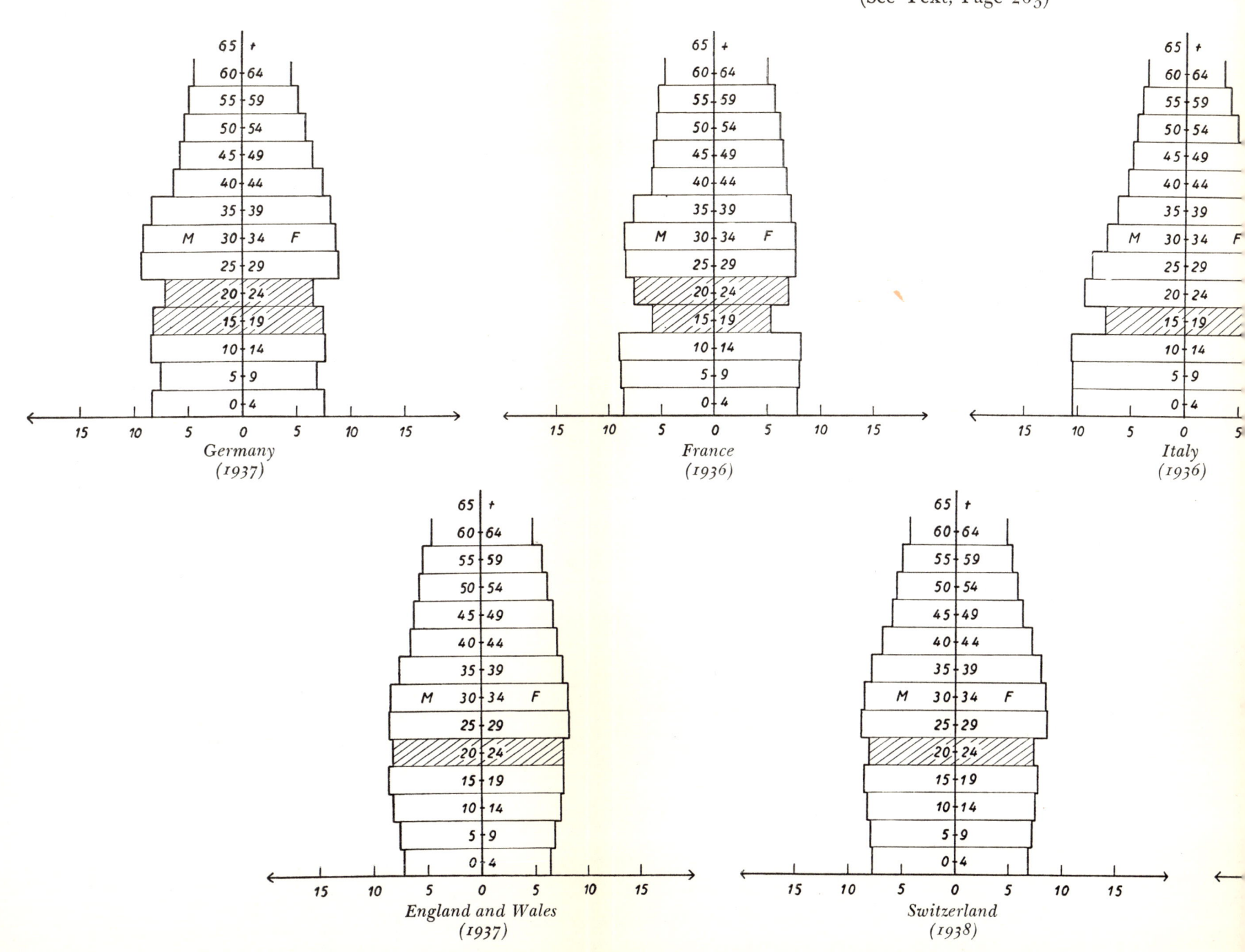

Germany (1937)

France (1936)

Italy (1936)

England and Wales (1937)

Switzerland (1938)

Index

A

Adams, T. S., 143
"Allies" (in first and second world war) (*see also* France, Great Britain, *and* U.S.A.):
  Allied Blockade Committee, 241
  Allied Maritime Transport Council, 216
  Allied Purchasing Commission, 94, 151
  control of neutral shipping, 236
  coordination of security sales, 65
  human war potential, 19
  imports, 205
  Inter-Allied Chartering Committee, 216
  Inter-Allied Trade Committees, 239, 241
  pooling of merchant marines, 216
  securities owned, 64–65
Andréadès, A., 134
Armaments, 54, 87, 88
Army and Navy Munitions Board, 25, 26, 46, 51
Asquith, Prime Minister, 72
Ayres, L. P., 87, 89, 95

B

Baker, C. W., 194, 196, 199
Balogh, T., 213
Baruch, B. M., 67, 93, 95, 117, 151, 152, 153, 161, 166, 167, 177, 285, 289
Bentwich, N., 219
Beveridge, W. H., 72, 173, 177, 182, 183, 184, 185, 186, 188, 199, 248, 276, 289
Bidwell, P. W. (*see* Tobin, H. J.)
Blanchard, R., 71
Blockade, 220
Bogart, E. L., 135, 143, 224
Bottlenecks in industry, 52

Bowley, A. L., 160, 175, 176, 178, 266, 268, 289, 301
Brandt, K., 22, 47
"Bulk line" price, 170–173
Bullock, C. J., 133
Burden:
  of war (*see* Financing of war)
  real, 121

C

Cassel, G., 31
Cherne, L. M., 79, 82, 117, 143, 178, 229, 250
Chlepner, B. S., 300
Clapham, J. H., 123
Clapp, E. J., 225
Clark, J. M., 20, 117, 143, 267, 268, 279, 289
Clark, J. M., Hamilton, W. H., and Moulton, H. G., 7, 67, 70, 82, 106, 117, 178, 199, 225, 289
Clarkson, G. B., 73
Clemençeau, G., 72, 269
Coal (*see* Raw materials)
Cole, G. D. H., 104, 105, 117, 289
Collective wants and costs, 31
Colm, G., 143
Conscription, industrial, 112, 115, 152, 194
Consett, M. W. W. P., 221, 223, 225, 231, 233, 238, 242, 250
Contraband of war, 218–221
Convoy system, 60
Cost of living (*see* Prices)
Culbertson, W. S., 51, 52, 215, 217, 289
Currency expansion (*see also* Financing of war), 298

D

Davis, D. F., 97
Dearle, N. B., 165

309

"Declaration of London" (*see* Maritime warfare)
Demand:
civilian, 90–92
military, 85–89
Demobilization (*see* Postwar economics)
Democracy, 76
Denmark:
economic dependence of, 288
exports of, 233, 241
food production of, 222
deWilde, J. C., 82, 114, 185
"Dilution," 104–108
Dixon, F. H., and Parmelee, J. H., 196
Douglas, P. H., 176
Durbin, E. F. M., 143

E

Educational orders, 54
Einzig, P., 65
Emeny, B., 21, 25, 27, 39, 40, 42, 47
Epidemics, 258–260
Excess profits tax, 134, 137–138, 292
Exchange control (*see* International trade)

F

Female labor (*see also* "Dilution"), 13, 14, 104, 266
Financing of war:
criteria for measures, 125
currency expansion, 128, 131–133
distribution of war burden, 121–143
gold stocks, 63–64, 122
Keynes plan, 139–142
loans (*see also* War debts *and tables II, III, Appendix*), 123–124, 129–135, 250
record of public credit, 66, 67
size of expenditures, 120 (table II, Appendix)
stocks of foreign securities, 63–66
taxes (*see also* Excess profits tax), 125–127, 249 (table III, Appendix)
termination of war finance, 291–292
Fisk, H. E., 120, 143, 205 (tables II, III, Appendix)
Fontaine, A., 107
Foodstuffs (*see* Raw materials)

France (*see also* Allies):
birth rate, 256–258
coal and iron, 41
death rate, 256–258
marriage rate, 256–258
mobilization, 71
prices in wartime, 161
Freight rates, 209
Friedensburg, F., 12, 21, 24, 27, 41, 47, 275

G

Garrett, P. W., 159, 165, 168, 170, 171, 172, 173, 178, 183, 225, 289
Germany:
birth rate, 256–258
death rate, 256–258
economic mobilization, 71, 73
exchange control, 210
food supply, 37
government operation of industry, 191
imports via adjacent neutrals (*see also* Neutrals), 221–223, 240, 242
iron ore, 41
labor, 109, 111–113
marriage rate, 256–258, 261–262
most-favored-nation treatment of Allies, 285
occupation of nonessential industries, 155–156
oil supply, 46
"pax germanica," 271
prices in wartime, 161
purchase permission, 188
railroads, 274–275
rationing, 183–185, 187–189, 283
special levy, 299
substitute production (*see* Substitutes)
super highways, 57
tribute payments, 278, 293–295
unemployment, 111
wages, 175, 177
war finance, 134, 136, 295
Gold, 63–64, 122
Goldenweiser, E. A., 64
Government buying, 92–95
Government control (*see also* Postwar economics):
costs of private business, 168

INDEX

Government control (*Cont.*):
  economic mobilization, 77-79, 82
  industrial development, 54
  international trade, 212, 271, 287
  labor conditions, 116
  prices (*see* Prices, control)
  railroads, 195-197
  strategic supplies, 154, 210, 246-247
  wages, 147, 174-177
Government operation of industry, 149, 189-198
  and expropriation, 189-190
Graham, F. D., and Whittlesey, C. R., 64, 67
Great Britain:
  blacklists, 238, 239
  bread subsidy, 173-174
  control of costs, 168
  conversion of war debt, 300-301
  economic mobilization, 72
  exchange control, 66, 210, 213-214
  exports, 211, 278
  food supply, 38, 181-182
  government operation of industries, 192
  government shipping control, 211, 212
  import monopoly, 154, 210
  imports, 206
  interference with neutral shipping, 234-237
  interference with neutral trade, 223, 224, 239-244
  labor, 14, 15, 98-101, 104
  merchant marine, 59
  national debt, 295-296
  navicert system (*see* Neutrals)
  "orders in council," 222
  prices in wartime, 161, 162, 167, 173, 175
  railroad operation, 196
  rationing, 182-186, 188, 283
  recruiting, 98
  securities, 64-66
  shipbuilding, 215
  shipping losses, 208
  strikes, 103
  unemployment, 113-114
  use of neutral ships, 209
  wages, 175, 177
  war finance, 134, 136-138, 292
Grebler, L., and Winkler, W., 103, 107, 109, 110, 267, 274
Groves, H. M., 138, 143

H

Haberler, G., 301
Hamilton, W. H. (*see* Clark, H. M.)
Harper, S. N., 70
Heckscher, E. F., 68, 231, 233, 248, 249, 250
Heimann, E., 47
Henderson, H. D., 155
Hersch, L., 255, 256, 257, 259, 260, 262, 268 (table IV, Appendix)
Hines, W. D., 197, 199
Hirst, F. W., 289, 296, 301
Hollander, J. H., 143
Hoover, H., 165
Hotelling, H., 126

I

Industrial mobilization plans, 79, 82, 167
Industries:
  adaptation to war, 110
  disproportions, 278-280
  essential, 128
  nonessential, 91, 106, 155-156
  readaptation to peace, 276-281
Inflation (*see* Currency expansion)
International subsidies, 123
International trade (*see also* Great Britain, Maritime warfare, *and* Neutrals):
  balance of trade, 205, 207, 245-246
  bilateral transactions, 215
  continental units, 287-288
  discount currency, 214
  exchange control, 66, 207, 210, 213
  exports of belligerents, 206-207
  import and export licenses, 209, 241, 247, 281, 286
  imports of belligerents, 203-206
  re-establishment after war, 284-288
Iron ore (*see* Raw materials)

J

Jessup, P. C., 251
Joergensen, J., 268
Joesten, J., 288
Johnson, E. A. J., 143, 289
Joseph, M. F. W., 126

K

Kähler, A. (*see* Speier, H.)
Keilhau, W. (*see also* Heckscher), 231, 236, 249

Keynes, J. M., 81, 138–143, 273, 301
Kindersley, R. M., 68
Kuczynski, R. R., 134, 144

L

Labor (see also Conscription, industrial, "Dilution," Military service exemptions, and Productivity of labor):
 hours, 106, 112, 281
 "leaving certificates," 103
 rights, 101–103, 107, 282
 training of war workers, 114–115
 turnover, 108
 unemployment, 111–114, 249, 265, 266, 272
 wages, 174–177, 248
Laissez faire, 50, 74–77
Lange, O., and Taylor, F. M., 157
Leith, C. K., 47
Litman, S., 165, 178
Lloyd, E. M. H., 164, 168, 170, 178, 181, 289
Lloyd George, D., 94, 159, 192, 269
Lutz, H. L., 131

M

Machiavelli, N., 40
McVey, F. C., 138, 144
Makower, H., and Robinson, H. W., 14
March, L., 161, 176
Maritime warfare, 217–224
Meade, J. E., 193
Meerwarth, Günther, and Zimmermann, 160, 176, 184
Mendershausen, H., 297
Merchant marine (see Shipping)
Middleton, T. H., 39
Military service exemptions, 98–101
Mitchell, W. C., 160, 178
Mobilization:
 economic, 69–82
 military, 16, 261
 under democracy and dictatorship, 79–82
Monopoly, 74, 146–147, 158, 193
Moulton, H. G. (see also Clark, T. M., etc.), 294, 302
Murray, K. A. H., 38

N

Navicert system (see Neutrals)
Netherlands war economy, 247–250
Neutrality Act of 1939, 224, 229

Neutrals:
 boycotting, 238
 "bunker pressure," 234–235
 concessions to belligerents, 232, 241
 economic invasion, 227, 228
 epidemics, 260
 manufacturing agents for belligerents, 222
 military invasion and appeasement, 227
 navicert system, 243, 244
 neutral war economy, 244–250
 rationing of neutrals, 235, 237–244
 ropedance of neutrality, 230
 scarce supplies, 245–250
 shipping losses, 236, 237
 tonnage agreements, 235, 236
 trade supervision, 238–244
 transit agents for belligerents, 221
 unemployment, 249
 war finance, 249
Newcomer, M., 131
Noel-Baker, P., 24
Norway (see also Neutrals):
 fish agreement, 230–233
 tonnage agreement, 236

O

Olphe-Galliard, G., 127
Orr, J. B., 38
Oualid, W., 5
"Overmobilization" (see also Military service exemptions), 70–71

P

Parmelee, J. H. (see Dixon, F. H.)
Passelecq, F., 12
Pasvolsky, L., 294, 302
Pigou, A. C., 31, 120, 144, 153, 178, 180, 199, 225, 290, 299, 302
Pinot, P., 183
Popper, D. H., 82, 114
Population (see also Epidemics):
 age distribution, 12, 13
 birth rate, 256–258, 261, 262
 colonial, 11, 260
 death rate, 255, 256–258
 density, 17
 "hollow classes" (see also Appendix diagrams), 260–264, 266
 importance in war, 11

INDEX

Population (*Cont.*):
  marriage rate, 256–258, 261
  occupational distribution, 13, 14, 16, 17
  sex distribution, 12–14, 266
Possony, S. T., 15, 47, 86, 88, 97
Postwar economics (*see also* Population):
  adjustment of industry to new customs frontiers, 277
  burden of reconstruction, 292–295
  care for veterans, 267
  consumption standards, 265
  continuation of government control, 281–284
  demobilization of men, 272–274
  depletion of capital equipment, 274–276
  employment, 272
  feeding of nations, 285–286
  international exchanges, 284–288
  plight of soldiers, 265
  public works, 273–274
  war-debt settlement, 293–301
Pratt, E. A., 68
Prices:
  causes of wartime boom, 162–163
  control, 146–150, 158–160, 163–174, 281
  in first and second world war, 160–162, 248, 250
  "parametric function," 157–158
Priester, H. E., 41, 46, 47
Priority system, 145, 150–154
Prisoners of war, employment of, 107, 293
Production, social criterion of economical, 32
Productive equipment, 48–55, 109, 110
Productivity of labor, 18, 108, 275
Profits (*see also* Excess profits tax), 30, 76, 132, 145–146, 160, 162, 237
  fixing of profit margins, 170, 173
Public debt and national well-being, 296–297

R

Railroads (*see also* Government control *and* Transportation), depletion, 274–275
Rathenau, W., 72

Rationing:
  consumers' goods, 149, 179–189, 247, 250, 281–283
  neutral imports (*see* Neutrals)
Raw materials (*see also* Substitutes):
  changing character, 22
  coal, 39–42, 275
  ferro-alloys, 42
  foodstuffs, 37
  iron ore, 39–42
  measurement of war potential, 35
  metals, nonferrous, 42
  military strategy, 46
  oil, 44
  regenerated substances, 26
  rubber, 29, 30, 44
  stocks, 24
  "strategic" and "critical," 25
  textiles, 43
  usability in wartime, 23, 24
Redmayne, R. A. S., 109, 170, 195
Ritchie, H., 221, 222, 239, 243, 251
Robinson, H. W. (*see* Makower, H.)
Rochester, A., 106
Rubber (*see* Raw materials)
Rumania, oil in, 45
Runciman, W., 72

S

Salter, J. A., 60, 180, 209, 211, 212, 215, 225, 235, 236, 237, 290
Sarter, A., 274, 275
Schumpeter, J. A., 290
Self-sufficiency, measurement, 36
Seligman, E. R. A., 133, 138, 144
"Shadow factories," 55
Shipbuilding, 215, 279
Shipping (*see also* Transportation):
  demand for, 208–209
  lack of tonnage, 208
Shirras, G. F., 302
Skaug, A., 250
Soldier-worker ratio, 15, 96–98
Sombart, W., 7
Southard, F. A., 214
Special levy, 298
Speier, H., and Kähler, A., 20, 22, 47
Standardization:
  of armaments, 113, 116
  of ships, 215
Stein, H., 144, 171, 172, 178
Storage of war stocks, 61

INDEX

Strikes, 102
Subsidization of production, 30–33, 146, 173, 247
Substitutes, 27–34, 44
Sundt, E. *(Eilert Sundt's Law)*, 263–264

T

Tansill, C. C., 220, 225
Taussig, F. W., 89, 171, 178
Taxation *(see* Excess profits tax *and* Financing of war)*
Tobin, H. J., and Bidwell, P. W., 79, 82, 117, 178, 192
Transportation, 55–61
  air, 60
  motor vehicles, 57
  railroads, 55
  shipping, 58–60
Tribute payments after first world war, 293–294
Trutko, F., 88
Turlington, E., 251

U

U.S.A.:
  agriculture, 229, 280–281
  bilateral trade, 215
  credits to Allies, 205, 229
  dyestuff industry, 51
  economic mobilization, 72
  Emergency Fleet Corporation, 279
  exports to European neutrals, 223, 224, 240–244
  Food Administration, 165, 168, 170, 173
  Fuel Administration, 166, 168, 170
  General Munitions Board, 94
  glass industry, 50
  gold stocks, 64
  government purchases, 93–95
  labor, 176
  neutrality, 224, 228, 229
  operation of railroads, 196–197
  price-fixing committee, 166
  prices in wartime, 161, 164–167
  priority system, 151
  raw material supplies in war, 25–26, 40, 42–44
  shipping in wartime, 224, 229, 230
  supplies for A.E.F. in first world war, 87, 89
  synthetic rubber, 30
  veterans, 266–267
  wages, 176
  war finance, 133, 135, 292
  War Industries Board, 93, 94, 151, 154, 168, 170
  War Labor Policies Board, 101
  War Trade Board, 210, 241
U.S.S.R.:
  economic mobilization in Old Russia, 70
  oil, 45

V

Van der Flier, M. J., 247, 248, 249, 250, 251
Veterans, 266–267
Viner, J., 120, 144

W

Walker, E. R., 68
War debts, 294–301
War economics:
  definition, 1
  origin, 2–4
War investments, 190
War potential (table I, Appendix):
  economic *(see* Raw materials, Productive equipment, Transportation, *and* Financing of war)*
  human *(see* Population)*
  political, 18, 81
Watkins, G. S., 106, 108, 117, 177
Whittlesey, C. R. *(see* Graham, F. D.)
Wilson, President, 171, 223, 269
Winkler, W. *(see* Grebler, L.)
Wolfe, H., 98, 102, 104, 105, 107, 118, 193
Wolman, L., 109
Wunderlich, F., 112, 118

Z

Zimmermann, W. *(see* Meerwarth)